Y0-BXD-381

GLOBAL SECURITY WATCH
SUDAN

GLOBAL SECURITY WATCH
SUDAN

Richard A. Lobban, Jr.

Foreword by Mahgoub El-Tigani Mahmoud

 PRAEGER

AN IMPRINT OF ABC-CLIO, LLC
Santa Barbara, California • Denver, Colorado • Oxford, England

Library of Congress Cataloging-in-Publication Data

Lobban, Richard Andrew, 1943-
    Global security watch—Sudan / Richard A. Lobban, Jr.
        p. cm. — (Global security watch)
    Includes bibliographical references and index.
    ISBN 978–0–313–35332–1 (hard copy : alk. paper) — ISBN 978–0–313–35333–8 (ebook)
1. Sudan—History. 2. Sudan—Strategic aspects. 3. National security—Sudan. 4. Regionalism—
Sudan. 5. Sudan—Politics and government—1985- I. Title. II. Title: Sudan.
DT155.6.L63   2010
355'.0330624—dc22   2010019799

ISBN: 978–0–313–35332–1
EISBN: 978–0–313–35333–8

14 13 12 11 10   1 2 3 4 5

This book is also available on the World Wide Web as an eBook.
Visit www.abc-clio.com for details.

Praeger
An Imprint of ABC-CLIO, LLC

ABC-CLIO, LLC
130 Cremona Drive, P.O. Box 1911
Santa Barbara, California 93116-1911

This book is printed on acid-free paper ∞

Manufactured in the United States of America

Contents

Foreword

Based on four decades' guru knowledge on the social cultures and structures of Sudanese society in the past and present times, Professor Richard Lobban, Jr., provides a unique evaluation of the current dilemma that continues to develop in long pursuit to bring about a consensual "national identification," or to end the twentieth century's longest armed conflict by peaceful co-existence of two separate states.

It is the first time, however, since national independence in January 1956 that a Comprehensive Peace Agreement (CPA) opens an internationally recognized constitutional path for the Southerners to make their own choice by referendum, in the year 2011. The Sudanese people are excited to see the outcome of the referendum following scheduled elections in 2010 in spite of many different expectations already adopted on the possibilities of optional unity vis-à-vis the two states' option. Key questions are specifically raised: whether the NCP/SPLM ruling parties would secure the settlement of these issues or whether the reemerging popular democratic opposition would finally bring a lasting and just peace by national elections.

Global Security Watch—Sudan is an intriguing volume on the urgent and most critical agenda of peace, unity, and development in contemporary Sudan, an essential guide to assess the national, regional, and international concerns regarding the present state of affairs and future prospects of the country, as well as timely analysis for the Sudanese community, with whom the author and his wife and lifelong research partner, Professor Carolyn Fluehr-Lobban, share a special passion for the history, archaeology, and anthropology of the social life, religious beliefs, and politics of Sudan. I would add to the Lobbans' works on the country a tremendous range of friendships that accumulated over the years with many individuals and groups.

Characterizing the South as "extremely complex [with] inherent ethnographic diversity, major disruptions and dispersals, slave raids and war, differing religions, migrations, and refugee situations, as well as complex interactions with neighboring peoples . . . ," Lobban highlights a most interesting fact about the North-South relationship despite the South's "heterogeneous record in glottochronology and lexicostatistics, which is coupled with a relatively weak record in ethnoarchaeology . . . The relationship with the North is perhaps even more complex, as many Northerners *have genetic links to the South through their maternal lines.*" [italics mine]

The Sudanese ancient civilization stands out as a challenging reminder of unity implications in the long run: "While this link is easy to verify by genetics and phenotypes, the cultural fact is one of deep denial, and so many Northerners are fundamentally linked to the South while simultaneously subjecting its population to violence and exploitation." Will the post-independence war-trodden Sudan prevail as a unified country, or will it move on by the 2011 referendum to exist as two neighborly North-South states? The CPA emphasizes rightfully the unity option, with due respect to the right of self-determination.

"The burial of Sudanese vice president John Garang brought grave concern that the CPA, ending two decades of civil war, might join him in the grave," notes Lobban. This and other negative views are justified with arguments that, nonetheless, are equally contested by unionist Northerners and Southerners. The *Summary's* political map entails several predictive scenarios on the possibilities of separation on the final episode, or some desirable settlement on the basis of optional unity. Still, the intratribal and intertribal powers, as well as contending armed and/or civil society groups in Darfur, might play a significant role in the possibilities of a far-sighted democratic solution of the crisis.

The NCP Northern beneficiaries' "supportive impression" about the government's stability and successful development, as reported in the *Summary* for the twenty-year repressive rule is counterbalanced with unrelenting struggles all over the country by the civil society democratic opposition (including the SPLM) to succeed the NCP/SPLM failing partnership. The uncertainties of the 2010 elections and the 2011 upcoming referendum might be removed by the Sudanese popular realities; "No Sudanese postcolonial military regime proved to be 'dynastic,' " this book eloquently stresses.

Earlier, William Adams's *Nubia Corridor to Africa* called for archaeological research on the North-South cultural anthropology. Since 1992, the late Sudanese archaeologist Usama Abdal-Rahman al-Nour discussed ideas on unraveled ancient connections that might stimulate further discoveries in the area. Dedicated research by the Sudanist scholar Richard Lobban, Jr., has advanced both historical and contemporary works on the issue, including explorations on linguistics, social change, and this masterpiece summary of a possible postelection Sudan.

In the final analysis, it is the Sudanese willpower that emerges decisively as the most powerful force of political change in the one Afro-Arab country that alone toppled dictatorial regimes by popular movements throughout the twentieth century.

Mahgoub El-Tigani Mahmoud
Nashville, March 2010
Professor of Sociology
Tennessee State University

Preface

This work is something of a summary of four decades of studying Sudan, first as a Ph.D. researcher, but then as a journalist, visitor to friends, extensive traveler, tour group leader, teacher, researcher, consultant, and founder and administrator of the Sudan Studies Association. From my first visit in 1970 during the Nimieri military regime, to a visit during the democratic administration of Sadiq al-Mahdi, to visits in 2008 during the military administration of Hassan Omer al-Beshir, forty years have passed. It is said of Africa and equally of Sudan that you will visit once and never again, or you will drink from the Nile and endlessly return. I am in the second category for sure. Yes, there are plenty of challenges to life in Sudan, first of all for Sudanese, but also for its visitors, but like your first love . . . you never forget.

There are other reasons that I am inspired to write this book; much of my Sudanist life was spent with my colleague wife, Dr. Carolyn Fluehr-Lobban, with whom we first lived on a houseboat floating on the Nile, just behind the armored river steamer that was used by General Kitchener to conquer Sudan. From our most recent travels to the South, and archaeology in the North, we have had virtually endless conversations about Sudan. Writing for the *Nile Mirror* and the *Sudan Standard* gave us firsthand journalistic views of Sudanese events. This conversation is essentially continuing here. Intellectually, Sudan is such a delightfully complex place that it is very stimulating to try to understand it. Human curiosity is certainly a factor to try to explain the marvelous Sudanese people, who live in such curious relations of sometimes glorious heroism and sometimes dysfunctional rivalries.

In order to make this work synthetic, analytical, and readable, I have kept notes at a minimum, but have provided an extensive bibliography for those seeking more sources and deeper study on Sudan. Much of my professional career as an anthropologist and an ethnographer of Africa I spent at Rhode Island College, where the curriculum featured non-Western studies that welcomed courses with African and Middle Eastern content. I often taught courses on Sudan with both ancient and modern orientations. As a Director of the Program of African and Afro-American studies for about thirteen years, and finally as the Chair of the Anthropology Department, I had the opportunity to appoint others who would teach about these regions. While earning the status of retired *Professor Emeritus*, I was contacted by the Naval War College in Newport, Rhode Island. It seems that the Department of Defense was about to reconfigure its command structure, dubbed AFRICOM (Africa Combatant Command); they wanted to hire someone to teach basic graduate-level courses on African culture and history, and African religion and politics, to civilians and military officers from around the world. Security interests of the Departments of State and Defense were added to our usual menu of discussion topics. These several roles added to the seamless conversations and reflections on Sudan that make writing this work a genuine summarizing pleasure.

In 2009, I was asked to join a winning grant as adjunct professor and SME (subject matter expert) with Carnegie Mellon University (CMU), which had received a grant from the Office of Naval Research (ONR MURI N00014-08-1-1186) to study the causes and resolutions of conflict in Africa in general, and in Sudan in particular. Believing in the moral and practical and moral importance of this project and that it could save lives and have wider application, I assembled a research staff of graduate students to assist in systematic data collection so that CMU's Computer Center leaders, especially Dr. Kathleen Carley, could formulate accurate models on conflict in which early proactive interventions might help spare the long-term bloodshed that Sudan has known so painfully.

I want to acknowledge the great help of the research team that has been assembled for this project. These include Adam Gerard, Erica Fontaine, Evgeni Riabovolik, Fred Fullerton, Agniezska Marczak, and Laila Wattar. Since this is all from open-source documents, all are welcome to make use of it: http://www.riresearch.net. As of this writing, this project is still underway, and this present book has benefitted from this data collection as well as papers presented at Sudan Studies Association's national meetings and at the International Sudan Studies meetings held in Pretoria, South Africa in November 2009 hosted by the University of South Africa (UNISA) and with the active participation of former South African president Mbeki, who is highly engaged in the diplomacy of Sudanese conflict resolution.

The many modern issues of global and humanitarian concern, such as ecology, environmental change, and climate change all converge on Sudan in general and on Darfur in particular, as it appears that desertification and declining rainfall have played some role in the crisis there. Not unrelated are issues of human rights, political asylum, refugees, foreign policy, gender, international law, and justice, which have attracted considerable attention as well. Parallel concerns with development, the evolution of regional autonomy in the South, and the relationship of Islam and the state in the post-9/11 era have also been very engaging. Tactical military issues of armed revolts by insurgent forces and counterinsurgency by the state are equally fundamental in Sudan's postcolonial history. Likewise, there are the uses of antipersonnel mines and their tragically lingering effects on civilian populations. More interest has grown about Islamic history, culture, and practices, sometimes linked with concerns about "terrorism" and global security, as well as increasing note of the major role of China in Africa and the world as its seeks ever-scarcer petroleum in a time of deep questioning about global energy supplies. Even issues of trafficking of small arms and people are raised in Sudan studies. With such a whirlwind of complex and confounding topics circling in and around the Sudan, it is clear that the Sudan that was ignored by the world when my career began is a Sudan that is now featured in multiple worldwide forums today.

INTRODUCTION AND GENERAL OBJECTIVES

This present work intends to look at Sudan's long history in all of its modern regions to determine the various strategic security issues that have been or are present. The fundamental assumption is that history shines a bright light on the present. This is either to be alert for age-old strategies and tactics that failed or succeeded, or to reveal when past patterns are over and new Sudanese security relations are established. The basic belief is that comparative analysis, over time, will give better chances of anticipating the future or, at least, more rapidly coming to the realization that something new in Sudanese security is unfolding. For a state that is so very large and internally diversified, it is equally necessary to deconstruct the regions of Sudan, since this political mosaic is, at least, the sum of its parts, or more. It is a state of juggled balance, or perhaps gridlock, with all the many actors and interests that constitute its modern form.

The analysis is also guided by the outlook of the discipline of anthropology, which is not only historical and comparative but assumes that all component parts of a state system are integrated and need to be viewed in a holistic, interactive, and potentially transformational manner. Here, old relations can be transformed into new, such as colonialism evolving to anticolonialism; expansive empires overextend to their own destruction, and systems of rich exploitation by one group lead to resistance and challenge to that group's own interests. Such is the flow of history, and with the Sudanese record so long, there is very much to be seen and understood.

DEFINITIONS

As a first step, some basic terms need to be defined, as well as the nature of conflicts with which they may be associated. When the term *state* is referenced, it implies a stratified political system having unitary central control with the basic goals of regime and state security supplied by an armed force to control the means of production and access to critical resources. The state is sovereign in the territory that it controls, and any threats to the state are considered existential and are resisted to the fullest possible extent. States are symbolized by their monumental works, iconography, and associated belief systems.

By centralizing control, a state seeks a monopoly of established and legitimate *authority* to adjudicate disputes, set standards, make decisive judgments, legitimate ownership of lands and property, regulate barter or currency, establish foreign pacts, maintain domestic order, and have unique access to the commanding heights of that state. Authority can be institutionalized by a system for formal codified law or by legitimate councils who maintain respected knowledge of the legal or customary past and of what are considered equitable and appropriate judgments that will be respected. Authority is very often, but not necessarily, wielded by a religious class and its institutions that bring supernatural forces into play to support the state.

If state authority fails to prevail in resolving issues, the state still has access to its instruments of *power* that can include bodyguards, palace retainers, a soldier cohort, militias, standing armies, and all the human and physical instruments of the military and police forces that can be mustered for offensive or defensive action. Power should be *legitimate*—that is, it should operate by established legally accepted rule and standards. *State power* is the ability to act with strength of force of arms, law, or legal sanctions that are either accepted, or so feared that they are not resisted.

The combined exercise of *authority* and *power* is the essence of the state as it seeks to govern public and private affairs, control commerce, exploit natural resources, make judgments, and control normal interactions with its proscribed territory. The study of these relationships is generally understood to be "political."

POLITICAL GROUPS

Political groups can include stateless, decentralized or acephalous *bands* that were autonomous, non-tribute-paying, and beyond state control. In ancient times, such groups existed in Sudan/Nubia/"Ethiopia," but they are virtually extinct at present, unless one might consider transitory insurgent guerilla groups to fall into this taxonomy. Bands can have short and spontaneous interpersonal conflicts, but group solidarity is so important for collective survival that major efforts are made to keep conflict minimized and quickly resolved.

Commonly, the state also regulates *tribes*, which by their name means that they are "tributary" or under state control and must pay "tribute" to the state on some periodic basis. Failing to pay can bring negative judgment in front of state "tribunals." Tribes usually have the reality or fiction of common values, descent, and origin, as well as other unifying features like language, religion, and territory to achieve internal cohesion or external administration. Many pastoral peoples of the northern

Sudan with clear patrilineal descent groups and lineage heads could be called tribes, especially during times of colonial rule with systems of "native administration." Bands can be rendered as tribes if they lose their autonomy, and tribes can become self-determining *nations* if they can topple the authority that subordinates them. Likewise, nations can become tribes if their state autonomy is crushed by colonial or imperial forces that are greater or stronger than they are. This was precisely the case when the term *tribe* emerged in the context of the expansion of the Roman Empire beyond the three "tribes" of Etruscans, Latins, and Sabines; imperial forces went on to absorb and conquer far more other traditional nations, which became *tribalized*. Also problematic is the casual or journalistic use of the term *tribalism*, in which the implication is that some "throwback" group of people are incapable of seeing beyond their circumstances and responding in some sort of instinctive fashion to wider events. Clearly, such application of this concept does more to "blame the victims" of their circumstances than to really explain or understand them. The important point is that these three terms are implicitly expressing some relationship to state power; in short, these three terms are relative and not absolute or fixed. Because of the contextual nature of the word *tribe* and because it can easily carry pejorative or even downright racist connotations, many anthropologists have abandoned the term and replaced it with the more neutral expression of *ethnic group*. Nations can use sustained and campaign warfare to acquire more territory, resources, or tribute payers.

Some sources and some circumstances make note of other political organizations, such as *chiefdoms* or ranked societies, in which the ruling authority is either a (sometimes hereditary) chief or a consultative council of elders that appoints or regulates chiefly functions. There are many examples of such societies in southern Sudan. Such entities are typically small-scale in territory and have authority in buffer areas where state power has not penetrated. Chiefdoms can also be used as an instrument of indirect rule, where local authority is granted as long as central authority is respected. Models of chiefdoms can be traced to ancient and medieval times, and the *ethnarchs* of Greco-Roman imperial administration, where all manner of personal-status issues were solved at the local level, but rights to control currency and taxation, and to raise armies, were exclusively relegated to a higher power. This ethnarch model prevailed through Turkish colonial rule with the "millet" system and with British colonial administration of Lord Lugard's "indirect rule," as was the case they tried to implement in the Closed Districts Ordinance in southern Sudan.

There were many cases of "kingdom" states in Sudan's political history. A kingdom is typically an amalgam of or unification of tributary-paying chiefdoms (or feudal lords), which have a defined territory with a usually hereditary figurehead who is linked to the royal religion of the state. Past state-level kingdoms in Sudan included Kerma, Napata, Meroë, the three Christian kingdoms, and the Sultanates (sultans are essentially kings) of the Funj and Darfur. While these are all concluded, there was a serious, but failed, postcolonial effort to make Sudan a kingdom, and the last ruler of pre-independence, neighboring Egypt was King Farouk, and there was a long line of kings in Ethiopia, also now concluded with the overthrow of Haile Sellasie. In southern Sudan, at least two kingdoms still have a titular existence, with the kingdom of the Azande and the Shilluk with its hereditary *reth*.

Then there is the *nation*—that is, a group of people associated with a particular territory that is aware of cultural, linguistic, and historical unity to mobilize, defend, or seek a government of its own interests and objectives. Under the framework of a colonial "nation," a spirit of anticolonialism or African nationalism was frequently born. This was all in the wake of the infamous colonial partition of Africa in the Berlin Congress of 1884 to 1885, which failed to consult with any Africans whatsoever as their continent was divided and conquered by force on the basis of European nationalism. In Arabic, the word *nation* can be quite nuanced, from the generic *umma*, implying the broad "nation of Muslims." It could also indicate national consciousness, with the term *balad*, which is more connotative of authenticity or the "country" that is in your heart and soul, to the term *wataniya*, which suggests something closer to the modern political entity of a nation-state. In addition, one could have irredentist "nations," such as the effort to achieve "national" reintegration of the five component territories in which Somali people were traditionally found. Since the Berlin Congress often divided people who were spiritually together and also unified people who had little in common, so the postcolonial nation in Africa has been a difficult construct to administer; this is particularly the case in the heterogeneous Sudan. There are also "national liberation movements" that sought freedom from European colonialism or, for some southern Sudanese, freedom from Arab domination and Islamization. For nations that ceased to function as normal states, the term *failed state* is sometimes used; this assumes that they were once an effective state and lost capacity, but it may be that they never properly functioned as a state at all.

Finally, there are *city-states* and *imperial states*. Typically, empires are conglomerates of "tribes," "kingdoms," and "states" ruled by a king or emperor and controlling a territory far more extensive than the one that began as a city-state or single nation-state. For Sudan (ancient Nubia), Kerma was a medium-sized imperial state, and Nubian Dynasty XXV was as extensive an imperial state as the New Kingdom Egypt that ruled over Nubia for five centuries. Napatan and Meroitic rule may be considered small-scale imperial states. The three Christian kingdoms of Nubia that never amalgamated fully may be considered city-states. The Funj and Darfur Sultanates may be considered large kingdoms or city-states (Sennar or al-Fasher) that advanced to considerable complexity and expanded to substantial territory. When the Turks and English came to rule Sudan, briefly in both cases, Sudan was conquered by military forces and made tributary to those external imperial states. In the case of the Turks, this intrusion launched the Islamic-nationalist revival or *jihad* of Mahdism that was essentially a nineteenth-century national liberation movement that had its own imperial ambitions, with blunted attacks on Egypt and Ethiopia. Across the eighteenth and nineteenth century, in the Sahel (sub-Saharan) region, there were a number of parallel *jihad* movements. Once Sudan regained its authority as a sovereign state in Africa, it was generally satisfied as a postcolonial state, but in the case of the training camps for units of al-Qa'eda, ambitions of reconstructing the Islamic "umma" were clearly in the minds of Hasan al-Turabi and his guest, Osama bin Laden.

Integral to this work are three additional terms—*security, strategy,* and *tactics*—that need amplification since they also carry multiple meanings. For "security," one can safely say that this is freedom from worry or danger, but when the security of a regime is the insecurity of an administered group, there can be serious misunderstanding. Moreover, one can have security in health, resources, human rights, civil rights, judicial or legal access, constitutional rights, private property, and investments, and with police, military forces, and so forth, so one must exercise caution with this rather slippery word. Generally, "strategy" implies the formulation of a general plan that uses appropriate resources to achieve specific results or end goals. This too can range from military strategy, to political and economic strategies, to cultural and linguistic strategies, to combinations of all of these objectives. Last, "tactics" indicates the specific ways, means, and forces mobilized to achieve strategic objectives. Economists might have tactical mobilization of capital for the strategy of development; politicians mobilize and market the vote to have strategic success in an election; and military leaders move forces, arms, and supplies with appropriate timing and placement to win battles.

Conflicts result when the existing systems of authority face certain contradictions that cannot be resolved by existing solutions provided by law, diplomacy, and force. Recognizing the holistic intersection of politics, economics, and military force, a neat distinction in reality is often difficult to achieve. Such conflicts are tracked, in this case, through Sudanese history to see how they have evolved and been resolved. Implicitly or explicitly, political entities such as those identified above do see *strategic* objectives of self-sustenance or growth that they seek to achieve by the *tactical* decisions and resources they have available at any point in time. As conflicts are resolved, the objective of *stability* and *security* can be achieved, at least until new sources of stress or conflict need to be addressed.

The following chapters move through the historical foundations of conflicts in Sudan to reveal central and persistent themes. Then, chapters on the South, the East and North, Darfur, oil, and China bring out the modern specifics of these critical but sometimes marginal parts of the Sudanese state. The final chapter integrates all of these parts into contemporary regional strategic concerns.

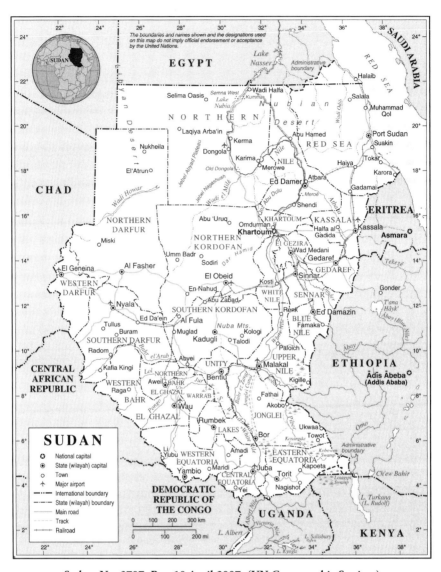

Sudan, No. 3707. Rev. 10 April 2007. (UN Cartographic Section.)

CHAPTER 1

Historical Foundations of State Security: Lessons from the Past

INTRODUCTORY ASSUMPTIONS

A basic assumption of this initial chapter is that the enduring strategic interests of modern Sudan can be seen in the political history of its previous states of Kerma, Kush, Meroë, and Nubia, and in its medieval Christian and Muslim states. From the dawn of this history for 5,000 years, there are remarkably persistent patterns between these "Sudanese" states and Egypt, the neighboring powerhouse to the north, as well as the western state of Darfur and Axum to the east, and the human and natural resources to the south. This historical span reveals enduring tactics and strategies that shed light from the past onto the security dynamics of today. As a second note, it is critical to recognize that modern Western security interests in Sudan (such as oil, stability, "terrorism," concern with China, human rights, and such) are not necessarily the shared strategic concerns held by Sudan vis-à-vis their own national interests. Indeed, it is mainly when strategic interests are shared that there will be progress in advancing such interests with mutual strategic advantage. Moreover, changing administrations in Europe or the West, the Middle East, and other African nations, and internal opposition groups in Sudan, complicate the picture considerably. Despite the variant forms of Sudanese governments—from kingdoms, to sultanates, to regional autonomy agreements, to multiparty parliamentary democracies, to various forms of military rule, to the present coalition of national unity—the Sudanese administrations function as "normal" states, that is, they need *legitimacy* that can be achieved by elections, religion, constitutional agreements, repression, coalitions, treaties, and such, and they behave, or try to behave, domestically and internationally as *sovereign entities*. This present work is not aimed at adjudicating the many complex conflicts in Sudan, but rather at understanding them with greater clarity.

Thus, linked to both *sovereignty* and *legitimacy* is that all Sudanese regimes from the past to the present manifest themselves essentially as *unitary states*, despite the various features that might bring this into question, such as models of failed states, unstable states, dysfunctional states, a state divided by plebiscite, or a state with ungoverned spaces. Because the political aim of being a state is so enduring, at least on an international level, one may conclude that the Sudanese strategic plan is to maximize, or try to ensure, a legitimate, sovereign unity government. Any external plans or policies that are, or are perceived to be, opposed to these foundational Sudanese strategic objectives will certainly face the strongest opposition and little hope of effective implementation. If Sudan is treated as a centrifugal or failed state, it is hard to hold it accountable for issues of management or mismanagement. In short, it is easier for the outside world to consider Sudan as a normal state, even when there is common agreement that it is not functioning effectively in this role. This is part of the problem that one faces in forming strategic policy for Sudan. Should we relate to Sudan as its wishes to be and as it is accepted in most political forums, or should we deal with Sudan as an entity that is not properly functioning, the outside world thereby being "entitled" to make up its own rules and policies that, in fact, undermine Sudan's capacity to be the state it pretends to be? Such strategic patterns are embedded in Sudan's extremely long history, and, in general terms, the present is not really that much different.

SOME REFERENTIAL TERMINOLOGY

Ancient Nubia no longer exists as a political entity, but its name only very recently disappeared between the borders of Egypt and the modern Sudan. Lower (northern) Nubia is incorporated as southernmost Egypt. Upper (southern) Nubia is incorporated within the northern Sudan. Its complex history has been obscured by many changes in reference names and territorial boundaries. Its peoples have had names for themselves and names attributed to them by foreigners. Moreover, these names have shifted from time to time, and their encompassed territories have also been adjusted repeatedly. At times, Egypt has controlled Nubia; on other occasions, Nubia has controlled Egypt; at different points, the two have been military rivals with a policy of détente and peaceful coexistence. Thus, ancient Nubia straddles significant cultural and political frontiers as well as ethnic ones. Historically, Nubia has served metaphorically as a filter, frontier, barrier, and pathway between these ancient and modern regions. It also served as a trade and transportation route between the ancient peoples of the Red Sea coasts and the peoples across the Sahel and savanna into West Africa. Occupying this strategic position on the world's longest river and connecting several climatic regions also means that ancient Nubia was a bridge for ideas, technology, and materials passing between ancient Africa and the Middle East.

The name "Nubia" (from the Egyptian word *nb*, the "land of gold") is the simplest term to define the region that lies between Aswan in modern Egypt at the first cataract (rapids) on the Nile and the confluence of the White and Blue Nile just above the sixth cataract. One must also include the banks of the river Nile, which interacted with the adjacent hinterland. Other early references were to the *Ta-Seti*, or the ancient Egyptian general reference to Nubia's being a "land of the bowman." Some sections of Nubia have more specific nomenclature. *Wawat* is the ancient Egyptian name for what is essentially the northern part of Lower Nubia. *Irtet* rested adjacent to Wawat but went to an indeterminate distance further south. Greeks and Romans used the term *Dodekashoenos* to describe the region of Lower Nubia that they sometimes controlled. Arab terminology provides the reference to the *Butn al-Hagar* ("belly of stones") for the section of the Nile from the second to third cataracts. Above the third cataract was the ancient Nubian state now known as Kerma for the small village of that name in the vicinity, probably known to ancient Egyptians as *Yam* or *Irem*. At the crossroads of river and land transport, Kerma became the political, religious, and commercial capital, and included the majestic royal burial ground for the Kerma kings. The term *Kush* must also be highlighted, as it certainly appeared in the Egyptian Middle Kingdom (2050–1850 BCE) and was part of an important dynastic title throughout the New Kingdom (1570–1090 BCE). *Kush* appears to be a broad term roughly inclusive of Nubia, but it too shifts in its territory from time to time. It is likely a term that Nubians used for themselves.

The Ptolemaic Greeks (332–30 BCE) referred to Nubia as *Ethiopia*, referring to the "land of burnt faces" anyplace south of the first cataract. Greek and Roman references noted the contemporary civilization on the Nile known as *Meroë* (270 BCE to 340 CE). At its height, Meroë incorporated the entirety of Nubia from the first to sixth cataracts; at the time of its collapse, it was primarily concentrated in the "Island of Meroë," or the savanna lands of the Butana steppe lying to the east of the Nile from the fifth to sixth cataracts. To abide by a standard convention, the word *Meroë* defines these ancient places, while *Merowe* (ancient Sanam) is the term for the modern Sudanese town just downstream from the fourth cataract and Jebel Barkal.

Christian Nubia refers to the three Kingdoms of Nobatia, Mukurra, and Alwa that covered this region, and *Nubia* was the reference to the region throughout medieval times down to the very end of the nineteenth century. It was then that the name "the Sudan" began to be used, coming from the Arabic expression *Bilad as-Sudan* ("the land of the blacks") essentially as an Arabic translation of "Ethiopia." In medieval Muslim literature, it was applied sweepingly to all of Africa south of the Sahara, meaning the broad belt of plains and savanna land stretching from the Atlantic to the Red Sea and lying between the Sahara and the forest areas.

Earlier in the nineteenth century, the region was either "Nubia" or "Turkish Nubia" when ruled by the Turco-Egyptian Khedive Muhammad 'Ali Pasha. Now, in English or Arabic, the term is used specifically to refer to the nation south of Egypt that formed the Anglo-Egyptian Sudan (1899–1955) and the contemporary independent Republic of the Sudan.

Ancient Nubia fluctuated in size over time, but its effective control was only about one-third to half of the territory represented by colonial or modern Sudan. The climate of Nubia for the last five millennia has been desert, and rainfall is light and rare. A semi-arid belt in the central plains extended much further north in ancient times. Moving south, the seasonal rainfall increases to sustain grasses, woodland savanna, and scrub and acacia trees. The Nile, and its tributary rivers, is the most dominant single feature of the physical landscape. The river system cuts across the climatic and vegetation belts, providing water for irrigation, a major means of transportation, and the locus for most of the settled agricultural life and economy of the country. The Nile is formed by the confluence of two great rivers, the Blue and White Niles at the Mogren in Khartoum. The Blue Nile rises from Lake Tana (Dambea) in the Ethiopian highlands and contributes most of the floodwaters, since the White Nile loses a great percentage of its water by evaporation in the Sudd. The only major tributary north of Khartoum is the seasonal Atbara River. The region can be differentiated as follows: (1) the Upper Nile drainage system in the north and center, where farming is by irrigation; (2) the regions of the Red Sea Hills and Kordofan that supported pastoral nomadism and rainfed agriculture; (3) volcanic uplands in Darfur; and (4) southern Sudan and highlands of the Nuba Hills that support various forms of agriculture and animal husbandry. Generally, Nubia is built upon a sandstone foundation with areas of volcanic and granite infusion, along with emeralds and gold also found in its deserts.

Nubian peoples have maintained a cultural distinctiveness and blend since ancient times. Lower Nubia has experienced repeated demographic and ethnic population fluctuations, as it was the Nubian meeting place of ancient Egyptians as well as other foreigners such as Assyrians, Greeks, Romans, and Arabs. In Upper Nubia, one finds the ancient kingdom of Kush or Napata. Napata was often the main royal residence for Nubian kings and was a prominent religious center just at the foot of the impressive Jebel Barkal plateau and its huge temple to Amun and other gods and goddesses. It controlled a strategic river crossing and could be seen for miles across the flat plains. Further south, in the former grasslands, was the extensive commercial kingdom and trade and religious center of Meroë. It was bounded on three sides by the Nile and Atbara Rivers and was known as "the Island of Meroë." Meroë was an important and early center for iron smelting and fabrication. Further up the river valley, the area between the Blue and White Niles came to be called the "Gezira" or "the island." The southern third of the country has, in the twentieth century, come to be spoken of as a separate region, "the South." This region included the former provinces of Equatoria, Bahr al-Ghazal, and Upper Nile. It may well have been that the territories of those Nilotic people extended much further north in antiquity, as the Egyptian depiction of "Nubians" is similar to those people of the Nuba Mountains in southern Kordofan who have probably retreated there as a refuge from millennia of slave hunters.

At the first cataracts on the Egyptian Nile are the Kenuz Nubians of Aswan. Further southward are the Fadicha Nubians, who occupied the region closer to the border with Sudan. This section of Lower Nubia also has an intrusive Arab group called the *al-Aleqat*. From east of the Nubian Nile to the Red Sea Hills is occupied today by the Bisharin people, who are the modern descendants of the Blemmyes, Medjay, and Pan-Grave stocks. At the third cataract, one finds the Mahas, Sukkot, and Danagla Nubians. To the west of the Nubian Nile, the populations were likely much lower but featured some oases, stone quarries, and desert trade routes. Linguistically, the peoples of modern Nubia speak five dialects of a related language stock that descends from the Eastern Sudanic linguistic family; these dialects are structurally unrelated to Arabic or ancient Egyptian. In ancient times, the populations and migrations of Sudan may only be estimated with reference to known settlement sites and their associated cemeteries. Then, the main population centers were at the successive capital towns or cities at Kerma, Napata/Sanam, Meroë or Faras, Dongola, and Alwa in Christian times. A particularly challenging issue in ancient demography is not only what is *not* known, but also how to interpret what *is* known, especially in terms of the modern ethnic composition of the settlements. A case can be made that other northern Sudanese are basically "Arabized" Nubians.

Since the several ancient Nubian states apparently did not exercise control south of the confluence of the Niles, it would not be fair to include the population of Nilotes who lived south of that point. In short, the ancient population was mainly northern and riverine except for those who lived along the oasis routes. It is hard to imagine that the entire population of the biggest ancient Nubian polity was greater than a half a million, and was likely much less. This speculation is based also on the ratio of existing modern populations of Egypt and Sudan, which typically favor Egypt by about three to one. But this modern ratio relies on very heavy use of irrigation in Egypt and much less for Sudan. In ancient times, the lack of extensive irrigation and less arable land in Nubia must have supported an even smaller population size there. Ancient Nubia has long been on a major route of north-south migration along the Nile and west-east migration across the Sahel by migrants and herders. Population shifts from famine, disease, migration, warfare, and climate shift were likely important demographic factors. There is no known population census during the ancient periods of Nubian history.

The "race" of Nubians is complicated by the very definition of the concept and by the combination of various groups in this region. To further complicate this matter, there is much confusion in the literature among race, ethnicity and culture, and language. One may consider Nubians to be "Negro" Africans, but this facile description belies the huge admixture into Nubia from southern Nilotic and Noba or Nuba peoples through the five millennia of north-south relations involving migration, relocation, and the slave trade, not to mention numerous foreign and Egyptian admixture from marriage, colonialism, and conquest from the north. Migrants from various regions are also known to have spread into Nubia at times, as well as withdrawing at others. As if this were not sufficiently complicated, there were certainly additional and ancient admixtures from the Libyans to the west and the Medjay to the east. Modern Nubians can vary from rather light to rather dark, from tall to short, and with straight hair to tight curls. This modern diversity has certainly been present for an extremely long period of time. Therefore, one can construct a special sort of a "Creole" population for Nubians, that is, neither Egyptian nor Nilotic, but somehow both. Amazingly, the cultural sense of being Nubian and of speaking Nubian dialects has persisted for many centuries and amid this great mixture along the Nile. Today, the ethnic composition of Sudan is very roughly one-third "Arab," one-third "Southerners," and one-third others (such as Nubians, Fur, and Nuba). Within these groupings there is considerable ethnic heterogeneity, admixture, and dispute about the population numbers. "Purely" Nubian peoples in Sudan today who still speak Nubian dialects are a minority of the riverine, far north from Dongola to Wadi Halfa, and in Egypt, from the border to Aswan, overlooking the great number of relocated Nubians and migrants to Egyptian and Sudanese cities.

ANCIENT PRE-COLONIAL STRATEGIC INTERESTS

The first lessons to be drawn are from the case of state formation and state dynamics from the empire which we now call *Kerma*. Kerma was most probably the state of Yam and its associated (Nubian) Nehesi people known as early as Old Kingdom Egyptian texts. The existing Mahas Nubians in the same area might have their name derived from this ancient root. Egyptian mineral prospectors reached the second cataract, as we know from rock inscriptions at this time, when the Old Kingdom pharaohs first began fortifying the region at Buhen. At its greatest extent, Kerma likely controlled the Lower Nubian administrative districts of Irtet, Wawat, and Setiu, which were not under effective Egyptian authority during the First Intermediate Period. Certainly, peaceful Egyptian trade expeditions took place at this time, judging from Egyptian-made alabaster vessels found at Kerma. The ancient site is known from today's village of Kerma. Thus, the first durable lesson is that Kerma/Kush/Nubia/Sudan and Egypt have had ancient trade relations while typically maintaining their own unique cultural features and politically defined territory.

Kerma controlled the riverine region from the second to fifth cataracts. There is less evidence that its strategic authority extended to the left (west) bank of the Nile; this might have been under the control of Libyans, or a different intrusive people.

In the adjacent eastern desert lands were the Medjay (or Blemmyes), who are the likely ancestors of today's Bisharin and Beja of the eastern Sudan, who are known archaeologically as the Pan-Grave group. The people of the east rarely had power to take over the center along the Nile valley, but they always had the power to disrupt it. These times are termed by some scholars as the Middle Kerma Period. Kerma was related to other Second Intermediate sites elsewhere in Nubia, such as the massive Egyptian defensive fortifications and warehouses. A parallel for today is that the tallest building at the first cataract in Aswan (from *syene*, for "trade") is the heavily guarded headquarters of the modern police department. The significance of Kerma rests upon its being the oldest major state in Africa south of Egypt. Its character is clearly not Egyptian in terms of burial and pottery styles, and domestic, political, and religious architecture. Along the Nubian Nile, the eternal rivalries are expressed in the relative strength of one regional power as a function of the relative weakness of the other. The shifting frontier of these power relations has often oscillated between the first and second cataracts. In short, Kerma is the oldest African state built on its *own* traditions, even though it had complex and sometimes contradictory articulation with Egypt in trade, military, and political relations.

The precise time of the rise of Kerma is not known, but it was at least 2300 BCE or several centuries earlier if one considers the so-called A-Group and the C-Group cattle people to be ancestral to Kerma. Certainly, the state of Kerma was formed before the First Intermediate Period in Egypt (2181–2050 BCE) and was contemporary with the rise of the state in Egypt. Whether the C-Group was ethnically distinct from Kerma or how they were politically articulated with Kerma is also not fully understood. Some aspects of the material culture of the C-Group are strongly similar to the modern Nilotics of the southern Sudan. This serves as another lesson: The ethnically defined territories of ancient or modern Sudan are always in a state of flux and contestation, and this is a very old and continuous pattern. One may speculate that the rise of Kerma in Nubia helped to hasten the collapse of Old Kingdom unity of the Egyptian Nile valley. By about 2050 BCE, Kerma had achieved considerable strength and autonomy. The archaeological reports of the huge grave tumuli and hundreds of human sacrifices to honor the Kerma kings suggest very substantial wealth, power, and social differentiation. The long history of slavery by the elites in northern Sudan dominating the peoples of the east and south is thereby established in antiquity. Of the many mysteries of this ancient state are two large mud brick structures known as *deffufa* ("ruins"). Without further investigation or texts, their precise function is not known, but their lack of major storage capacity for goods or troops and their connection with royal residential structures has tipped the consensus toward a politico-religious function. Their immediate proximity to the royal palace and African-style audience chamber most certainly correlate such awesome structures with aspects of state legitimacy.

The massive western *deffufa* is a central part of the royal town site of Kerma that now consists of a simple-chambered unfired mud brick ruin. It is still of impressive size, some 65 feet (19.8 meters) high, 170 feet (51.8 meters) long, and 88 feet (26.8 meters) wide, but it was likely larger when in use. In Egyptian measures, its length comes very close to 150 cubits, the standard of the time. The forward portion bears some similarity to an Egyptian temple pylon, and the whole structure may have been fully faced with stone. Probably the last change was late in the Classical Period, just prior to New Kingdom conquest. From side stairs, it appears that one could enter the rather small interior and by way of an interior stairway reach the roof with its commanding view. The huge amount of labor required and the proximity to the royal "audience chamber," "palace," or "reception pavilion" suggests that it had an iconic political, religious, or ritualistic function. The round, un-Egyptian palace was rebuilt many times, judging from the series of postholes. It likely had a large thatch roof very similar to those of the Shilluk of southern Sudan or the Buganda of the Great Lakes Region.

The slightly smaller eastern *deffufa* is associated with the cemetery of Classical Kerma and was likely funerary in nature. It measures 132 feet (40.2 meters) in length, 66 feet (20.1 meters) in width, and 40 feet (12.2 meters) in height. The relatively rich material culture, human sacrifice, and massive monumental works underscore the considerable wealth and autocratic power of Kerma. Given the persistent need for slaves in Egypt, it may have been that Kerma's wealth was largely derived from a profitable exchange with Egyptians that included slaves, ivory, ebony, incense, animal skins, ostrich feathers, and livestock, based on Kerma's raids and trading further south. Impressive burial structures, especially *qubbas* (tombs), remain a significant part of the Sudanese landscape in later Muslim times, in which the spirit of the prominent deceased still confers supernatural powers or *baraka*. The royal family retinue, craftsmen, and bodyguards were located within the royal quarter of the city. Even though the population of Kerma cannot be ascertained with precision, there was certainly an extensive residential area beyond the defensive and ditched walls. Unlike Egyptian cities, especially in the New Kingdom, the streets of Kerma were not orthogonal, but wandered in the fashion of traditional Sudanese towns. Houses consisted of one to three rooms, with provisions for holding domestic animals and storing grains.

During Egypt's Middle Kingdom Period (2050–1786 BCE), Kerma, the lands upstream of Semna, became known as *Kush*. Kush, or Kerma, experienced further growth and established standard classical styles for royal burials, polished beaker pottery, and *angareb* (bed) burials, similar to those of the Nubians and northern Sudanese still today. During the Middle Kingdom Period, Egypto-Nubians continued their extensive relationship of trade and interaction. A resident Egyptian trader community was probably in place at Kerma, but it had continued autonomy. Indeed, the southern borders of the Middle Kingdom incorporated a series of massive and garrisoned fortifications on strategic choke points and islands on the Nile to the southern end of the *Butn al-Hagar* at the second cataract. While we lack great detail about the internal dynamics of Kerma, it is implicit that it was a very strong and potentially threatening state to Egypt. When the Middle Kingdom collapsed in about 1786 BCE, this ushered in the Second Intermediate Period (1786–1567 BCE), which offered still more relative autonomy for the Kerma kings.

A major bilateral strategic security lesson is to be drawn here. When Egypt is strong, Nubia is weak; and when Egypt is weak, Nubia/Sudan can be strong, then and now. Indeed, the disappearance of Egyptian authority allowed Kerma to achieve its greatest "Classical" phase, ranging from about 1700 to 1500 BCE. While the intrusive Hyksos ("Shepherd Kings") rulers of Egypt controlled the Delta and Lower Egypt, they did not control Thebes and could not directly reach Nubia, yet trade seals and small jugs from the Hyksos have been found in Kerma. In a celebrated case of an intercepted message, the Hyksos king Apophis wrote to the ruler of Kush (Kerma) to propose a joint alliance against the Egyptian pharaoh Kamose of Thebes. Thus, it is clear that the Hyksos and the Kerma rulers were politically allied in their convergent aspirations to undermine and reduce the Egyptian power at Thebes. The adage that "the enemy of my enemy is my friend" also holds true, then and now. In the first Gulf War, Egypt was allied with the United States, while Sudan was allied with Iraq.

As long as Egypt was divided and occupied, Nubians from Kerma were presented with a great opportunity for the aggrandizement of their state in Lower Nubia as far as the first cataract and thereby to control the gateway at Kubban to the valuable gold mines of Wadi al-Allaqi. This was of course, a very different Lower Nubia from that of today, and it was under the leadership of Kamose's successor, Ahmose, the river commander, that the grand New Kingdom reconstituted a united Egyptian state, which has left so many monuments down to the present. It was Ahmose who returned to Thebes with the dead body of a Kerma king hung upside-down from the prow. His precise identity is not more clearly known. Kerma was assaulted and burned in the late sixteenth century or early fifteen century BCE; perhaps this happened more than once. All further traces of Kerma are lost early after the rise of the Egyptian New Kingdom (1567–1090 BCE). Thutmosis I may have sent his soldiers to overrun Kerma in about 1520 BCE. By the time of Thutmosis III (1504–1450 BCE), the Egyptians had fully conquered Lower and Upper Nubia, had destroyed Kerma, and had placed a boundary *stela* above the fourth cataract at Kurgus. Since the New Kingdom authorities termed the general area *Kush* and installed the king's viceroy (or *Son*) of Kush to administer this area of Nubia, one may also conclude that Kerma people persisted as Kushites, but now as a colonial population of Egypt rather than their former sovereign state. When the New Kingdom withered after Dynasty XX, Kushites slowly reemerged in this power vacuum and probably reestablished a small and weak state someplace between the third and fourth cataract. Finally this political process culminated in the emergence of Dynasty XXV at Napata when Nubians were able to seize the entirety of the Egyptian state. In this rather sweeping sense, Dynasty XXV might be considered as the renaissance of the descendants of Kerma, but in a rather Egyptianized form, at least during the period that they ruled from the Delta and Thebes.

Like most ancient civilizations known archaeologically, our awareness is skewed toward what has been preserved over the centuries. Organic remains of items of wood, plant, bone, and fiber have broadly vanished, and important grave goods were looted, or remain undiscovered under the Nubian Desert. Kerma's material culture is mainly known from cemeteries, including multicorridor grave tumuli and modest graves. The town site has produced other evidence, including the "royal palace," defensive structures, workshops (for local bronze and faience production), and the *deffufa*. Kerma's material remains can be grouped into categories: (1) human skeletal remains; (2) animal and bird remains (e.g., skeletal bone [of cattle, sheep, dogs], leather [for garments, burial coverings, and sandals], ivory [for handles and inlays], feathers [for head decoration and fans]); (3) wood products (e.g., tool and knife handles, zoomorphic bed legs, carvings); (4) metal (bronze, gold, and silver) goods (tools, daggers, razors, toilet articles, and jewelry); (5) pottery, brick, and stone (of varying styles, quantities, and qualities at varying periods) for clay trade seals, construction, vessels; and (6) minerals used decoration (faience, carnelian, mica, porphyry, and quartz). Pottery from Kerma is especially well-preserved, and the typologically distinct type is the fine-walled, flared "tulip beaker," which has a black top, red bottom, and white stripe running horizontally in the midsection.

Although our awareness of Kerma's material culture is incomplete, our knowledge of the religion of this nonliterate society is even more speculative. The major concentration of Kerma's economic and human resources in supporting its king at his palace and in his tomb suggest that he was likely given divine status to ensure his legitimacy. This is a common pattern of early African states and is a reasonable assumption. Whether access to power was through patrilineal or matrilineal descent cannot be clear, but the use of matrilineal metaphors allows for the hypothesis that matrilineality and perhaps queen mothers played a role. There is no doubt that a part of the religious belief system was built around the idea of an afterlife, as subsequent and neighboring societies all had such beliefs. But the Nubian nature of Kerma contrasts with Egypt in burial styles (bed burial, tumuli, and flex burial), and funerary offerings of humans, cattle, and sheep for royal personages. Stellar and zoomorphic images in the faience wall tiles in the tombs and the well-known zoomorphic deities of Nubia make it reasonable to assume that these were integrated with the religious system of Kerma. One zoomorphic form, the fly, was apparently not specifically religious, but was a military badge suggesting the tenacity of Nubian flies. The funerary goods such as offering bowls were typically placed on the east side of the tombs, with the heads of the deceased also oriented to the east, and cattle and decorated ram skulls were placed to the south. Such depictions were highly convergent with similar C-Group practices. Yet Kerma's religion also had a mix of Egyptian religion in statuary, perhaps some deities, and in the use of the winged solar disk icon.

After Dynasty VI, there is little record of Kerma-Egyptian trade relations, but it is likely that Nubians as individuals may have sought military service in Egypt, since they are depicted as archer battalions in the tomb models of the immediately following Middle Kingdom. At the same time, Kerma was clearly a military and commercial river threat to the Middle Kingdom. In Dynasty XII, Senusret I and III campaigned in the region and set up a strict military frontier at Kumma and Semna, just upstream of the second cataract, indicating that they had reconquered Lower Nubia and that Nubians were not free to travel or trade beyond Semna. A *stela* of Senusret III at Elephantine (first cataract) states his contempt for the "vile" Nubians who needed constant monitoring and control in his estimation. Other forts at Buhen (opposite Wadi Halfa), Uronarti, Mirgissa, and Quban (to prevent access to the gold mines of Wadi al-Allaqi) all featured in the complex military network of massive mud-brick walled forts. Some of the forts have strong defensive ditches, archer loopholes, and fortified entrances protecting inner storerooms, craft workshops, small chapels, barracks, and Nilometers. These fortifications were often placed at strategic points or on islands and also defended the Egyptians from desert attack by Medjay (Pan-Grave?) peoples. Fragments and broken sculpture from Dynasty XII are found at Kerma. So, our knowledge of Kerma's military comes by implications from these elaborate measures made by Middle Kingdom Egyptians to control the military and trade potential of the soldiers of Kerma.

Our knowledge of Kerma's defensive or offensive capacity comes from the defensive walls and ditches at the town site, which might foreshadow the parallel structures of Omdurman in the late nineteenth century. For male burials, it is not uncommon to find injuries of a violent nature, and for many "soldiers," we find burial with their bows, arrows, stone arrow looses, and handsome daggers, of a style reminiscent of that of the Hyksos. It is likely that there were soldiers for both regional military defense and offense for Kerma, as well as royal bodyguards for the king's personal protection.

In sum, the economic, political, and military power and security strategy for Kerma is illustrated by several factors: (1) a stable, long-term, and continuous state; (2) a complex division of labor, including military and craft specialization; (3) centralization of power at a fixed location; (4) extensive and reciprocal regional trade with considerable wealth in livestock, slaves, and primary goods; (5) construction of large-scale monumental works including the *deffufa* and tumuli; and (6) fairly well-defined borders that fluctuated over the centuries. Overlooking the ancient time period involved and focusing just on the structural aspects of a state, one can see that it abided by rather conventional rules and political order. Its strategic concerns were to ensure, protect, and celebrate its ruling class with institutionalized ideology. Its objectives were too secure trade routes, to defend its borders to raise a military force, to conduct punitive raids against the desert neighbors and raiders, and to conduct slave raids further south. Its main foreign policy concern was with Egypt to the north since the two states shared mutual contempt, respect, admiration, fear, plotting, and tactical alliances. Relations with Egypt were typically stalemated with caution, military balance, and an extensive series of a score of massive mud-brick fortresses linked by visual communication that were strategically placed on promontory points or defensive islands to keep the parties apart but functionally connected by well-ordered trade. In these respects, it is remarkable how little has changed over the passing millennia.

In Intermediate Periods, when the Egyptian imperial state collapsed, the balance of power shifted to Kerma, as shown by texts found in abandoned Egyptian forts that proclaimed loyalty to Kerma. Kerma kings confiscated Egyptian sculpture to bring it back to their capital and royal tombs. After 1100 BCE, a Nubian state again emerged with vigor and even became a refuge area for Egyptians fleeing civil war and foreign conquest. By 950 BCE, the Sudanese city of Napata had become the site of the major temple for the Nubian worship of Amun, the god of the most important priesthood, and a distinctive Egyptian-Kushite culture evolved. Napata became the capital of Kush, and its kings even conquered Egypt for a time, forming Dynasty XXV in the late eighth century BCE to 664 BCE. The famed leaders (three are noted in the Old Testament) of Dynasty XXV reverted to alliances with the Jewish state and supporting counterinsurgency in Phoenicia (Lebanon) to try to block Assyrian advances. This again follows the principle of "the enemy of my enemy is my friend." When the Assyrians conquered Egypt in about 664 BCE, the Kushites were pushed back to their independent Nubian state. A Kushite fortress in Wadi Howar in the western desert was discovered in 2006 that attests to their military defense in this area. Later attacks on Napata from Egypt by Psamtik II in 591 BCE caused the capital to be temporarily moved south. When the enemy withdrew, Napata was restored for three centuries before seeking strategic defensive depth by permanently moving the royal capital to Meroë.

Vibrant and independent Meroë was influenced by Greek, Roman, and ancient Egyptian ideas. Relations between Meroë and Ptolemaic (Greek) Egypt were broadly collaborative in areas of science, technology, and trade. However, when the last Greek, Cleopatra VII, was toppled, the balance was lost, and regnant Meroitic queens mounted military attacks against Roman Egypt to reset the Lower Nubian boundaries (*limes*) between colonized Egypt and independent Meroë. Like Kerma, Meroë developed its own syncretic cultural traits. It was a gateway and marketplace for ideas, writing, resources, and technologies into and out of Africa. Major advances in iron/steel technology provided durable tools and weapons that gave regional supremacy to the expansive Meroitic state. Meroë began to meet pressures from ecological degradation and from the state of Axum in Ethiopia. Meroë came to an end around 350 CE following an Axumite invasion from the southeast that found it already much weakened and vulnerable. Much less is known about the following period of disorganization following the collapse of the state of Meroë.

ANCIENT STRATEGIC SECURITY

From this rapid survey of the ancient past, the lands that became the modern Sudan had fluctuating and contested borders to the east and west, and the south was a sources of slaves and livestock to accumulate the wealth of the ancient states. Kerma, in particular, had strategic depth from Egypt that provided its best defense, while Egypt had a series of strong houses and fortifications that protected it from attack from the south. Generally, this was a stable situation with mutual trade benefits until tipping points in antiquity meant colonial intrusion into Nubia/Sudan by Egypt and at least one occupation of Egypt by Nubians. Both ancient states had to deal with their own domestic security issues as well as foreign relations, and for Nubia in any case, they made an ancient strategic alliance with the Hyksos, who occupied the Delta and lower parts of Upper Egypt, to try to tap Egyptians in their weakened state in Upper Egypt at Luxor and Karnak. The takeaway observation is that there is a generally manageable rivalry or détente along the Egyptian-Sudanese Nile, but even at times of imbalance with imperial overextension, it will ultimately fail. Applications of these patterns today are apparent in that both nations are endlessly rebalancing this security equation by negotiation, periods of discord, some attacks, and harsh words, but there is enduring economic interaction and generally a concern with the political and resource stability in their respective nations.

STRATEGIC RELATIONS IN MEDIEVAL TIMES

Out of the confusion, three states emerged: Nobatia, Mukurra (Mukuria, Muqura), and Alwa. Their rulers converted to Christianity between 543 and 580 CE, and Nobatia and Mukurra merged into the kingdom of Dongola by about 700 CE. Old Dongola rose on the east bank of the Nile and commanded a view of the northern plain, the river Nile, and the eastern desert. The best-known aspect of the history of these states is their relationship with Egypt, which became one of the early Islamic conquests in North Africa in 640 CE. There were battles, treaties, attacks, and counterattacks, with the long-term trend in favor of the Muslims. Tradition holds that the first Muslim became king of Dongola in 1315 and that Soba, the capital of the last Christian Nubian kingdom of Alwa, fell to the Funj Sultans in 1504. Soba was situated on the Blue Nile, with camel and horse trade routes across the Butana plain and river traffic to Ethiopia and points south.

THE FORMATION OF CHRISTIAN STATES OF EGYPT AND NUBIA

Convention has it that Christ was born on 25 December 4 BCE in Bethlehem, during the reign of Caesar Augustus. This new prophet would present a historical challenge to the legitimacy, and hence the security, of Imperial Rome. Christ and his parents presumably fled through Gaza and al-Arish, Egypt, as noted in

Matthew (2:13–15). Then, they went on through Roman Old Cairo (Babylon) and on to a Jewish synagogue at Ma'adi, where they boarded a small boat to go to Upper Egypt. At their most southerly point in Upper Egypt, a church was later built and is now known as Deir al-Muharaka (Monastery of the Flight). Egyptian, Ethiopian, and (most probably) Nubian Copts have been attracted to this spot, believed to have curative values. The first Nubian convert to Christianity may be the official of Meroë who was exposed to Christianity in about 37 CE. In the Acts of the Apostles (8:27–39), a ranking eunuch of "Candace queen of the Ethiopians" was converted to Christianity by the prophet Esaias. There is no record of others who might have followed this faith at this Nubian city. When the disciple Saint Mark returned to Egypt from 61 to 65 CE, one may say that Coptic (Orthodox Egyptian) Christianity reached the Nile in a more organized way. Mark was born a Jew in neighboring Cyrenaica, where he received a religious education that attracted him to this new faith. During these perilous early decades under such repressive Roman Emperors as Caligula, Claudius, and Nero, the Gospel was first introduced, especially in Alexandria. Saint Mark was savagely martyred in 68 CE on Easter Monday after being dragged through Alexandria by a mob of Roman soldiers. Coptic Christians, often converted Jews, continued to suffer from religious and political persecution under the imperial Romans in the second and third centuries. Under the rule of Septimus Severus (193–211 CE), during a visit to Egypt from 199 to 200 CE prohibited Romans from accepting rival Christianity. Despite this persistent repression, Patriarch Dionysius actively sought more Egyptian converts to Christianity from 247 to 264 CE. A result of his work was a period of major conversions of Egyptians to this faith. Coptic monasticism in the eastern desert developed especially at this time under Saints Paul (228–343 CE) and Anthony "the Great" (251–356 CE). Further percolation of Christianity into Nubia took place from about 260 to 300 CE.

These hardships continued during the reign of Roman Emperor Diocletian (284–304 CE), who continued to feared this threat to Roman polytheism. The Coptic "Calendar of Martyrs" (AM) is put at 29 August 284 CE to commemorate those who died during his particularly repressive rule. The repression by Diocletian against Egyptian Christians in 302 CE is said to have taken hundreds of thousands of lives. Diocletian was also threatened by the division of the Roman Empire into its eastern and western sections. The Christians were easy scapegoats in his reign of terror against them, their books, and their properties. Christians in the late third and early fourth centuries, such as Saint Anthony, struggled to survive in isolated desert retreats, caves, and monasteries. Christian disciples of this "secret religion" came from throughout the eastern Mediterranean, Armenia, and Nubia ("Ethiopia") in the third century CE. The Church of the Forty Martyrs in Wadi Natrun, Egypt, commemorates the test of faith of Christians in 313 CE. By the fifth century, Egyptian churches dedicated to Saint Sergius (Abu Serga) and Saint Barbara were constructed to memorialize these many early

Christian martyrs. The battle for state security through religious legitimacy was over—for a while.

EGYPTO-ETHIO-NUBIAN CHRISTIANITY AIMING FOR STATE POWER

Galvanized and legitimated by their iconic cross, Christians spread their theology and territory. After the Roman Emperor Constantine accepted Christianity as the official religion of the Roman Empire, the faith spread widely in Egypt, Nubia, and Numidia. The first Christian basilica in Rome was under construction from 313 to 322 CE. Increased missionary activity from Egypt is recorded in 324 CE in Nubia. This represented a "pincer movement," as this mission was synchronized with the Axumite (Christian) King Ezana of Ethiopia, who destroyed the remnants of Meroë. In the same period, Bishop Athanasius of Alexandria ordained the Ethiopian church. The collapse of Meroitic polytheism and the rise of state Christendom in Egypt and Ethiopia created a religious vacuum into which the missionary activities could begin to take place throughout the entire Nile and Blue Nile valleys. The so-called X-Group tried to fill this void with a pre-Christian syncretic blend of Egyptian, Kushitic, Meroitic, Greco-Roman, and Nubian beliefs, practices, and architecture from about 350 to 550 CE. A hint of the early Christian influence is seen in X-Group grave goods, including crosses and other icons. This transitional period of weak state security featured intense rivalries and military attacks against the settled people in Lower Nubia by the semi-nomadic Blemmyes.

SCHISMS IN EGYPTO-NUBIAN CHRISTIANITY: STRUGGLES FOR LEGITIMACY

Despite—or perhaps because of—its early successes in the fourth century CE, Egyptian Christianity very quickly entered into a schismatic religious debate that continues to the present. State power needs ineffable legitimacy to be sustained, so in 325 CE, more than three hundred eastern bishops met at the Council of Nicaea, called by Emperor Constantine to "resolve" the issue about the "oneness" of Christ and give further momentum to the Christian missionary movement. The followers of the "heretical" Egyptian theology of Arianism had rejected the idea that Christ had a divine nature, which they reserved for God alone. Thus, their position was that there were separate "natures," one for God and one for Christ. Pope Alexander of Alexandria sought support at the Nicaean Council for his view that Christ and God were one. The view that Christ had a "single person with two natures" succeeded, and the Egyptian Bishop of Alexandria was sustained. The Arian (as well as Jewish and "pagan") creeds were rejected. The Eastern Greek Church has followed the Nicaean credo since that time.

However, the sectarian division persisted within Egypt over the Arian and subsequent Monophysite interpretations of the status of Christ. But this early

Christian schism served to isolate the Egyptian, Nubian, and other eastern Orthodox branches from the western (Roman) branches of the Christian church. The Alexandrian Coptic Church sought to follow the Nicaean credo, led by patriarch Saint Athanasius, who had attended the Nicaea conference as an observer. After he returned to Egypt, he served as the pope of Alexandria from 327 to 373 CE. The bloody struggles between the followers of Athanasius and the Arians continued in Egypt after the Edict of Theodosius in 384 CE declared that Christianity was the official religion of Egypt. But it was in 391 CE that Coptic (Monophysite) Christianity became the state religion, and the divisions continued.

Athanasius served as pope and assisted with the growth of Egyptian monasticism and the cautious encouragement of Nile Valley Christianity. Around 400 CE, Saint Jerome introduced a Latin version of the Bible to Egypt and set the stage to spread the Gospel to the south. However, the division between the official Monophysite view and that of the Arians continued, so Emperor Theodosius sought to "resolve" this matter once again in the 381 CE Council of Constantinople. This was viewed as a political threat; to shift the official center of Christianity from Alexandria to Constantinople would marginalize the historic role of Alexandria as a center for learning and religion, and this Council only added more to the divisions that continued to the third Ecumenical Council in 431 CE and thereafter. In 451 CE, these festering divisions descending from the Council of Nicaea were only reaffirmed with the Council of Chalcedon (near Constantinople). Emperor Marcian and Pope Leo called this council to try again to "resolve" the doctrinal, political, and national differences between the Roman pope of Byzantium and Patriarch Dioscoros of Alexandria. The Dyophysite view that Christ was a single person with "two natures" (one divine and one human) was upheld. The Monophysite ("one-nature") view of the Egyptian patriarch Dioscoros was defeated, and he returned to Egypt. Although the theological dispute was "resolved" by declaration, another dimension of the conflict was introduced when the Council of Chalcedon sought to resolve the matter by force rather than further debate. The Melkite (royal) or Antiochian authority appointed by the Emperor not only represented the Dyophysite view but also was given legitimacy to restore the unity of the church, by force if necessary, to bring this "rebellion" to an end. Specifically, the effort to land in Alexandria and install an official Melkite priest, Proterius, in place of Pope Dioscorus was the final blow. The Egyptian and Ethiopian Copts could not accept this forceful intrusion into their religious lives. This offended their deeply rooted Christianity as well as their own proud nationalism.

Despite this isolation, the Orthodox Church in Egypt and Nubia then made a more aggressive attempt to spread the Christian message from Egypt to Sudan that can be dated to 452 CE, and perhaps the initial construction of a mud brick church at Faras. This was a time when rivals on the Nile were not only Egyptian Copts and Romans, but also the Blemmyes and Nobatae of Nubia, who had attacked Romans and taken hostages that Roman general Maximinus fought to release. This turbulent time was patched together with the 453 CE Treaty of Philae that gave non-Christian Nubians and Blemmyes the right to continue to worship the goddess Isis celebrated at that temple. Ironically, the role of Isis and Horus reemerges in a new conflated form as Mary and Jesus in Christianity. Meanwhile, Egyptian Christian converts also traveled to Europe and the Middle East to spread the Gospel. Not surprisingly, it was this confused context locally that saw the formal end of the entire Roman Empire in 476 CE, although as late as 515 CE, Romans were still weakly seeking to negotiate a treaty with local Blemmye and Nobatae leaders if they would just leave the Romans in peace.

The security lessons to be drawn here are many. Religion is usually about the struggle for power and land, even when the issues are projected as theological. Internal divisions in a given religious community can serve to weaken it in the longer term. Religion can be a potent force for political mobilization, acquiring economic resources, and rallying military strength. The security and stability of such features in state relations can be powerful and enduring, or fissile and ephemeral, as in medieval Christian Nubia or modern Muslim Sudan.

THE CHRISTIAN MISSIONARIES ARRIVE IN NUBIA

Thus the seeds of the Christian kingdoms of Nubia were germinated in Egypt but were transplanted to Nubia between 350 and 550 CE with the formation of the kingdoms of Nobatia, Mukurra, and Alwa. At its height, Nubian Christianity would connect the Alexandrian church with its Nubian affiliates and finally deep into the heartland of Ethiopia, where it still remains. With the Roman Empire in active retreat by 524 CE, a political, religious, and military alliance was established between Copts in Egypt and the Axumites in Ethiopia. Blemmye and Nobatian mercenaries also saw action in Yemen in support of Axumite ambitions there.

When Emperor Justinian (527–565 CE) and Empress Theodora came to rule Byzantium, this movement gained even greater force, while taking an odd turn in the royal family. The Emperor naturally favored the Chalcedonian (Melkite) perspective about this simmering religious debate. Remarkably, his independent-minded Egyptian-born wife Theodora supported the anti-Chalcedonian Monophysite view that was still widespread in Egypt. Jacob Baradai actively pros-elytized this view in about 530 CE, earning the anti-Chalcedonians the label of "Jacobites." The struggle continued when the Monophysite patriarch of Alexandria, Theodosius, was forced out of his church and was banished to Thrace for his anti-Chalcedonian position. Since Theodora had supported Theodosius, his death in exile only embittered the "marital" and political relations between Byzantium and Alexandria. Egyptians consistently rejected the three successive Melkite appointments to patriarch of Alexandria. Not surprisingly, the Melkites and Jacobites also sent out rival missionaries to Egypt and Nubia to win recruits for their respective positions.

During Justinian's reign, several pivotal events are recorded relative to Nubia. First, he officially closed and suppressed the Isis cult at Philae. It is believed that much of the defacement of this Ptolemaic temple took place at this time. Second, in his alliance with King Silko of Nobatia, the Blemmyes were militarily subjugated. The famed inscription of King Silko written in poor Greek at the Roman temple built by Augustus at Kalabsha records this moment. Here, Silko declares that his victory was the result of a singular god, thus establishing an official start of Nubian Christianity at about 536 CE. In 542, Silko was approached by an official delegation of papal authority, but he indicated that he was quite content with the Copts, who were already among the Nobatae, and that he wanted no further intervention from Egypt.

During the period of 543 to 569 CE, the first Monophysite Christian kingdoms were formally organized in Nubia to consolidate and legitimate the military victory in Nubia, along with a flood of Coptic immigrants escaping the troubles in Egypt. The leader of this missionary effort was Julian, a priest deeply loyal to Patriarch Theodosius and who had been with him in his exile. In memory of Theodosius, Julian was committed to gaining new converts among the "Barbari" Nubians. This religious campaign was secretly backed by Theodora and secretly blocked by Justinian, who wished to win the new followers to the Chalcedonian position. If the pro-Jacobite accounts are to be trusted, it appears that Theodora was the temporary victor, as Julian reached the region of Nobatia first to establish in 543 CE the town of Faras as the capital of Christian Nobatia. Perhaps the declaration of King Silko is a veiled reference to the arrival of Julian to Nubia close to that time. Mukurra and its capital of Dongola, situated further upstream on the Nile, were converted to the Chalcedon Council in 569. In 579 to 580 CE, missionary Longinus dodged Melkite opposition and intrigue in the Chalcedonian kingdom of Mukurra by taking a circuitous desert route to the south. Reaching Alwa, Longinus was instrumental in its conversion to Monophysitism. With this event, the period of growth and consolidation of Nile Christianity was complete; but in only six decades, new Muslim religious rivals challenged these Christian kingdoms.

THE MUSLIM RIVALS ARRIVE IN CHRISTIAN NUBIA

Following the death of the prophet Muhammad in 632 CE, his followers spread his message to Syria in 636 CE, and in 639 to 640 CE, Arab Muslims easily conquered Egypt and immediately began to move across North Africa. This new faith was quite welcome in Egypt for four reasons. First, it promised freedom to "all peoples of the book." Second, it was bent upon the conquest of Byzantium, which had been such a bothersome burden to Egyptian and Nubian Copts since the divisive Council of Nicaea way back in 325 CE. Third, it cleansed Egypt of the brief Persian occupation of 623 to 628 CE. Fourth, fractious disputes in

Christian Egypt prevented any effective local opposition. Clearly, there are more strategic lessons to be learned from this easy access to such a rich land.

Islam also spread quickly southward to Lower Nubia. By 641 CE, the forces of Amr ibn al-As reached the plain just north of Dongola, but they failed to capture the Christian capital of Mukurra. Frustrated by this barrier, these earliest Egyptian Muslims tried again in 646 CE to penetrate Nubia, but without further success. At last, in 652 CE, a famous *baqt* (treaty) was established between Nubia and Egypt under Abdallah ibn Sa'ad ibn Abi Sahr. The Melkite patriarch left Egypt at this time. In the areas of Lower Nubia under Muslim control, the Nubian populations were forced to pay an annual tribute of 360 slaves and livestock and to promise no aggression against Egypt. Muslim Egypt would provide 1,300 "kanyr" of wine to Nubia in return.

Although Christian Nubians were pressurized to accept this tributary status, there were active conflicts between Mukurra and its northern neighbor of Nobatia. Apparently, this détente seemed to be a satisfactory outcome, and, amazingly, the principles of this *baqt* were to last, more or less, for some six centuries. Under the Umayyad dynasty in Egypt (661–750 CE), a renewal of a similar *baqt* in 720 CE between the Egyptians and the Blemmyes did not fare nearly as well. Under the military threat from its northern Muslim neighbors, and strife with each other, the two Nubian Christian kingdoms of Nobatia and Mukurra were finally merged to form the kingdom of Dongola under King Merkurius (697–707 CE). It may have been at about this time that the existence of a combination of Greek, Arabic, and Coptic languages signaled the final end of Meroitic writing, to be succeeded by Old Nubian, especially for religious purposes.

The Egyptian efforts to project their power did not always result in success at this time. In about 745 CE, Cyriacus, king of Dongola, countered the Umayyads, then under Khalifa Marwan, by besieging his capital at Fustat (Old Cairo) in protest of the Muslim imprisonment of the Coptic pope. At some point in the eighth century, some Nubian Christians are believed to have constructed a small church near the Church of Ma'adi believed to have marked the place where Jesus and his parents had embarked to Upper Egypt. This building was pulled down by Ibn al-Hafez a Fatimid (Shi'ite) Khalifa. While Cyriacus failed to restore Christianity to the Egyptian state, the Umayyad dynasty collapsed in 750 CE to be replaced by the Abbasids until 870 CE. During this dynasty, the emir of Egypt corresponded with the king of Nubia. And, in 819 to 822 CE, the Christian king of Dongola (George I, 816–920 CE?), his Bishop Yoannes III, and the Beja all refused to pay *baqt* tributes to the Abbasids. Nubians and Beja also mounted joint attacks on Upper Egypt. At his death, Yoannes was entombed at the cathedral at Faras.

The degree of mutual respect, trust, or autonomy between Muslim Egypt and Christian Nubia may be seen after the coronation in 835 CE of King George I (816–920 CE) of Mukurra. In 836 CE, King George traveled safely to, and through, Cairo to Baghdad. During the independent reign of 'Amir Ahmed ibn Tulun (868–884 CE) in Egypt, the relations between the two states were such that thousands of Nubians enlisted in the Tulunid army, probably to pay a service tax. No doubt some were converted to Islam at this time and earlier, but still, the two religious states coexisted separately. During the time of the Alexandrian patriarch Gabriel I (909–920 CE), the famed "Door of Symbols" in the Virgin's Church in Wadi Natrun was constructed in 914 CE with ebony and ivory from Nubia. In 920 CE, the allied Christian King of Dongola, King Zakaria III, could begin his rule in peace. But by the mid-tenth century, some Muslims were reported as far south as Soba, the capital city of the Christian kingdom of Alwa. Was it anxiety about the Arab presence that caused Nubians to conduct raids into Upper Egypt in 951 and 956, and as far as Akhmin in 962 CE?

The ancient pattern of rivals on the Nile resumed in 969 CE, when the Fatimids came to power and Fatimid military leader al-'Umari initiated attacks on Nubia. Ironically, this may have been with some Nubian soldiers, since up to 50,000 Nubians served in Fatimid army. Coming to power at this same time, in 969 CE, King George II of Dongola is reported to have attacked Egypt. Reports written between 975 and 996 CE by the Egyptian official Ibn Selim al-Assuani noted that Alwa was a Christian city of splendid buildings and gold-endowed churches. Its economy was built from an extensive fertile land based on agriculture and livestock. The bishop of Alwa was ordained from Alexandria, and their books were in Old Nubian. Certainly, Faras in 999 CE was equally splendid in church architecture, as we see in the portrait of Bishop Petros.

A footnote to this history appears with the marble tray now found in the Cave Church at Wadi Natrun. This stone was presumably a gift brought by Nubian monks under the reign of King George IV of Nubia (1106–1158 CE), who had been enthroned in 1130 CE. A small Christian kingdom of Dotawo (or Daw) is also reported at this period (in the 1140s).

In 1171 CE, the Ayyubid Dynasty (1171–1250 CE) led by Sultan Saladin replaced the Fatimids. One of his first tasks was to force Nubians to withdraw to Upper Egypt and Lower Nubia, then under Christian King George IV. Playing upon the hope of a tactical Christian alliance, the European Crusaders sought to link with Nubian Christians in Upper Egypt in 1163 CE. This Nubian-Crusader alliance against Ayyubids actually resulted in clashes in Cairo and Delta towns in 1172, but with subsequent counterattacks by Ayyubid military leader Turanshah in Nubia. In 1173 CE, Turanshah attacked Saint Simeon's monastery in Aswan; its Coptic bishop and priests were sold into the slave market. He also sacked the church at Qasr Ibrim at about the same time. This was also a period of Egyptian Coptic flight to Nubia to escape this turmoil; Jerusalem had fallen to Saladin during the contemporary crusades. In 1204, various Nubian and Crusader leaders met in Constantinople, but finally failed in their plans to topple the Ayyubids; in 1235, the last recorded priest was sent from Alexandria to Nubia.

Christian Nubia and Islamic Egypt had fought to a standoff with the Fatimids and Ayyubids, but a different fate was in store for them during Mamluke rule. Under the Bahri Mamlukes (1250–1382 CE), especially during the reign of Sultan Al-Zahir Baybars (1260–1277 CE), Nubians were again forced to pay *baqt* tribute. Documents from 1268 CE show such tribute reluctantly paid by Dongola King Dawud. King Dawud II (?) showed his opposition with raids organized against the Mamlukes in Aswan in 1275 CE. In 1276 CE, the Mamlukes, under Shekanda (?), organized a punitive attack that captured King Dawud and sacked Dongola. Its citizens were forced to convert to Islam. Resistance continued, so in 1289 CE, the Mamlukes waged still another major attack upon Dongola.

The Nubian king Kudanbes may have first come to power in 1309, but in the first decades of the fourteenth century, skirmishes continued. In 1317 CE, the first mosque was built at Dongola in a former church. 'Abdullah Barshambu was installed as its first Muslim king to replace Kudanbes, who had returned to serve as the last king of Dongola in 1323. *Baqt* payments to the Mamlukes were reestablished under Al-'Amir Abu 'Abdallah in 1331. With these events, the formal presence of Christianity in Nubia was at an end, although Christian symbols and some communities of believers lingered on in Nubia. There is some record in the mid-fourteenth century of the king intervening on behalf of Pope Mark IV, who had been jailed by Mamluke king Saleh II. Even as late as 1372, the Bishop of Faras was officially consecrated by the Alexandrian patriarch, and in 1438 to 1439, the Synod of Florence was held to try to resolve the differences among Rome, Alexandria, and Ethiopia. It too failed.

NUBIAN CHRISTIANITY IN DECLINE

When the Holy Roman Empire of the East finally fell to Islam in 1453, it was only a matter of time before Muslims would advance further in Nubia. A passing reference to Joel of Dotawo hints that some Christians were still extant in 1464. But at last, the southernmost Nubian Christian kingdom of Alwa collapsed in 1504 CE during Burji Mamluke rule in Egypt to the north. Alwa was brought to an end by the rise of the Islamic Funj Sultanates further south at Sennar. Although the Christian kingdoms had been defeated, isolated Christian communities in Nubia were still reported to have appealed for religious support from Christian Ethiopia as late as 1520. Such was the case during the visit to Ethiopia of the Portuguese missionary Francisco Alvares. Another visitor, in 1522, was the Jewish traveler David Reubeni, who visited both Soba and Sennar and later met with the pope and Spanish king with a plan to resist the Ottomans, who had only come to power in Egypt a few years before.

For much of the following two centuries, Christians in Ethiopia, backed by the Portuguese, sought to avoid Arab control of the Eastern Mediterranean, and managed to maintain a rather stable frontier between Funj and Ethiopia. A variety of religious Christian missions and contacts took place during the sixteenth and seventeenth centuries. In 1541, there was a mission to neighboring Ethiopia. In 1624, Bishop Christdoulous, an "Ethiopian" monk at the Monastery of the Forty Martyrs, died in Egypt, where he was buried. In 1647, a visit to Sennar was undertaken by the Portuguese priests Giovanni d'Aguila and Antonio da Pescopagano; the period from 1699 to 1711 saw three papal missions to Ethiopia, all of which passed through Dongola and Sennar on the way to Ethiopia.

ICONIC AND LEGITIMATING ARCHITECTURE IN CHRISTIAN AND MUSLIM NUBIA/SUDAN

A detailed treatment of this huge topic of Byzantine religious art is impossible in this present work. However, some of the basic features can highlight the long evolution of Christian architecture in Nubia. First, it is critical to recognize that, as with much of Nubian history, there are features that range from the unique to diffused and syncretic traditions. Also, there has been a very long historical evolution in art, iconography, and architecture in addition to buildings that were reused for purposes not originally intended. Moreover, many religious structures in Nubia were periodically modernized, replaced, and rebuilt. Notable thick-walled castles and monasteries were heavily fortified and garrisoned, and this single physical feature stands as mute evidence to the concerns that they had about the north. For these reasons, the study of Christian architecture in Nubia is particularly complex and sometimes controversial in interpretation, and has become a specialized field in ancient Nubian studies, like those of ceramics and textiles. Much of the same may also be said for Islamic art and architecture from the introduction of Islam to the present.

The most extant and accessible monastery of Lower Nubia that is still *in situ* is that of Saint Simeon in the western desert at Aswan. It appears to have been initiated in the fifth century CE, or even earlier if it had been a Roman border fortress for the region. This structure mostly dates to the seventh century CE and later. Some reconstruction took place in the tenth century, and it was finally abandoned in the thirteenth century for reasons that are not clear. It has huge defensive walls, corner towers for observation, and an internal water supply, as well as chapels and facilities for food production, dining, sleeping, and monastic life. Large-scale religious celebrations were held in a grand arched hall, where some original paintings still exist.

Gradually, Arab Muslim merchants and teachers settled into Sudan, where they married and became Afro-Arab Nubians. So, at the end of the medieval period, the spread of Islam and the Arabic language in Sudan was more a gradual transition and conversion than a result of conquest. Christian Nubians interacted with Egyptians Muslims for six hundred years. The three centuries between the traditional date for the fall of Alwa and the Turco-Egyptian conquest of Sudan in 1820 to 1821 are of great importance in Sudanese history. The movement of people and establishment of new institutions confirmed both the Islamization and Arabization of much of the northern Sudan or former Nubia. During these times, the major movement of Nilotic peoples into the south was undertaken, and the Azande kingdoms were firmly established. Other regional sultanates in Darfur and Kordofan were emerging within the area of modern Sudan, and ancient Nubia was terminated as a sovereign region. In Darfur, the Daju gained control over part of the area before 1200 and were followed by the Tunjur. They were succeeded in turn by the Keira dynasty, which created a sultanate controlling most of Darfur from the mid-seventeenth century until 1916.

Islam was firmly established in northern Sudan during the Funj rule of Sennar in central Sudan and the Daju, Tungur, and Keira dynasties in independent Darfur. Traveling merchants and teachers opened the region to the rest of the Islamic world. Local schools were created, and the great Islamic orders or *turuq* gained a firm foothold. Holy men and their families came to wield important influence in all areas of life. Nubians, especially Mahas in the central Sudan, were much involved in the spread of Islam as religious sages and teachers. In this way, the basic Sudanese Islamic pattern was focused on individuals in a personalized socioreligious order. The religious brotherhood joined the primary ethnic group, kin, and family as the bases for social identity.

Postmedieval experience created the foundations for modern Sudanese society. The major states of both north and south had provided more than simply a localized ethnic identity. In Nubia, the Islamization of society was confirmed, and its Arabization was far advanced. Yet Nubian culture and language persisted. Even when it was time for the Sudanese to resist and overthrow the hated Turco-Egyptians, it was a Nubian boatman, the prophet Mohammed Ahmed al-Mahdi, who was the leader of this successful anticolonial and Islamist revival movement.

From this long historical survey, there are a core set of three intersecting strategic objectives: (1) preservation of territory from aggression, (2) mutual benefit in trade relations, and (3) securing access to human and natural resources. This pattern is deeply woven into Sudanese history and accounts for the relatively long and stable states and empires that prevailed. However, in the modern postcolonial nation-state of Sudan, these earlier traditional objectives are almost all no longer attainable or are seriously subordinated to a new set of modern strategic interests: (1) regime security, sometimes linked to territorial security, (2) economic benefit to core elites residing—ever more stratified—in the central urban areas, and (3) neglect of the periphery and marginalization to the point that the security of natural resources is put in jeopardy by severe structural instability and repeated revolts in insurgencies.

STRATEGIC CONCERNS IN THE TURCO-EGYPTIAN COLONIAL PERIOD

The Imperial Age of Ottoman Conquest can be dated to 1517 with Sultan Selim I, but it was not until 1821 that the Khedive Muhammad 'Ali turned his attention and interests to the south to acquire slaves for sale, slaves for domestic service, and especially conscripts to his army. He made no effort to conceal that the financing of this mission would be by force to acquire these slaves, gold, ivory, livestock, and whatever other natural and human resources would come into his hands by this military invasion. Promptly, Sudanese expressed their opposition with the famed attack on Turkish military leadership including Isma'il Pasha, the son of the Khedive, by Mek Nimr at the town of Shendi. Mek Nimr escaped to Ethiopia, but the Turks, led by the Daftardar, unleashed a punitive campaign through the central Sudan. Since the Turkish conquest objectives were clear, their first strategic task was to occupy and dominate the former Funj state at Sennar, which also gave control of the Blue Nile access to the Ethio-Sudan borderlands for slaves and gold. Promptly, their interest in oppressive taxes, slaves, and ivory turned further south, and White Nile access was also needed, so they began to construct their permanent colonial capital at Khartoum, where the two Niles converge. Their strategic security was built with a river barrier to the west, north, and east, and a gated and thick mud brick wall to the south side of the administrative and garrison town. In general, this served them well for six decades. Developing little in Sudan and leaving remarkably small traces in Sudanese history, the Turco-Egyptian gained as much wealth as they could for their ambitious "modernizing" projects in Egypt, from urban architecture to their U.S.-trained military and for the major development of the ambitious reopening of the Suez Canal.

MAHDISM HAS ITS OWN IDEAS

It almost looked like they could achieve all of this, when a Nubian ascetic-turned-divinely-guided-prophet grew tired of their abuse, done in the name of Islam, and determined to stage a small act of resistance at Abba Island on the White Nile in 1883. Thinking this would be easily put down, the Turco-Egyptians did not send adequate forces and instead returned to Khartoum in defeat. Wanting to check this alarming development, the British mercenary General William Hicks was sent back in pursuit to track down this self-styled Mahdi and his Ansar followers into the scrub forest lands of Kordofan. At the battle of Sheikan, the Turco-Egyptians were to face a second defeat that brought substantial arms into the Mahdist *jihad* as well as a great deal of political capital for the insurgent forces, which were soon organizing a strangulation siege on the provincial capital of al-Obeid in Kordofan. With promises of loot and treasure, Ansar forces grew as the Turco-Egyptians shrank back and lost the strategic initiative at this tipping point. Steadily, the insurgency expanded and the ever more desperate Turco-Egyptians were increasingly trapped in their garrison town of Khartoum, only escaping for foraging missions to sustain the beleaguered forces and civilians. The dire situation called for a Christian messiah as well, and the

Khedive called upon already experienced General Charles Gordon to get to Khartoum to evacuate the colonial town. Instead, General Gordon hung on until it was too late, a weakness in the western river side wall appeared, and the Mahdi took the chance to assault the now-vulnerable Khartoum. Close hand fighting brought the Ansar to Gordon's place, and a spearman brought his life to a close on 25 January 1885. His head was delivered to the Mahdi across the river in Omdurman, which had become his base of military operations. An ill-conceived British relief mission reached Khartoum a few days too late. This significant anticolonial military achievement for the Sudanese is made even more significant by the fact that major European powers concurrently meeting in Berlin in 1884 to 1885 were organizing the great colonial partition of Africa—the European scramble for Africa.

IMPERIAL AGE OF BRITAIN

In the very month of the European colonial division of Africa, Gordon's head was being removed as a trophy of the Mahdist war. Clearly, the British ambitions in Sudan needed rethinking and retooling after their grave setback. A strategic imperial policy of containment was developed to maintain a toehold in Suakin on the Red Sea and to block expansionist Mahdist ambitions in Ethiopia, Egypt, and to the southern Sudan. Internal dynamics in the Mahdist state played their own role. Ironically, within six months of Gordon's death, there was also the mysterious and sudden death of the Mahdi himself. His follower, the Khalifa 'Abdullahi, a Ta'isha Baggara, did not have the same charisma as the Mahdi. Moreover, running a successful military insurgency is not the same as running an Islamic state. In other words, coming to power and staying in power are quite different things, as the Meroitic kings and queens, the Christian Nubians, and the Sennar sultans had all found out. The British containment policy, coupled with famine, military adventures, political repression, and economic mismanagement in Sudan, gradually remade the regional political terrain in the 1890s.

The stiff Sudanese resistance to the British imperial dreams of railways and corridors of control from the Cape to Cairo was in reality a temporary diversion. Little by little, the British re-officered and retrained the Egyptian military, since their own forces were spread throughout the world "where the sun never set." Steadily, too, the Egyptian railway, roads, and communications could deliver troops and material to Aswan. With Mahdist troops withdrawn from Wadi Halfa at the second cataract, the Anglo-Egyptian forces could begin to mass in that town, and the next phase of the so-called "Reconquest" could be advanced in the form of a military railway across the eastern Nubian Desert. Missing a tactical opportunity, the Mahdist Ansar were not successful in sabotaging this railway project that could deliver soldiers, material, horses, weapons, ammunition, and the important dismantled armored steamers. The history of the "River Wars" is very well-known;

essentially, infantry and cavalry units advanced to clear Mahdists from the next tactical objective of the railway and a chance to assembly the military steamers. This methodical drive by General Hubert Horatio Kitchener was met with skirmishes and notable battles at Atbara and finally at the killing fields of Karreri just north of Omdurman, where some tens of thousands of Mahdists were killed to some scores of British and hundreds of Egyptian soldiers. While the Mahdi was able to escape with some of his followers, they were finally hunted down and killed where they prayed; their bodies were buried in unmarked graves. The Mahdist state was over, and the way was open for the joint condominium conquest of Sudan by Egyptians and English. Though these two flags were flying in reclaimed Khartoum, it was only British Governors-General who ruled in Sudan with British officers, colonial officials, and Egyptian regular troops. The Egyptian and English crowns still wanted revenge for Gordon's death and their defeat in 1885, but their major aspirations were to control the Nile waters and develop Sudan's great agricultural potential, especially for high-quality cotton for the textile industries in Britain.

The same military railway that brought troops southward to Sudan was now returning northbound with hundreds of thousands of bales of cotton. A remarkably small number of British district officers applied the Lord Lugard strategy of indirect colonial rule in northern Sudan; as long as resistance was curbed and production was up, they had rather little cultural impact. But in two areas—railways, posts, and telegraphs, and creating a civil service infrastructure—they laid the future seeds of their own destruction. From these roots was born the strongly nationalist trade union movement as well as the intellectual forces of the Graduates Congress. As before, lessons from this colonial era can certainly be drawn that have parallel application for today.

STRATEGIC CONCERNS IN THE POSTCOLONIAL AND CONTEMPORARY PERIOD

Other chapters in this book will break down Sudan's strategic concerns in much greater detail, but the struggle to maintain territorial integrity has clearly been the preoccupation of domestic security, with civil wars consuming huge resources and the majority of the independence period. While there have certainly been tensions with some neighbors and the use of proxy insurgencies, there have been no sustained interstate conflicts. Foreign relations of modern Sudan have also engaged it politically and militarily with the wider Middle East conflicts, including the Arab-Israeli conflicts, with Iraq, and even with al-Qa'eda, but these have all been essentially reeled back in. Even the Cold War period involved extreme fluctuations, from being ardently pro-West to being supporters of the Soviet Union. Now, Sudan is much engaged with the Peoples' Republic of China as well as with other Asian powers. Just as this long historical survey has shown that the principle ancient concern was with defense of the state, Sudan likewise got caught up in the religious and ideological debates of the ancient, medieval Christian, and Muslim worlds. Sudan also took sides on various issues, but in general, it retreated from those concerns once they were shown to be unproductive politically or militarily. Even the postcolonial military governments have kept (Arabized) Nubians at the centers of power, to the great chagrin of those at the periphery. And while, happily, the trade in slaves, ivory, and gold has been replaced by oil and the value of the Nile waters, a new "gold rush" is presently underway in Sudan. The strategic depth, large size, and abundant human and natural resources of Sudan have from ancient times to the present kept it relatively immunized from external sanctions. Aside from Egyptian colonialism in the New Kingdom, foreign military interventions (of the Turks and British) into Sudan lasted only decades and not centuries. Similarly, Sudan's abilities to have long-term external projections of its power are also limited.

As savants have long noted: *Plus ça change, plus c'est la même chose!*

NOTE

Many parts of this chapter are drawn from my two-volume history of Sudan: *Historical Dictionary of Ancient and Medieval Nubia* and *Historical Dictionary of the Sudan* (London and Lanham, Maryland: Scarecrow Press, 2002). Reprinted with permission.

CHAPTER 2

The South

The long cultural and political history of southern Sudan ("the South") is extremely complex for a variety of reasons, including inherent ethnographic diversity, major disruptions and dispersals, slave raids and war, differing religions, migrations, and refugee situations, as well as complex interactions with neighboring peoples. On top of this, there are cyclical patterns of seasonal transhumance in rotating searches for grazing areas. This complexity can be seen in the heterogeneous record in glottochronology and lexicostatistics, which is coupled with a relatively weak record in ethnoarchaeology that could help to resolve some key questions of Southern chronology and ethnogenesis in the precontact period.

Also key to understanding the South on its own terms or in relation to other regions, especially northern Sudan, is its extreme isolation and marginality. Climatological differentiation and the presence of malaria and the *tse-tse* fly, as well as the vast barrier swamp, the Sudd, also added to the relative isolation of the South. All together, these features meant that its positive exposure to the wider world was delayed and that traditional beliefs and practices were remarkably persistent. However, among the many Southern cultures, there are also important distinctions to be made. Two Southern societies, the Shilluk and Azande, reached a level of centralized power that could be called a kingdom of small state. This political organization either protected them from predations of slave raiders or engaged them in this trading and raiding practice. Some areas in the South, such as Dar Fertit and the Ingessana hills, were known by outsiders simply as slave resource areas, overlooking the fact that these hapless victims had their own strategic interests of preserving their families, dreams, and local economies.

The only way this could be dismissed was by systematic beliefs and practices of racism, which were especially intense when directed against Southerners in order to subject them to extremely harsh and oppressive treatment.

The most numerous single group in the South is the Dinka, concentrated in Bahr al-Ghazal, followed by the Nuer of Upper Nile and the Bari in Equatoria. Practices of raiding for women, children, and cattle caused tensions among these people, but also created many connections. The modern presence of political and economic resources, especially oil, is sometimes viewed with a Southern lens, seeing traditional rivalries for traditional resources. The relationship with the North is perhaps even more complex, as many Northerners have genetic links to the South through their maternal lines. While this link is easy to verify by genetics and phenotypes, the cultural fact is one of deep denial, and many Northerners are fundamentally linked to the South while simultaneously subjecting its population to violence and exploitation. While this term is not typically used in Sudan, one could speak of a "creolization" of the entire society in this respect.

As centuries, if not millennia, of this relationship continued, the enmity, stereotypes, and isolation became deeply institutionalized. But in a very contradictory way, the more the South was isolated, the more it was victimized and, thus, the more it became connected to the North. This *yin-yang* relationship is why so many reduce the North-South issues in Sudan to simple polarities when the more essential fact is that the regions are irrevocably and tightly connected. The present debates about regional autonomy and independence can only be understood within this fundamental tension. Indeed, it is with some considerable irony that the strategic goal of the Anya-Nya rebel movement (1955–1972) was total independence from the North, and it achieved regional autonomy, while the Sudan Peoples' Liberation Army (1983–2005) had the objective of secular and democratic unity of Sudan, and a referendum is now on the table for 2011 that could separate the country into two nations, one of which is ruled by principles of Islamic law.

BIRTHPLACE OF CONFLICTS

With the above relations kept in mind as a primordial cause of the modern conflicts in southern Sudan, there are many other factors in its history of isolation and exploitation, especially the savage form of slavery that persisted for millennia; all ancient and medieval states in Nubia (northern Sudan) were regular users and transporters of slaves. This history can be glossed by emphasizing the heroic historical achievements of Kerma or New Kingdom Egyptians, or Napatans, Meroites, Christian kings, or Muslim sultans, but nonetheless, this all sits very painfully in the consciousness of Southerners, who understandably want to bring such relations to a total conclusion and even receive some compensation for these ancient wounds. How many tens of thousands of Southern women and children went through Sennar, Khartoum, and Suakin along the "forty-days road" will never be known, and how many tens of thousands of men lost their lives in trying to protect their families will equally be lost to history, except in the Southern genes that flow strongly through northern Sudan. With slavery being a virtually universal experience for state-level societies, particularly imperial ones, there are few people globally who have not been affected in one way or another.

During the centuries of the Sultanates of Darfur and of the Funj of Sennar, regular slave raids went south to acquire slaves for export, domestic labor, and concubines. The historical records are adequate to detail some measures of the endless numbers of Southerners who went north, never to return home. The Turco-Egyptians (1821–1885) put an end to the Sennar Sultans in 1821, but by no means did they end slavery. After facing violent challenges to their rule, the Turco-Egyptians gradually expanded their pursuit of slaves, initially in the borderlands, and by 1839, they probed and penetrated the South to acquire ivory and slaves from that region, even though the barriers of climate and distance still prevented them from reaching the source of the White Nile at the time. The Turco-Egyptians managed to occupy and manipulate Darfur for their owns ends, but if anything slavery probably increased during the Turkiya, with their heavy desire for slaves in the royal courts as servants, concubines, and entertainers, and great demand for slaves in their armed forces and Sudanese (Nubian) gold mines, as seen in the repeated *razia* (slave raids) to the south. So, even this major modern political transformation of Sudan left slavery solidly intact and Southerners much victimized. Since most Sudanese suffered under burdensome Turco-Egyptian taxes and punitive missions here and there, there was a period during the Mahdiya (1883–1898) when the Southern and Northern Sudanese struggled together to expel the Turks, led at the end, ironically, by a crusading Scot, General Charles "Chinese" Gordon, who made some efforts to curb slavery. However, this probably inflamed as much Northern opposition to his rule as it did to free Southern Sudanese from slavery.

Because of the political and military isolation of Mahdist Sudan, the export business of slaves declined during that time, but Mahdist *jihadist* attitudes of racio-religious supremacy continued slavery but on a smaller scale. As the Mahdist state withered away under Khalifa 'Abdullahi because of his territorial overreach, famine, mismanagement, and Western policies of imperial containment, all of Sudan suffered again from dislocation, famine, death, and destruction, with a massive net loss of population. Mahdist forces effectively controlled parts of the riverine south in the 1880s and early 1890s, but their roots were never deep. In the late 1890s, the suffering was perhaps greater in the North, and with Northerners so distracted, this was a brief period where Southerners were left more to their own regions and devices. Ultimately, it did not matter; the British and their mechanized military forces crossed the desert by military railway and armed river boats, and steadily advanced into Sudan to execute two sons of the Mahdi and shoot down the Khalifa. That era was over.

COLONIAL POLICIES AND PRACTICES

Once the Mahdiya was violently deposed by Anglo-Egyptian military forces invading Sudan in 1897–1898, there was another opportunity to change policies and practices regarding the South. In some important ways, things changed, and in some other important ways, things stayed the same. Needing moral legitimacy to create a "civilizing" mission for the colonizing Anglo-Egyptian condominium land grab, the British launched an antislavery campaign, which certainly weakened this very old Sudanese institution. They deserve praise for this pioneering move. At the same time, the incessant slave raids that were required to support slavery meant disruption and potential challenges to their authority. This also had to be stopped. Also, the British wanted colonial taxes that unpaid slaves could not provide, and they needed labor for their massive agricultural schemes in the South and near North, such as the Gezira and Azande schemes. So, one leg of the colonial authority took a strong step in the right direction, while the other leg marched to keep the restive South under colonial management by sending "district officers" and anthropologists to the region to conduct cultural and military intelligence, and to try to implement the system of "indirect rule" that British Lord Lugard had successfully developed for the city-states in northern Nigeria. Unfortunately, the majority acephalous or decentralized peoples in the South could not be so easily ruled and regulated, so countless punitive expeditions were mustered against extensive anticolonial resistance to keep these colonized people under British control.

In due course, the British advanced from their commissioners' rest houses, local jails, and militias, and included mission schools as part of their plan to administer the South, while also advancing elsewhere in Sudan, such as Sir Hubert Huddleston's campaign in which he assassinated Sultan 'Ali Dinar of Darfur in 1916 and annexed that formerly independent territory. By 1918, Sunday, rather than the Islamic Friday, was the official day of rest in the South, as missionaries brought Southerners under Christian influences and simultaneously blocked the spread of Islam to the South as part of a global strategic objective of Islamic containment, particularly fearing that Muslims would rise up against Western expansion. This "thin-entering wedge" into Southern Sudanese colonial policy to isolate the South from the North in the well-known practice of "divide and conquer" appeared to be functioning fairly well when, in 1924, the British received a major shock. The first part of this blow was the assassination in Cairo of Sir O. F. M. Lee Stack (1868–1924). Stack was appointed military Governor General of Sudan in 1917, and he was in office during the Egyptian revolt of 1919, just two years after the Russian revolution.

The augmented cause of colonial panic in 1924 was that the White Flag Society (League), led by Ubayd Haj al-Amin, 'Ali 'Abd al-Latif, and 'Abd al-Fadil al-Maz, moved into a revolt of solidarity with the Egyptians. The last two leaders were Southern converts to Islam who represented what the British most feared: symbolic North-South unity aimed against them. In 1921, 'Abd al-Latif formed the United Tribes Society, and he was arrested and imprisoned in 1922. He went on to form the White Flag Society in 1924, which promptly held an anticolonial demonstration in Khartoum in June that caused him to be arrested again quickly (Collins and Tignor 1967, 125). Tensions mounted, and in August, the military school cadets in Khartoum also joined the growing chorus of protesters, along with a group of Egyptian workers stationed in the Sudanese railway town of Atbara. When Sir Stack was killed, this launched the heroic revolt of two platoons of the 11th Sudanese Battalion, which sought tactical unity with Egyptian forces in Sudan with the strategic objective of removing colonialism from the Nile Valley. While the revolt might have not have been adequately planned and while the Egyptians never joined the Sudanese in Khartoum, they did revolt in Atbara, and it is clear that the revolt along the Nile in Khartoum was finally put down by the same Sir Hubert Huddleston.

Needless to say, this was an anxious region in anxious times, and Egyptian troops were soon substantively removed from Sudan. For the South, the now very nervous British also introduced a more formal statement of the plan that had already been in evolution, namely the 1930 Closed Districts Ordinance. This official proclamation sought to seal hermetically the South from the North in all possible ways—culture, language, dress, trade, and religion. If one sought the "smoking gun" of divide-and-rule legislation, this was it. Despite the arbitrary colonial fiction that Sudan really was a naturally political formation of the Nile Valley, the Closed Districts Ordinance artificially dismantled this fiction. The 180-degree turnabout from national unity to national separation is historical evidence that the British were running out of administrative options.

Essentially, the colonial administration of "indirect rule" adopted by Lord Lugard from its "successful" application in northern Nigeria could be applied in Northern Sudan with various types of centralized polities, but in the South, the "hands-off" indirect rule for the acephalous people meant barely any control at all. Even when they expanded the provisions in 1940 to eliminate all Arabs in the South and all proselytizing of Islam in the South, they were essentially running upstream not only in geographical terms, but also against historical trends. By 1943, victorious but severely damaged from World War II, the British took a fresh look at their colonial administration of Sudan by created an Advisory Council of the Northern Sudan (essentially creating indirect rule through lineage and ethnic leaders), and in 1946, they reversed the Closed Districts policy for the South, where they *never* had a parallel Advisory Council.

The British confusion about which colonial policy to pursue was matched by the 1947 Juba conference that officially determined that there would be a united Sudan rather than have those regions joined with East Africa, to which they were more akin culturally, linguistically, and in other terms. Since Southerners were barely consulted and their views were essentially dismissed, the Juba conference is typically considered, by Southerners, as a betrayal of their interests. Such suspicious Southern views were maintained in the 1951 constitutional commission, which had one Southern representative. By 1952, the British realized that their colonial mission in Sudan was increasingly not worth it, and a proposal for self-government was put forth. However, with steady frustrations and deepening fear of Northern domination, the Southern elite created the Southern Party in 1953, which managed to win twelve of twenty-two Southern seats in the elections for the House of Representatives; Sudan was moving on toward independence according to the Anglo-Egyptian Agreement of 1953. In 1954, this party was renamed the Liberal Party.

In the model of gradual transition from colonial to independent nation, the British also advanced in 1954 with the "Sudanization" of the armed forces. But Southerners did not find themselves in top leadership positions, despite the fact that there was still hope about building a new and integrated nation, especially in the far South in the Equatoria province, which was rich in agricultural products and more closely linked, culturally and economically, to East Africa than to Northern Sudan. Close to the border and east-southeast of Juba, in Torit, the provincial capital of Equatoria, the fears and hopes reached a critical level of tension; on 18 August 1955, the Equatorian Corps of the Sudan Defense Force mutinied at Torit, with many Northern merchants and Southern killed. Thus, on the eve of independence, on 1 January 1956, the South was already in a revolt that presaged four decades of war to come.

THE SOUTH IN THE POSTCOLONIAL PERIOD

The political temperature in the North was also rising with the second Arab-Israeli clash over Egypt's nationalizing of the Suez Canal on 26 July 1956; with intense Arab (secular) nationalism along with broad enthusiasm about the end of colonial rule, the last thing the British wanted was an internal revolt. This was sometimes projected in racist terms and as a plot of the West and Israel against the struggling Arab world. This was not a theoretical concern when Britain, France, and Israel invaded Egypt and only American intervention could restrain them on 29 October 1956. In this context, the Torit revolt was considered to be a marginal, short-term problem that could be "resolved" with a military "solution." Moreover, the first weak, compromise government of Prime Minister Isma'il al-Azhari and the Ashigga Party lasted only seven months. The struggles between the Khatmiya and Umma turned to dominate (and divide) the Northern political landscape as 'Abdallah Khalil became the new prime minister. The new Sudanese government took over the mission schools in the South in 1957 and began a long and steady process of Arabization and Islamization that found, by 1960, Sunday replaced in the South by Friday as the official religious day of rest.

With Southern fears increasingly realized and Northern politics being diverted, the South was neglected and left to fester, with the main issues still unresolved. Southern leaders determined that the situation was hopeless, and a struggle for secession from Arab "colonialism" was their only recourse. In 1963, the Sudan African National Union (SANU) spun off the Anya-Nya (I) to proceed on a military "solution" themselves. Infighting among Southerners and Northerners slowed their progress, with a popular, massive revolt over Southern policies in October 1964 and a failed Round Table Conference in 1965 to address the "Southern problem," followed by the assassination of SANU leader and Parliamentarian William Deng in 1968 after his frustrated participation in the Round Table Conference. By 1969, the Anya-Nya (I) leader Joseph Lagu was under effective control of the renamed Southern Sudan Liberation Movement (SSLM).

In this same year, amid the state of confusion in the North, a military coup was launched on 25 May that brought Ga'afar Nimieri to power with the important backing of the Sudanese Communist Party (SCP). He realized that the "Southern problem" was destroying national unity and expending scarce national resources; it had to be solved. The first step was to create a Ministry for Southern Affairs headed by a Southerner, Joseph Garang, and the second step was to proclaim the 9 June 1969 declaration of regional autonomy. At last a political solution seemed to be at hand, but there were some important "bumps" in the road, with the Abba Island and Wad Nubawi revolts against Nimieri in March 1970, which he saw as a test of his authority and which were put down violently. The death of Egyptian leader Gamal 'Abd al-Nasser on 28 September left the world of Arab nationalism in a state of confusion. Yet the socialist program of Nimieri advanced with bank nationalization in May and the effort to unite with Egypt and Libya in November 1970, and the first steps to create the single ruling party Sudan Socialist Union (SSU) in May 1971. A significant challenge to Nimieri came from the traditional Northern parties as well as from the left with the July 1971 coup by Hashim al-Atta that briefly toppled Nimieri and brought about executions of many communists he believed had plotted against him. Among those executed was Minister of Southern Affairs Joseph Garang. It would have been reasonable to imagine that the nation would turn back to full-scale civil war, but a September 1971 referendum voted "yes" for Nimieri (no other options were available), and the SSU resumed its course. As 1972 began, the SSU was officially established in January with a new constitution and SSU Political Bureau, with work still to do on the South. Behind-the-scenes negotiations finally reached fruition with the March 1972 Addis Ababa Accords that brought the war to an end and integrated the Southern fighters into the Sudanese national military and other services, while also granting major autonomy in managing their own regional affairs in the South. After so much violence, failed efforts, and false starts, this was truly a heroic achievement that drew worldwide acclaim and a rich sense of optimism among Sudanese from both North and South. There were unfounded rumors that General Nimieri would be nominated for the Nobel Peace Prize. The wonderful thing about these accords, built on mutual hope, was that they worked; the tragic aspect is that they were not institutionalized and that the arbitrary rule of Nimieri that brought them into reality was also the unique reason that he brought them to failure after functioning for more than a decade.

So, for this period, a cool but functional peace prevailed; the war was over, but military rule in Sudan left little room for broad debate among traditional parties and political negotiation among contesting forces mostly suppressed. The 6 October 1973 Yom Kippur war reminded all that the conflict between Egypt and Israel was not resolved, while Sudan, still under Nimieri's rule, sought to solidify relations with Egypt and Libya. Essentially, this was a second Nimieri, after his socialist first start was terminated after the 1971 coup brought that epoch to a close. His next incarnation was as a "capitalist" and Arab nationalist, but this too was brought to a sudden end when Libyans were charged with trying to overthrow Nimieri in May 1974, and especially when Libyan military forces attacked Khartoum in 1976. Closer ties to the United States and with Saudi Arabia were advanced, along with military pacts and economic development schemes. By February 1979, there was a new turning point in the Nimieri administration, with an attempt for national reconciliation that brought Sadiq al-Mahdi (from the Umma Party) and the Muslim Brothers into the government in order to broaden his political bases. Now-"Islamist" Nimieri slid into his third phase, his elusive quest for legitimacy in the North that took him to "Islamism" and "Arabism." Cynics noted that "Imam" Nimieri had exhausted his other political alternatives and wanted mainly to instill a repressive regime to quell his now many opponents. He turned to Islam, which had not previously been close to his personal political philosophy. Southern perceptions of this move rested on serious concerns about "backsliding" on political autonomy and fears of a return to Islamization that would challenge the secular and Christian leaders of the South. The formation of a committee to conform Sudanese secular law and Shari'a (Islamic) law added substantially to these worries. A short-lived mutiny at the Juba Airport was indicative of rising tensions.

When Nimieri dissolved the Regional Assembly in 1980 to try to regain decentralized political power at the center in Khartoum, this was "crossing the Rubicon" from the perspective of many skeptical Southerners. When more promising discoveries of oil in the South were also made in 1980, the Northern elites began a series of gerrymandering of the borders that, in principle, meant the "North" went further south. Needless to say, this only deepened the suspicions that Southerners already broadly held. In this context, Southern leaders also regrouped to form the Anya-Nya II, clearly named for the parent organization, Anya-Nya, that represented Southern interests at the Addis Ababa meeting— interests that were steadily unraveling by this time. The original goal had been separation, and the present objective was the same. The Southern perception was that any serious engagement to build national unity would simply not be accepted by Northerners. They concluded that it was simply hopeless, and the Arab-Islamic North never abandoned racial stereotyping and their Islamic mission for the South. Whether by democracy or military coups, the possibility that a Southern non-Muslim could rise to leadership of Sudan proved to be impossible. As if to rub salt in these political wounds, in 1982, the Nimieri government appointed a Muslim Brother as the Vice Chancellor of Juba University. This exiled university, ironically, had long been based in Khartoum, but there were Southern aspirations to return it to the South and to have it fulfill the dream of secular, modern education. A Muslim Brother as the appointed head of Juba University was seen as brazenly provocative.

This watershed year of 1983 finally brought Shari'a from its calm and widely accepted past of personal status law into full state power, complete with the harsh *hudud* penalties that Nimieri introduced and did not hesitate to apply; hands and feet were amputated, and lashings were applied to Muslims and non-Muslims alike. These "September Laws" became the last tattered banner of the Nimieri regime. One could argue that Nimieri's outright abrogation of the Addis Ababa Accords in 1983 was just an honest statement of the fact that these dreams had completely deteriorated. The few voices of Northern sentiment to bring them back could not be heard in the context of the lack of consultative democracy.

By the time of mutiny at Bor in 1983, the situation was very much out of control. It might be symbolic that while the Torit revolt in 1955 was just over the Uganda border, the Bor revolt was well downstream (north of Juba), on the main river route to the North. This was not to be a marginal revolt at all, but was to aim at the heart of North-South relations for years to come. One Southern officer named John Garang was back from American military training as well as a Ph.D. in economics. He gained his elevated position as part of the integration of forces that descended from the Addis Ababa Accords. He was intelligent and trustworthy; what better assignment than to send him to Bor to crush the revolt by any means required?

Instead, in the turbulent world of Sudanese politics, Garang went south to form the Sudan Popular Liberation Army/Movement (SPLA/SPLM). He did essentially stop the Anya-Nya II by swinging its secessionist objectives around his progressive program of liberating all of Sudan in a movement of secular democracy, regional autonomy, national unity, and mutual respect for regional differences. Easily said, but decades would pass before this agenda was to be negotiated. Moreover, the twists and turns of the Nimieri regime were also about to run out; he had started as a socialist, tried out Arab capitalism, and turned to extreme Islamism that antagonized not only Southerners but also Northern democrats.

As his final assault on secular Sudan, "Imam" Nimieri ordered the execution of Mahmoud Mohammad Taha, the seventy-three-year-old leader of the fresh and imaginative Republican Brother movement. As the "Gandhi of Sudan," Taha had stellar intellectual and historical credentials for his progressive *Second Message of Islam*. Needless to say, he was a strong and steadfast opponent of Nimieri's September Laws. He and seventy followers were arrested to try to clamp down on the movement that questioned Nimieri's legitimacy. To intimidate them further, Taha and several of his closest Republican associates were sentenced to death for "apostasy" after being "tried" by Nimieri. If they would only recant their "mistaken beliefs," they would be pardoned, said Nimieri. Under this extreme pressure, the followers understandably bent to Nimieri's dictates, but on 18 January 1985, Taha was hanged at Kober prison, dying for his beliefs. This extreme punishment for personal beliefs was painfully unsettling to democratic and secular Northerners and Southerners alike. This last major act of Nimieri soon became the last nail in the coffin for his own political career.

In a popular revolt reminiscent of the 1964 revolution, President Ga'afar Mohamed Nimieri was toppled, mostly by broad sentiment and demonstrations in 6 April 1985, but also by the military move of General Sawar ad-Dhahab, who promised democratic elections in a year. These were delightful, optimistic, and turbulent times; the SPLA calculated that the two-year war was over and that democracy would prevail to address the fundamental issue of regional autonomy and the creation of a secular state. This political item was at the top of the SPLA's "to-do" list, even if it required some patience for a year of custodial military transition back to democracy. Certainly, they hoped and thought, the next promised democratic regime would withdraw these Islamist measures. Meanwhile, in May 1985, the National Islamic Front (NIF) was formed as the Sudanese descendant of the Muslim Brotherhood in Egypt by the wily Hassan al-Turabi, survivor from the Nimieri regime and instigator of the Islamic law measures in the first place. His tour through Sudanese political life was far from over. The excited atmosphere was spurred on by the March 1986 Koka Dam meetings in Ethiopia between the SPLA and several Northern parties, excluding the Democratic Unionist Party (DUP) and the NIF. While lacking teeth, their agreement set a reasoned and fair charter for peace in Sudan. The 1986 formation of the Inter-Governmental Agency for Drought and Development (IGADD) provided another open forum to discuss the serious issues that had hobbled Sudan for so many years. Many looked toward IGADD as the neutral political playing field in which damaged trust could be rebuilt.

For about a year, this all seemed possible, even when ad-Dhahab stepped down and elections took place in April. Elections were suspended in thirty-seven

Southern electoral constituencies for reasons of "security." So, this truncated democracy brought back the "old guard" in May 1986 from the Umma Party as the new prime minister, in the form of Sadiq al-Mahdi. This Western-educated democrat would certainly cure the problems of Sudan, it was thought. Yet this was only a possibility, not a probability. Al-Mahdi struggled within his own party for legitimacy, and bickering among the traditional political parties paralyzed him. He could take none of the required initiatives; not least of all, he could not quite find the political will to suspend the *Shari'a hadud* measures of Islamic law that so annoyed many Northerners, provoked Southerners, and brought out voices of protest from human-rights organizations around the world. This transformational moment was slipping away.

As if the bitter distrust needed any further nudge, at the ad-Da'ien railway in southern Darfur in March 1987, a group of Rizeigat Baggara militias (later to be known as the *janjaweed*) provocatively attacked Southern civilians and killed some thousand people, according to reports by human-rights workers. Despite this horrible setback, former U.S. president Jimmy Carter struggled to blow life back into the IGADD talks (now named, more simply, "IGAD"). Amazingly, there was still hope, especially when the SPLA endorsed the Koka Dam Agreement, signing an accord with the Anya-Nya II and with the southern Union of Sudan African Parties (USAP) while fresh from military victories on the battle field.

The new NIF was becoming nervous, impatient, and fearful that it would be isolated in this whirlwind, and changed course in May 1988 to join the coalition DUP and Umma government to play its cards and protect its interest in preserving a measure of the Shari'a law that was emblematic of its Islamic image and objectives. Under these conditions, with the North politically divided and the Southern insurgency carrying on, the Khartoum government was almost literally hamstrung. It could not go forward with the pressing issues, and the baggage of the past was dragging it ever downward. Most major parties, except for the NIF, agreed on a seven-point peace program in 1989. The SPLA insisted simply on 1 June that Shari'a should be withdrawn, and they would be ready to return to peaceful engagement with the North. The "tipping point" toward a progressive and democratic society seemed to be virtually at hand. Under similar conditions to those of the 1958 Abboud coup, the 1969 Nimieri coup, and the 1985 Ad-Dhahab coup, the situation was teetering into a crisis of gross indecision and paralysis, with the unresolved war in the South and confusion in the North again being the common and persistent features.

Instead of realizing these hopes, the Islamist factions in Sudan panicked and feared a loss of their mission. As much as many thought, wished, and believed that a new Sudan was about to be born, on 30 June 1989, another coup took place, led by Hassan Omer al-Beshir, an army general with long military experience in the South. The indecisive but democratic regime of Sadiq al-Mahdi was abruptly terminated. At first, it looked like "just another Sudanese coup," when all political parties were abolished and solutions about the South were aired. But when "ghost house" detention centers, arbitrary arrests, and executions began, it was clear that it was a different situation. Then, when Islamist Hassan al-Turabi came out of Kober prison and into the center of the political arena as the "king-maker," it was increasingly clear that there was a totally new agenda in the Sudanese government. Briefly, al-Beshir flirted with the ideas of separation and federalism, but very soon they devolved to a return to war, with former U.S. president Carter doing his best to resume IGAD and negotiations. The moment of building a new Sudan was lost. A reported massacre of some six hundred Shilluk at al-Jabalein in 1989 brought the short political honeymoon to a braking halt. In addition, the overthrow of the Ethiopian government of Mengistu Haile Marium in 1991 meant a serious blow to the SPLA, which had received great support from Addis Ababa. Sensing this weakness, the Southern Sudan Independence Movement (SSIM), encouraged by Khartoum, began its own civil war against the SPLA by 1991. Opti-mism for democratic secularism had been turned on its head; more violence and the Islamist agenda was on the rapid rise. A full-scale *jihad* was declared against the South and its rebellious "infidels" by 1992, with thousands of conscripted "martyrs" sent on this one-way mission.

To be shockingly clear about this new direction, a "guest" from Saudi Arabia was welcomed in Khartoum to begin many ambitious construction, develop-ment, and banking enterprises. This same "guest" was also committed to a sweeping new global Islamic agenda. Enter, in 1990, Osama bin Laden and his al-Qa'eda organization. Enter, as well, the blind Egyptian Sheikh Omer 'Abd al-Rahman, his *Jama'a al-Islamiya*, and underground groups from the Maghreb to the Mashraq and from west to east in the Arab world, people and groups who felt comforted by the political atmosphere in Khartoum and especially by its chief ideologue, al-Turabi, and his Egyptian comrade, Dr. Ayman al-Zawahiri, who had been identified as a conspirator in the assassination of President Sadat in Egypt in 1981.

A sample of some of the more prominent events that were perhaps conceived in Khartoum are the first World Trade Center bombing and the attempts on the life of Egyptian Interior Minister Hassan al-Alfi and the Egyptian Prime Minister Atef Sidqi in 1993. Also in 1993 was the battle in Mogadishu that was immortalized in *Black Hawk Down*, with a training role possibly played by an Egyptian police offi-cer allied with Dr. Zawahiri. Then there was the attack on the Egyptian embassy in Islamabad in 1995. In 1996, President Mubarak narrowly missed assassination in Addis Ababa by killers who flew in from Khartoum. This was enough for the Sudanese to ask him to leave, but in 1997, tourists were murdered in Luxor, Egypt. In August 1998, the U.S. embassies in Kenya and Tanzania were targeted, with great loss of life. Given the advance planning typical of al-Qa'eda, most if not all of these acts of violence were apparently hatched in Khartoum, built upon an extremist version of holy war against the West and its allies. Notably, it was not the Sudanese government but their legal guests who overstayed their welcome. In 1999, Zawahari was sentenced to death in Egypt, *in absentia*, for his many acts against the state. In circumstances that are not totally clear, the U.S. ambassador in Sudan encouraged bin Laden and Ayman al-Zawahiri to leave, or perhaps bin Laden felt it was time to go, so he moved on from his attractive houses in the Ar-Riyadh section of Khartoum back to Jalalabad, Afghanistan, where al-Qa'eda was first founded. There, with his Taliban hosts, he planned the attack on the U.S. Navy destroyer *Cole* in October 2000, and the second, even more devastating, attack on the World Trade Center on 11 September 2001, now known simply as "9/11" or "September 11th."

The previous paragraph gives a brief sketch of the political life and rumors in Khartoum in the first half of the 1990s, but turning back to southern Sudan, it is not hard to imagine the sense of discouragement and the intensification of the struggle to rid Sudan of these people and to move toward a democratic, secular state. Generally, Southern people accepted Islam; there were certainly Southerners who were Muslim, but Muslim extremism and violence was unfathomable and tended to fulfill the worst stereotypes of Islam and brought back some of the negative experiences they had had in resisting Islamic extremism in their own land. By 1993, this bloody and volatile situation in Sudan took another aim at peace with the principle-setting Chukudum Accord that affirmed the option of separation of the South when both the National Democratic Alliance (NDA) and the SPLA signed the Asmara Declaration. But with the NDA weak and in exile, and the SPLA still in military rebellion, Khartoum could just ignore them for the time being. However, this principle of the right to national separation was now seriously on the negotiating table once again. In 1994, IGAD presented this Declaration of Principles as a positive starting place for any serious peace negotiations to begin.

Accordingly, while the literally explosive plots were being concocted by bin Laden, the "guest" of the North, Southerners, in the form of the SPLA, had by 1995 been fighting for twelve long and bloody years. The SPLA joined in 1995 with the NDA, which was composed largely of like-minded Northerners. By the following year, the NDA, SPLA, and Beja Congress from eastern Sudan met in Asmara to consolidate their position of unity, but Khartoum still refused to listen or collaborate. Yet al-Beshir and Uganda's Yoweri Museveni did agree to meet in South Africa to try to find a way ahead. By this time, post-apartheid South Africa was seeking a wider and stronger role in African affairs, and the governments of Presidents Mandela and Mbeki gave a strong support to this meeting in the spirit of African unity. Certainly, it seemed that rational and reasonable people could bring these difficult times to an end. But, Sudanese politics being what it is, a split emerged in 1997 among the Southerners, with Riak Machar's group SSIM thereby breaking away in armed revolt against the SPLA leadership. Moreover, Machar actually joined forces with the Khartoum ruling elite of

Omer al-Beshir and Hassan al-Turabi. Some estimate that more people were killed in Nuer-Dinka clashes than in many previous years of North-South fighting. While these numbers are debatable, the divisions were very real. Complicating the situation further, Paulino Matip joined the revolt against Garang and the SPLA in 1998. However, these very damaging fissures could not be sustained, and in 1999, there was finally a Nuer-Dinka peace accord that managed to patch things back together. Yet the lessons of South-South infighting were clearly in focus, and this did not include rivalries between Equatorians. A political wild card was introduced into this mix when U.S. president Bill Clinton, amid a domestic sex scandal and impeachment charges, received some questionable intelligence that a pharmaceutical factory in Khartoum North was secretly making chemical weapons. Cruise missiles were launched, resulting in one death and the destruction of this alleged facility. This momentary diversion from the "Monica Affair" was great political capital for al-Beshir, who easily mobilized anti-American sentiments not far beneath the surface.

Despite such events and twists and turns, the al-Beshir government began to realize that it was running low on political options, and their Islamist direction was in need of fundamental course correction, as it was isolating them more than bringing in useful allies. An in-house coup was launched against al-Turabi in 1999 to make this critical adjustment. Back on a more or less stable footing once again and with Southern unity refocused,Khartoum believed that its plan for dividing the South had failed and that the SPLA was regaining strength. Now the approach between Khartoum and the SPLA was to negotiate a Memorandum of Understanding (MoU), signed in 2001, that could at least get some discussion of the principles needed to have lasting peace at some point. Another optimistic sign was the 2002 signing of a regional cease-fire in the Nuba Mountains, which had seen serious combat and military action against civilians as the SPLA fought to take the war north, and the North, using its militias and regular forces with air support, fought to push the war back south. As in the African saying, "the grass is trampled, when elephants fight," in this case, the "grass" represented the misfortunes of the marginalized people in the Nuba Mountains, who suffered terribly during the previous period. More significantly, the Sudan Peace Act was signed by U.S. president George W. Bush in 2002, which sought to apply more leverage against the Sudanese government and push all parties toward peace in southern Sudan. Actually, the situation appeared to be heading in a number of optimistic directions. This was all to change in the following year, when a short-lived coalition of Darfur rebel groups, the Justice and Equality Movement (JEM) and the Sudan Liberation Army (SLA), opened a military offensive against Khartoum government military targets in Darfur. This will be covered more fully in Chapter 4, but there were direct implications for upsetting the slow but steady progress toward peace in southern Sudan. Not only was the world distracted by the high levels of violence and broken cease-fires in Darfur, a variety of world powers and organizations were, on the one hand, trying to support Khartoum and the SPLA in the move toward peace, while, on the other, simultaneously criticizing and sanctioning Khartoum for the rapidly deteriorating rebellion and counterinsurgency situation in Darfur. Sudanese politics are never simple, but they just became more complicated, with a whole new area of interconnecting and changeable conflict unfolding.

THE SOUTH AND THE CPA: A CRITICAL TURNING POINT

Amazingly, amid the very rough terrain of this evolving diplomatic, humanitarian, and tactical situation, the North-South peace accord meetings limped onward to a sort of finish line in a neighboring resort in Kenya at Naivasha through much of 2004. They were on again, then off again, old barriers were crossed and new hurdles appeared, and there were periodic news leaks that the accords were failing or, alternatively, almost ready to be signed. Perhaps with divine providence descending from the inspired but exhausted religious communities involved, the Naivasha Accords finally drew together all of the principals, and witnessing world leaders as well, on 9 January 2005. With the Darfur conflict about to conclude its second year of strife and disruption, the Naivasha Accords were signed and became more broadly known as the Comprehensive Peace Agreement (CPA). While rightly, widely, and enthusiastically heralded as a fresh start and an end to conflict, it was soon apparent that the agreement was not comprehensive in two significant areas. First, there were other factions and elements in the South aside from the sole Southern signatory, the SPLA, and likewise in the North, for the NIF had been sidelined, along with all the other traditional parties that were sometimes grouped under the NDA. Second, two very thorny issues about the Upper Nile and Abyei were left unsolved, and these were the most contentious of all in terms of oil resources and the deep intercultural Sudanese divide. At the time, the level of goodwill was so high that it was devoutly wished and then believed that these issues would somehow solve themselves in due course. So, the "comprehensiveness" of the CPA was problematic at the start, and even the Sudanese "peace" aspects certainly had their shortcomings, as grave tensions prevailed in the East, the far North was falling into serious underdevelopment (see Chapter 3), and the war in Darfur was still expanding in 2005. Just as one faces war with the resources and circumstances at hand, Sudan went to peace in a similar fashion. Bumpy and imperfect, but still, it is hoped, heading in a peaceful direction.

The first bump in the road to peace was soon to occur. It almost threw the entire process into a political roadside culvert, as had been the case before. It brought much deep distrust quickly back to the forefront. On 30 July 2005, a mere six months after the Naivasha signing, the stalwart and surviving leader of two decades of war, Dr. John Garang, was tragically killed in a helicopter crash in southern Sudan. Cynicism about "assassination by plane or car crash" was not unknown in various African states, and many Southerners jumped to that conclusion.

The burial of Sudanese vice president John Garang brought grave concern that the CPA, ending two decades of civil war, might join him in the grave. The loss of Garang's charismatic diplomacy supported this view. The vast crowds that had met Garang in Khartoum just weeks earlier on his triumphal return had mounted speculation that he could be elected president in elections mandated by the accords. With Garang's sudden death, this all came to an end, but there are reasons for cautious optimism. First, the spontaneous violence in Khartoum and other cities soon abated. Salva Kiir Mayardit was appointed as Garang's successor, making him both head of the SPLM and technically vice president of all of Sudan (in the Government of National Unity [GNU]), as Garang had been for three weeks. Kiir was co-founder of Garang's SPLA/SPLM rebel force in 1983 and was his loyal deputy. Perhaps his commitment to the unity of Sudan is slightly less than Garang's, but rumors that Garang had been about to fire him do not seem well-founded given Kiir's intimate role in the peace negotiations in Naivasha. This story continues to unfold.

True, South-South politics can make North-South relations look simple. Salva Kiir is deeply rooted in his branch of the Dinka in the eastern Bahr al-Ghazal province. This is strategically close to the valuable Hegleig, Bentiu, and Unity oil fields, and to the sometimes tense borderlands with the Rizeigat and Misseriya sections of the Baggara cattle-herding Arabs, as well as the Abyei region, which stays very tense, volatile, and not fully resolved. Kiir played a critical role in negotiating with some of the Southern movements that were opposed to Garang in the late 1990s and early 2000s. He is an experienced military commander and is politically sophisticated, despite his relative lack of prominence, because he is a team player rather than any lack of diplomatic, political and military experience.

It was essential that an independent U.S. Federal Aviation Administration investigation of the helicopter crash in the Imatong Mountains in Eastern Equatoria along the Sudan-Uganda border finally confirmed that it was an accident caused by bad weather, since foul play could have played a role. Garang had many detractors, not the least of whom was Joseph Kony, the Acholi leader of the Lord's Resistance Army (LRA), whose movement Garang had promised to end only days before the crash. The LRA is based in this area and in past times had been supported by Khartoum. Kony's episodic insurgency was aimed equally against Garang and his ally and personal friend, Ugandan president Museveni, in whose sophisticated, Russian-made, military helicopter Garang was flying when he crashed.

The death of Garang changed the pace but not the dynamics of Sudanese politics. The implementation of the peace agreement has carried on because there is simply too much international pressure on the government of Sudan from the African Union (AU), the United States, the United Nations (UN), and the European Union, as well as neighboring African countries, for the historic peace to be reversed. Sudan has run out of options, short of the separation that is still possible within the CPA agenda. The opponents of the peace agreement, such as Hassan al-Turabi's Islamist forces and the LRA, are extremists who are presently isolated. Southern sentiment in favor of separation runs high, so the first test of Kiir's leadership is to continue to negotiate the very rough CPA terrain of separation or unity to keep Garang's lonely mission alive. Already, Shari'a law is withdrawn from the South and from millions of non-Muslims in the North, and the CPA survives, with a new constitution already approved.

Garang's SPLA has considerable national appeal among marginalized Sudanese of Darfur, Kordofan, Nubia, and the East, and there was, and is, a potential for the development of a national "movement of the marginalized" that received a spark of life following Garang's death. Kiir's leadership aims to broaden the SPLM and expand Garang's political legacy into a national movement may have a long-term effect in transforming Sudanese politics from chronic militarism. Conflicts rooted in marginality could be resolved by applying the model principles of the CPA, as in the Darfur peace negotiations at Abuja, Nigeria, or in the February 2010 negotiations in Qatar that may have brought JEM back into the peace equation. So far, the transition of Salva Kiir has been relatively smooth. The external forces unanimously favor the peace accords, as do most Sudanese, and the internal spoilers are presently too weak to undo the peace. Will the considerable oil reserves (see Chapter 5), perhaps a million barrels a day, lubricate the peace or fuel further war in the tough days ahead?

As this book is being written, the national election slated for 2009 is already postponed to 2010 for lack of election funds, adequate preparation, or other reasons. If the election is substantially delayed, the potential for the breakup of the CPA is increased. If the election does take place and the results are questionable, as is likely, with so much of the nation not governed in a stable or transparent way (such as in Darfur, where it would be close to impossible to have an election at present), the 2011 referendum for unity or separation becomes more questionable itself. Among the questions are: Will the CPA survive? Will the GNU survive? Who will be in charge in Khartoum with the International Criminal Court (ICC) pressures mounting? Who will be in charge in the South, with numerous fissile South-South cleavages? Will democracy be restored? Will war break out again? Will there be a broader peace settlement in Darfur than can stick? Clearly, there are many more serious questions than clear answers.

The results of the Abyei Boundary Commission were drafted, concluded, and then rejected by Khartoum. The town of Abyei was largely evacuated in fighting in 2008, and SPLA units have withdrawn further south while Khartoum-backed militias forces are not far to the north. Oil is pumped and piped from the South to the North to be shipped to China. Is the South getting its fair share? What will

*SALW: Small Arms and Light Weapons

Figure 2.1 General Assumptions: Sources of Conflict

be left by 2011? As if these questions were not ominous enough, Khartoum is rearming with state-of-the-art Chinese weaponry, not to mention becoming a significant arms producer because it was pushed into self-sufficiency because of the sanctions against it. With its share of Chinese oil funds, the SPLA is purchasing heavy armor and tanks and is rearming for what could prove to be a third regional war and a war of complete secession that would undermine the present leadership of both North and South.

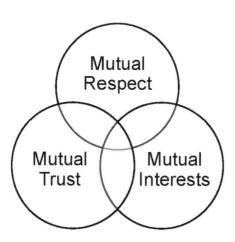

Cultural context:
Sulh vs. Salam;
Mediation vs. Adjudication

Figure 2.2 Recipe for Peace

THE SOUTH AT THE START OF 2010

Anyone attempting to predict the immediate future of Sudan is probably foolhardy. Already, the CPA-provided 2009 elections have been shifted to 2010. Absent a crystal ball, the question still remains: What is going to happen in the 2010 elections? The best answers can only be found by viewing the options provided by postcolonial Sudanese history conditioned by such realities. Political polling is mostly guesswork. Some constituencies cannot be reached at all, and despite the various open forums, publications, websites, and chat lines, the military government has its limits on public political expression and challenge. Registration took place in 2009 and, at least in peaceful areas, was not marked with violence or irregularities. Issues of eligibility were hotly debated, but mostly resolved. Some issues are still in the process of evaluation and adjudication by the Electoral Commission. Speaking with a wide variety of Sudanese on two visits to Sudan in 2009, this author's impression is that the Northern opposition groups have not consolidated a unitary position. The National Congress Party (NCP), especially in the central core area of Sudan, is perceived as having developed Sudan more in its two decades than has any other party at any other period. Roads, dams, income, import substitution, commercial and real estate opportunities, and industrialization are all widely seen as worthy of support. The ICC charges against al-Beshir are projected as a "hypocritical Western plot," since neither the United States nor Sudan is a signatory, and a broadly anti-Arab and anti-Islamist policy has been adopted by the United States amid the attacks by al-Qa'eda and American military engagement in Iraq and Afghanistan. Some history of free and fair elections by the several democratic governments, coupled with conflict fatigue and some already reconciled to the possibility of separation, all suggest that al-Beshir could well win the elections in the North. In the South, the SPLA is facing a variety of rather disorganized political opponents as well as the ongoing LRA insurgency, but few imagine an electoral defeat of the SPLA in the South. The wild card here might well be the potential electoral strength of the SPLA in the North. Given regional discord about elections and security, it is hard to predict a contagious effect in Sudan; will this mean a bigger effort to avoid the post-election controversies of, for example, Kenya? As a security regime, quick to use its many armed forces, a scenario of relatively peaceful elections is not to be excluded, despite the four military regimes that gained power by *coups d'etat*. Also tempering these realities is that all three military regimes (Abboud, Nimieri, and Sawar adh-Dhahab) were followed by democracy. No Sudanese postcolonial military regime proved to be "dynastic," unlike that of neighboring Egypt. The longest-lasting military regime had been seen in the three political incarnations of Nimieri (1969–1985). These sixteen years have already been exceeded by al-Beshir's regime (1989–2010), now entering its twenty-first year. Presumably, all governments have their beginnings and ends.

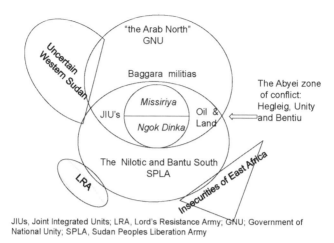

JIUs, Joint Integrated Units; LRA, Lord's Resistance Army; GNU; Government of National Unity; SPLA, Sudan Peoples Liberation Army

Figure 2.3 The North-South Borderlands

Since the 2009 elections were already postponed to 2010, the possibility also exists, as the stakes and tension are high, that security concerns could be mobilized for another postponement. A long postponement could also mean different political problems. Then again, the elections may not be transparent, since both the NCP and the SPLA have come to their positions of power by military means and not by elections. Problematic elections could easily degenerate into organized or spontaneous violence, given the long history of armed conflict and revolt in unsettled and contested areas such as Abyei and Upper Nile. Triggers for violent opposition have punctuated Sudan's postcolonial history. At the same time, the respective leaders and parties of the North and South certainly know that the oil pipeline in the North and the oil resources in the South have a convergent and mutual interest. So, although elections may or may not take place, and they may be free and transparent (or not), a hidden force may suddenly arise from a Sudanese barracks, as has already happened four times in the postcolonial period.

THE 2011 REFERENDUM FOR SEPARATION OF THE SOUTH

If the results of the 2010 elections are hard to predict, the outcome of the 2011 Referendum on North-South unity/separation provided by the CPA is even more difficult to forecast. This prediction rests upon four assumptions: (1) elections take place; (2) the CPA remains intact; (3) voter eligibility is satisfactorily determined and effectuated; and (4) war has not returned to Sudan. Given past history, these are all big assumptions. The Referendum could be canceled or postponed unilaterally or bilaterally, with military options exercised by the North or South.

Naturally, it is also possible that the Referendum does takes place, with mutually acceptable results. As 2009 closed some of the thorny issues about eligibility and the required margins for victory have been resolved. While there is a desire for unity, there is also a desire for peace and closure. Even with "separation," the North and South are not really going anywhere; the following day, they will still be neighbors, still with similar issues, and a loose future confederation cannot be ruled out. The South and North still have enduring and divisive issues. The regions will not have moved. The issues of oil, grazing land, trade, and water will remain contentious. Foreign powers have strategic interests that are threatened, weakened, or strengthened. Proxy wars, militias, and cross-border trespass and raiding can continue. The respective arms races grow. The AU gains a state; the Arab League loses territory. But to be optimistic, peace, justice, and development are also possible.

Many of these reflections were brought to the surface in November 2009 at a historic conference on the future of Sudan held in Pretoria, South Africa, hosted by the University of South Africa (UNISA) and the South African government. The significance of this conference, focused on African perspectives on Sudan's conflicts and future, was underscored by the presence of former president Thabo Mbeki on two occasions, one of which was his keynote address based on his experience heading the AU Task Force on Darfur. The fundamental realities of geography and historical connections between North and South were acknowledged by clear heads on both sides of the divide. For better or worse, whether the South secedes or does not, their ties to each other will remain. The sense that separation may solve many problems is buffered by the fact that the neighboring peoples, resources, and ecology will be the same. Unity has not been made attractive by the Government of Sudan (GoS), as its implementation has been weak and lacking in political will. As recent incidents indicate, there is little trust between the principal parties and the peoples they represent. Whether unity or secession, there is a significant need for trust-building based on mutual vested interests, common experiences, language, and contiguous borders. In the context of some alarmist domestic U.S. agendas, this international strategic balance of forces is not well-considered. The UNISA meeting underscored that there is much more to Sudan than Darfur.

The decision on the Abyei boundary dispute by the International Court at The Hague is a model of conflict containment to be studied. Based in political compromise rather than legal precision, the decision was welcomed by both the GoS and SPLM, thus pouring water rather than gas on the inflamed Abyei conflict. The Hegleig/Unity/Bentiu oil fields were detached from Abyei region (rejecting the initial report of the Abyei Boundary Commission placing them in the South), while the South gained significant fertile land and freshwater resources in the Misseriya area. Final status of the boundary is left to the two parties to establish through compromise and mutual interest (it is hoped), rather than renewed conflict.

The South appears to be broadly determined to have its independence, and from its long, bitter, and bloody struggles, its right to self-determination is well-earned. However, as the election and referendum dates draw near, hard-line positions are softening, and novel ideas are being discussed. The possible outcomes of secession depend upon whether the "divorce" is amicable or bitter. Phrases such as "hard landing" or "soft landing" have also been employed.

Option 1: Amicable divorce ("soft landing"). Southerners in the North and Northerners in the South and along the borders are vulnerable in each other's "territories"; amicable divorce favors their security over interethnic and religious conflict. Southern Kordofan (Nuba Mountains), Blue Nile, and Upper Nile are highly strategic in this respect, as they would be the likely areas of renewed war if the referendum is postponed or called off in 2011. Until things are different on the ground, the South needs the pipeline and the North needs the oil, with the bulk of the proven reserves mainly in the South. Oil finds in Uganda and connection to East African transport infrastructure could change this.

Codification of customary law in the South—presently underway—will ulti-mately result in more parity between the legal systems of North and South, and better outcomes over land disputes, if land registry claims can be dealt with judi-cially. A South without interethnic violence will continue to be elusive, so care must be taken not to consider any violent act indicative of the CPA failure. Vio-lence management and containment are more reasonable measures of relative success.

Option 2: Bitter divorce ("hard landing"). This outcome cannot be ruled out, given forty years of war to date, much higher stakes, notable tensions, and low levels of trust. However, it is in no one's interest to have a bitter divorce and a return to military "solutions" for the intersecting issues. Both sides have fought each other to a stalemate, and few would imagine that a military "solution" will gain much. Former Republic of South Africa (RSA) president Mbeki made it very clear that, from an African perspective, unity is the most preferred option, but failing that, separation on good terms permitting the regions/states to live and work cooperatively is still a more desirable outcome.

However, a bitter separation is not impossible to conjure. What little trust remains could be further eroded if elections are widely perceived by Southerners not to be free and fair, or if the referendum is either postponed or canceled for "security" reasons. This could increase the possibility of a unilateral declaration of independence (UDI) by the South and renewal of war, this time not a civil war but a war between unequal nations.

It is clear that both sides are preparing for war—not its inevitability, but its possible necessity. Northerners have a degree of war fatigue, while Southerners are not about to give up on the hard-fought gains of the CPA. The CPA allows both sides to be armed and to rearm, and there is something of a miniature arms race presently going on, with the North now self-sufficient in small arms, light weapons and heavy armor, armored personnel carriers, tanks, and even light military spotter planes. The North also has a modest air force with Chinese ground attack and fighter jets, and Soviet Hinds and Antonovs. The battle-experienced SPLA is acquiring heavy armor (such as T-55 tanks from battle capture, Ethiopia, and open arms purchases). Thus, the regional African implications for a new war are dire and potentially catastrophic. As President Mbeki said at the UNISA conference, "If Sudan succeeds, all of Africa succeeds—if it fails, all of Africa fails." Military brinksmanship is a subsidiary option in this framework. "Playing chicken" in this context can be risky, but could also be ameliorated with ongoing separation functions of the Joint Integrated Units (JIUs) in the most volatile areas. The antiwar/pro-peace objectives of the AU, Arab League, and UN, plus the presence of thousands of international military and police peace-keeping missions, should continue to help.

Option 3: Confederation. Although this option is not provided in the CPA, a compromise solution of independence for the South with a loose confederation of the North and South could be placed on the future political drawing board. This is being discussed in some Khartoum academic circles. The Regional Autonomy Agreement of the 1972 Addis Ababa Accords functioned well until abrogated unilaterally by Nimieri in 1983.

Observations

- Millions of Arabic-speaking Southerners in the North will remain where they are, unless they are forcible removed, an unlikely option at this time. Many favor unity, as they are a vulnerable minority in the North, although their numbers and historical grievances make Northerners fearful. They recall the days after the death of John Garang in July 2005, known as "Bloody Monday" (more like a week), when violence and property destruction erupted all over greater Khartoum. The "three towns" were in lockdown, as Southerners raged over the loss of their leader, blaming Khartoum for his death. If there is an "amicable divorce," the position of Southerners is not in jeopardy, and many will vest their futures in the North, where there is at present better educational opportunities and health and human services.

- Restoration of a secular state. SPLM General Secretary and co-chair of the Juba Alliance Pagan Amum is publically calling for this, while NCP Deputy Chairman Nafie 'Ali Nafie says the opposition wants "to impose secularism on the North." This remains a symbolic flash point for the more fundamental issue of unity or separation of religion and state. Although falling short of a full secular state, amelioration of strict and harsh Islamism has already occurred, and the trend will likely continue through the elections and referendum.

- It is estimated that a quarter to a third of the nation's population resides in Greater Khartoum. These are refugees from chronic conflicts and ecological crises, and those seeking better socioeconomic opportunities. The demographic aspects of modern Sudan, with a burgeoning youth population, need to be brought into the equation whether united or separate.

- Egypt is profoundly affected whether there is unity or separation. Only belatedly has it taken Southern secession seriously. Kenya and Uganda will likely support separation and be advantaged by it. The long insurgency of the LRA, often believed to be secretly supported by Khartoum, could receive greater attention rather than have SPLA troops diverted to the oil fields. Already, the Uganda Peoples' Defense Force (UPDF) is active in the Sudan/ Democratic Republic of Congo (DRC)/Central African Republic (CAR) borderlands in support of the SPLA as well as for its own security interests to keep the LRA from returning to Uganda.

- At this point, in January 2010, outcomes are still in question, and many twists and turns are to be expected. The election registration process went rather smoothly after some initial contestation about regulations and constituencies. In the absence of scientific polling, opposition groups are beginning to congeal and unify, but holding this strategic unity will be difficult. Speaking with a range of Sudanese from all parts of the country and from various walks of life, the sentiment is that al-Beshir will fairly win the election in the North unless a unified opposition mounts a strong platform and candidate for president, such as Yasir Arman or Pagan Amum. Salva Kiir, the first vice president of the GNU and the president of the GoS lacks the charisma of John Garang and is manifestly waiting for the opportunity for succession.

- The South is experiencing ethnic divisions and continuing LRA attacks in Western Equatoria and Bahr al-Ghazal. The two major political forces, NCP and SPLM, have internal divisions, and their respective capacities to link with, or marginalize, other forces will be critical, especially for Darfur, Nuba Mountains, and Eastern Sudan, as well as the complex demographic forces in the capital city region.

- The influence of Hassan al-Turabi seems to have come to an end, except for his protégé, Ibrahim Khalil, in the form of the Darfur rebel movement JEM, which is presently moving back into some tactical alliance with al-Beshir. Popular Islam and Sufism can never be discounted as democratizing forces in Muslim Sudan. Darfur's lingering issues are more manageable and less violent with a stable presence of AU/UN forces, and most rebels are laying down their arms or just resorting to banditry and warlordism.

- Recent contentious military interaction between Ndjamena and Khartoum appears to be on the mend, and the political relations with Sudan's eight other neighbors are relatively stable and unproblematic. Indeed, Ethiopia now gets the majority of its oil products from Sudan. The LRA is out of Uganda. Eritrea is consumed by its domestic issues and Somalia. The borders with Libya, CAR, and Egypt are calm. True, cross-border interethnic conflicts about trespass and grazing persist, but they remain local.

Reflections

- Sanctions should be eased or reconsidered. The U.S. policy has been counterproductive, with not enough credible "sticks" and many global sources of "carrots," while Darfur is substantially calmed. Apparently, the punitive sanctions were motivated more by domestic American pressures rather than by incentives for Sudan. The undesirable result was that Sudan's massive oil reserves were transferred from a Western monopoly to an Eastern one of China, Iran, India, and Malaysia. The fact that neither Sudan nor the United States is an ICC signatory weakened the acceptance of the ICC charges against President al-Beshir. With anticolonial and nationalist sentiments strong in the Muslim North, the ICC charges are broadly taken as a "Western conspiracy" against a defiant Sudan. With the United States diverted in Afghanistan and Iraq, and U.S. Africa Command (AFRICOM) in early evolution, the Sudanese leadership has expertly played a strong hand.

- Aside from oil, Sudan's huge agricultural potential (200 million arable *feddans*) is over-looked by Western interests, while *rentier* investors—again from China, India, and Muslim nations—have contracted lands for decades all over the arable North, with new dams providing water. Whether Sudan divides or does not, the demographic process of class formation is intensifying everywhere, with a small but very wealthy merchant and military class growing, along with landless subsistence farmers and herders struggling to survive in the face of global climate change and desertification.

- Capacity-building in the South urgently needs to take place, from basic infrastructure to political, legal, and military organization. These are fundamental necessities for a stable and secure South no matter what the referendum outcome.

- Transparent democratizing and engagement with the North needs to be supported by all possible means. The political situation within the North is in as much need for a "soft landing" as is the South. The political temperature is rising, with increasing expectations for change.

NOTE

See related sources on the South in the bibliography. This chapter was organized with reference to the historical chronology in Richard A. Lobban, Jr., Robert S. Kramer, and Carolyn Fluehr-Lobban, *Historical Dictionary of the Sudan* (Lanham, MD: Scarecrow Press, 2002) and Robert O. Collins and Robert L. Tignor, *Egypt and the Sudan* (Englewood Cliffs, NJ: Prentice-Hall, 1967). The inherent analysis was founded on my travels throughout Sudan over forty years, work in the Ministry of Southern Affairs in the early years of the Nimieri government of Sudan, work on political asylum cases, and regularly following, writing about, and teaching Sudanese history and current events.

CHAPTER 3

Sudan's East and North

THE CASE OF EASTERN SUDAN

Reflections on the History of Eastern Sudan Security Dynamics

The strategic interests of the many historical powers in central Sudan have been, for millennia, to secure the east-west trade from the center to the Red Sea periphery and to block or resist attacks from that region. This was usually possible by defensive retreat and remoteness. On the other hand, as external powers became more interested in the resources of Sudan in general, the peoples of eastern Sudan were often trapped between these struggles for power. In addition, there were local interests to consider in eastern Sudan as they sought to resist external powers as well as conduct their livelihoods in an area of marginal ecology and rainfall. These virtually eternal verities mark most periods of the history of eastern Sudan. This expansive area ranges from the Red Sea and the Ethiopian plateau on the east, the Blue Nile on the south, the Nile proper on the west, and the territory of Egypt to the north. The mountainous spine of the Red Sea Hills demarcates the territories of the Blemmyes, Medjay, Beja, Beni Amer, and Hadendowa peoples. Amid this sometimes grassy plain is the Butana, the dry "belly" of eastern Sudan. Over a very long period, this area has been much neglected by most.

These political realities are central to understand their perspectives looking from the periphery back to the political core or heartland. Strategic interests for most of this time, whether in eastern or northern Sudan, revolved around three principle concerns: (1) territorial defense and occasionally offense, (2) securing trade routes, and (3) securing access to resources, especially gold, slaves, hides, ivory, and other wild and domestic animal products.

Ancient Times

The earliest references to the peoples of the Red Sea shoreline and adjoining Red Sea Hills are the visits by Dynasty XVIII New Kingdom Egyptian traders. Among these, the sailors of Queen Hatshepsut (1503–1482 BCE) stand out not only in their vivid pictorial records at her majestic Deir al-Bahri temple in the Theban Assasif, but in the detail of the relationships between eastern Sudan and Ancient Egypt. The northern portions of eastern Sudan adjoining Egypt were occupied by the Blemmyes, who fluctuated as border patrol police (Matoi or Medjay) or as nomadic raiders threatening Upper Egyptian trade routes to the coast and, in particular, the highly valued Nubian gold mines in the eastern desert at Wadi al-Alaqi and elsewhere. The general coastal region of the western Red Seas was termed the land of Punt, located somewhere between north Somalia, Eritrea, and eastern Sudan. The Egyptians came as armed visitors and traders, but did not come as conquerors. This was just too far from the colonial presence they had in Sudanese Nubia. It is clear that they acquired plants, foods, hides, wild animals, and ivory. Precisely what the eastern Sudanese got in return is less clear, but their sovereignty was not at risk as early as 3,500 years ago. Coastal trade and smuggling have remained a constant pattern over the centuries until the present.

When Nubians were able to recover their Nile Valley lands from the New Kingdom pharaohs in the Kushite ("Ethiopian") Dynasty XXV, they were more concerned about security issues to the north, especially from the Assyrians (modern Iraq), and with maintaining political and military alliances with the Judeans (especially King Hezekiah). At the same time, eastern Sudan of the eighth and seventh centuries BCE required sending out punitive expeditions to crush nomadic attacks from eastern Sudan and to take slave captives from that region. In the fourth century BCE, for strategic reasons of increasing their buffer between Persian- or Greek-occupied Egypt and themselves, the Kushites withdrew their capital from Napata at the fourth cataract to Meroë, between the fifth and sixth cataracts. As such, their contacts with the eastern region of the Butana (the area between the Nile and the Red Sea) intensified substantially. Not only did Meroë represent an aggressive upgrade of regional economic control of the long-distance trade in the Butana from the south to the north, but especially from the Nile Valley to the Red Sea coast. As iron production increased hugely, the presence of Meroë had a major ecological effect of depleting acacia forest for fuel.

Greco-Roman Times

The Ptolemaic Greeks entered the Nile Valley in the fourth century and arrived at Meroë, and relationships became even more complex with foreign culture-bearers, game-hunters, and traders. Of great interest to the Greeks were the militarily significant elephants of Meroë. This was the great age of major land battles (e.g., Rapha) using armored elephants, used by Phoenicians, Ptolemies, Seleucids, and Romans. Mainly, the elephants were captured in the forest areas of the Butana and adjoining highlands of Eritrea/Ethiopia and were exported to ports on the Red Sea coast. The frequent presence of elephant images and sculpture at Musawwarat es-Sufra in the Butana is ample proof of their significance, even with images of the Meroitic kings riding handsomely decorated elephants. This ancient arms race of elephants brought the peoples of eastern Sudan into association with major world events more than two thousand years ago. Gradually, Greek and Roman map-makers (Agatharchides, Claudius Ptolemy, Diordorus, and Strabo) reported on the "troglodytes" (cave-dwellers) of eastern Sudan, who were differentiated by what they ate: ichthyophages (fish-eaters), acridophages (locust-eaters), strutophages (ostrich-eaters), and spermatophages (seed-eaters) attracted their attention in the region, and further south, they noted the more alarming and supposed anthropophages (human-eaters). Intimidating inscriptions of Meroitic kings at al-Geili suggest that the central Butana was still being contested for control.

Eastern Sudan gained greater recognition in the famed Roman seafarers' manual known as the *Periplus of the Erythraean Sea*, probably published in Alexandria; this guide indicated navigational references, commodities to exchange and trading towns in the region. Tensions mounted in Roman times when they established their *limes*, or defensible border, at Aswan and in the western Egyptian desert at Dush along the "forty-days road" to Darfur and Kordofan. In the eastern desert, they used the Medjay to police and patrol their southern security perimeter.

Medieval Times

When King Ezana accepted Monophysite Christianity in Ethiopia, one of his early missions was to send his armies westward across the Butana and down the water course of the Atbara (*Takkaze*) to destroy an already feeble Meroë (Kush) in about 340 CE. On this conquest journey along the Nile (*Seda*), he noted the brick town of Alwa while taking treasure and captives along the way. Even when Nubian King Silko accepted Christianity, he had to drive out the eastern desert Blemmyes from Nobatia in about 536 CE to accomplish this. By 579 CE, the third Christian kingdom of Alwa at Soba in Sudan was converted, and a vast swathe from the Mediterranean to the Highlands of Ethiopia was brought under Christianity. The people of eastern Sudan returned to relative subordinance vis-à-vis the central Nile powers.

When Islam entered Egypt in 639 CE, the Christian Nubians kept it out of Sudan, both along the Nile and in the eastern desert just across from the holy sites of Islam at Mecca and Medina. By 652 CE, a *baqt*—peace and trade treaty—was established between Christian Nubia and Muslim Egypt under 'Abdallah ibn Sa'ad ibn Abi Sahr. Nubia would provide 360 slaves each year and promise no attacks;

Egypt would provide 1,300 *kanyr* of wine. The origin of the slaves was presumed to be lands further south and east. By 720 CE, another *baqt* was established between Egyptians and Beja of eastern Sudan. In 758 CE, the ruling Abbasid dynasty (750–870 CE) in Egypt complained of no *baqt* payments and that the Blemmyes of the eastern Red Sea Hills had attacked Upper Egypt. This complaint was repeated from 819 to 822 when the Beja again refused *baqt* payments and attached Upper Egypt. Such raids were repeated endlessly in the ninth and tenth centuries. By the mid-eleventh century, some 50,000 Nubians served in the Shi'ite Fatimid (969–1171 CE) army that intensified its attacks against Christian Nubia, making a strategic alliance with the Crusaders, who continued attacks on the Sunni Ayyubids (1172–1250 CE) in Cairo and Delta towns. From 1250 to 1382, the Bahri Mamluke Dynasty ruled in Egypt and were a serious military threat against Nubia, which by 1284 was again compelled to make *baqt* tributes. By the time of the defeat of the last Christian king in Nubia and the first Muslim king, 'Abdullah Barshambu, being placed on the throne in Dongola, the *baqt* was reestablished and the first mosque built at Dongola. The peoples of eastern Sudan were left in comparative peace as major military struggles took place along the Nile.

The Turco-Egyptians, the Mahdists, and the Modern Era

The next epoch of Nile Valley history opened with the massacre of the Mamlukes in Cairo by the Ottoman Turks (1517–1805). Muslim Nubia was left on its own, with the Funj Sultans ruling from Sennar on the southwestern edge of eastern Sudan. As long as they controlled the trade networks from central Sudan to the coast and had an adequate supply of slaves from the East and the South, there was a relatively stable state. A few medieval travelers, such as the Portuguese Francisco Alvares, visited Ethiopia in 1520 and passed though Nubia; Jewish traveler David Reubeni visited Soba and Sennar in his plan to resist Turkish expansion. Their records tell us little about the people of eastern Sudan at the time, but by 1610, the Funj Sultans made a tactical alliance with the 'Abdallab to prepare for anticipated Turkish aggression against Sudan. Clearly, this was still an unstable world in 1647, when Portuguese priests Giovanni d'Aguila and António da Pescopagano visited Sennar. At least, they hoped, these Sudanese Muslims would be prepared to block further Turkish expansion. However, by about 1660, the Shayqiya along the east bank of the Nile revolted against the 'Abdallab, who a century later, in about 1770, themselves revolted against the Funj Sultans. Shifting alliances and a persistent struggle to maintain central power along the Nile are recurring themes of the region. Scottish explorer James Bruce visited Bejrawiya, Qerri, Sennar, and central Sudan.

The long-standing fear of Turkish "superpower" aggression was finally fulfilled in 1820–1822 when the Ottomans from Egypt conquered much of Sudan, ending the Funj Sultanate and establishing the Turco-Egyptian regime. This imposed a very heavy tax burden in domestic and military slaves on the riverine Sudanese. The first Sudanese response was rapid when the retinue of Isma'il Pasha, the son of the Pasha Muhammad 'Ali, were all killed in November 1822 at the key trade town of Shendi by Mek Nimr and his Ja'aliyin followers. The Turkish response to this revolt was even more brutal in 1823–1824 when Muhammad Bey Khusraw ("Daftardar") harshly put down the uprising, burning towns and massacring their inhabitants throughout the Nile Valley and eastern Sudan. Amid a sea of blood, by 1824–1825, the Turk 'Uthman Bey governed this land with the assistance of professional slave soldiers (*jihadiya*). This was the beginning of Khartoum as a military, later administrative, center. Harsh taxes, drought, smallpox, and famine prompted the flight of riverine Sudanese from the Nile and into remote areas away from this authority. By 1826–1828, the situation had calmed and taxes were reduced, cultivation was increased, fugitives from the regime were granted amnesty, and some Sudanese served as advisors to government. Khartoum developed, trade increased, and prosperity returned. The Turks continued with some slave raids in the South and East to the Ethiopian borderlands. By 1838–1843, with Turkish Abu Widan as Governor-General (*hukumdar*), there were further attempts at fiscal and land regulation that were resisted by the Shayqiya of western Butana. The Turks pushed hard to extend government control to the east toward the Red Sea coast; this was always very uncertain, and they began to be content with the Nile trade (in ivory and slaves) that passed through Khartoum and Shendi; gradually, this trade reverted to the Ja'ali and Shayqiya merchants who were generally termed *Jallaba*. In 1844, a tiny seed of their undoing was born on Labab Island, near Dongola, with the birth of Muhammad Ahmad (the Mahdi). In further attempts to modernize their administration of Sudan, some European Christians were placed in government employ:Samuel Baker (1869–1873) and Charles Gordon (1874–1876), as well as American military trainers and cartographers. Government steamers were introduced on the Nile and a telegraph system linked Khartoum to Egypt in the north, across Butana to Kassala and the port of Suakin on the Red Sea coast, and to el-Obeid in the west. Suakin and Massawa were ceded to Egypt by the Ottoman Empire in 1865. Things were looking bright for the Turco-Egyptians, and when the Suez Canal opened in Egypt in 1869, it appeared that the Turkish colony in Sudan would be productive and stable for years. Advancing their cause in 1873–1874, Zubayr Rahma Mansur was governor of Bahr al-Ghazal, conquering Darfur for Turkiya. And there were some further attempts to suppress slave trade. Even a Christian presence was tolerated with the appointment of a bishop of Nubia and Khartoum, established in Khartoum in 1879.

But this rosy picture from the Turco-Egyptian perspective was about to be challenged when, in 1881, Muhammad Ahmad revealed himself to be the "Expected Mahdi" and invited followers to Abba Island on the White Nile.

A government force that was sent to arrest him was defeated, and Mahdists (Ansar) made their famous emigration to Jabal Qadir in the Nuba Mountains. A second government force was also defeated, resulting in Ansar recovering booty and arms, and mounting Mahdist prestige. In 1882, a third government force under Yusuf Pasha al-Shallali was destroyed. While the Mahdists initially failed in their attack at el-Obeid ("Friday Battle"), they now included *jihadiyya* soldiers armed with rifles; finally, in 1883, Bara and el-Obeid capitulated to Mahdi. In growing desperation, the military expedition of Colonel William Hicks was sent out to put an end to this, but he was also annihilated at Shaykan, with more weapons going into Mahdist hands. Slatin Pasha, governor of Darfur, surrendered; Mahdi controlled virtually all territories of the west.

Meanwhile, in eastern Sudan, the clever tactician and slave-trader 'Uthman Digna joined the Mahdist revolt in the east, aided by Majadhib of al-Damer and Hadendowa people. Digna promptly laid siege to the eastern towns of Sinkat, high in the Red Sea Hills, and Tokar on the Red Sea coast. The situation was growing more and more desperate by 1884 when in January, General Charles "Chinese" Gordon left Cairo for Sudan as the newly appointed Governor-General. His mission was mainly to evacuate Khartoum, but already a veteran of Sudan, Gordon was also motivated by a religious and political mission. By February, Gordon reached Berber, now much closer to Khartoum, and there he publicly revealed Egypt's intention to abandon Sudan and revoke the ban on slavery. Sudanese loyalists were alarmed and feeling very vulnerable, so by the time Gordon arrived in Khartoum, he was determined to "smash the Mahdi." However, the noose was tightening, and in May 1884, Berber, the town he had just passed, was taken by Mahdists. Khartoum was almost completely isolated to the north, it was blocked to the west at Omdurman, and had little access to the south along the Blue Nile, and most of the east was under Mahdist control. Sinking further into fear and despair, the British parliament authorized the "Gordon Rescue Mission" during the late summer of 1884, but for political and logistic reasons, this mission-oriented task force was delayed in Egypt and slow in sailing up the Nile. The Mahdists were not waiting, and Khartoum was placed under full siege, led by one of their strongest generals, 'Abd al-Rahman al-Nujumi. The Mahdi himself was encamped just south of Omdurman on the other side of the Nile. In early January 1885, Fort Omdurman capitulated; taking advantage of a weakness in Khartoum's defense, that city was taken by the Mahdists and Gordon was killed, just days before the rescue mission arrived and glumly turned back in failure. Notably, the doors of the Berlin Congress—in which the contemporary European powers determined to partition the African continent and demonstrate "effective control" by means of "pacification"—had just closed the same month. Apparently, the Sudanese had other inclinations.

Among the ironies of this struggle was that the Mahdi died in Omdurman, probably of typhus, only six months later; most of the Mahdist period was actually administered by 'Abdullahi al-Ta'aishi (his Khalifa), who succeeded him as ruler of the Mahdist state. Consolidating his rule, the Khalifa defended his territory against Egypt, neutralized Nubian opposition in the north and in Khartoum, and suppressed revolts in the west; by 1888, the zealous Mahdist Ansar crossed eastern Sudan to Gedaref and through Gallabat to invade Ethiopia as far as the city of Gondar after killing King John IV in March 1889. Overextension and insufficient food supply can slow or stop any army, and the Mahdist army were soon to face failed harvests and famines in Sudan in 1889, in which thousands died and more civilians began to oppose the administration. Whether of military necessity or diversion from his problems, the Khalifa turned to attack Egypt at Tushki in Lower Nubia on August 1889; al-Nujumi was killed, and the Mahdist *jihad* to the north was ended. Such failures exposed the Khalifa to still more opponents in Omdurman, especially among the family of the Mahdi, and he turned more and more to domestic problems, at least until 1894, when the Italians thought to take advantage of the Omdurman confusion and extend their colonial rule of Eritrea by attacking the eastern Sudanese town of Kassala. King Menelik had other plans for the Italians when he organized a stinging military defeat at Adowa that kept them out of Ethiopia.

Seeing the weakness of the Khalifa, nursing the desire for revenge of Gordon, and needing raw cotton for their textile mills, the British began their own plans to retake Sudan. As early as 1896, the mechanized, organized Anglo-Egyptian invasion of Sudan commenced, spawning local revolts against the Khalifa as it progressed with river steamships and a railway across the desert from Wadi Halfa via Abu Hamad and on toward Khartoum. By September 1897, the methodical force led by General Kitchener had reached Berber; by April 1898, Mahdist General Mahmud Ahmad's army was bloodily defeated at Atbara. Then, on 2 September 1898, some ten thousand Mahdist soldiers were killed at the "Battle of Kereri" near Omdurman. The Khalifa fled with a small following that was hunted down and killed at Umm Dibaykarat in Kordofan. The Mahdiya was ended, and British colonial occupation began.

Historical Patterns Become the Present: From Colonialism to Postcolonialism

Consistently, over these centuries, tactical actions in eastern Sudan figured in the strategic goals of those in the core of power along the Nile. At the same time, the people of eastern Sudan were more often than not pawns in power relations at the core. It is this dynamic that defines the plight and issues of eastern Sudan in the colonial and postcolonial period as well.

During the Anglo-Egyptian condominium colonial rule (1898–1856), there were endless revolts in the West and the South, but for eastern Sudan, there was some development, such as the construction in 1905 of the Atbara–Port Sudan railroad that linked the Red Sea to Khartoum for the first time. This was in conjunction with work begun to build the new town of Port Sudan, replacing Suakin as the major Sudanese harbor on the Red Sea. The colonial economy was aimed at self-sufficiency, and along this line, the Sennar Dam was completed in 1925 to supply water for the vast Gezira agricultural scheme. Italian forces based in Eritrea were still seeking revenge for their defeat at Adowa, so they invaded Ethiopia in 1935, while Sudan remained under British control. During the course of the war, Italians invaded Kassala on 4 July 1940 and bombed Khartoum, while the British backed Haile Sellasie and gradually advanced to liberate Eritrea from Italian occupation. By 1941, suffering reverses in Europe and elsewhere, the Italians were driven out of Kassala. Most of the major events of the colonial era, such as annexing Darfur and repressing revolts in the South, had little apparent effect in eastern Sudan. However, immediately after Egyptian independence in 1952 and the nationalization of the Suez Canal on 26 July 1954, the access to the Red Sea was destined to be much contested in the five Arab-Israeli wars. Even Egypt's plan to construct the Aswan High Dam had an effect in eastern Sudan when thousands of displaced Nubians were resettled at Khasm al-Girba and New Halfa between Kassala and Gedaref. Neither the Nubians nor the local nomadic populations were very much pleased about this major change in their lives, history, and territory. The marginalized status of both left few avenues of protest. Even the contest for power in Khartoum among democrats, the military, and the ruling elite left the peoples of the East more observers than participants. The chief exception to this was the dominance of the Unionist *Khatmiya tariqa* and its stalwart al-Mirghani family, long tangling with the Mahdists, both of whom pulled on the levers of power in Khartoum—during democratic times, at least. During the military regime of Colonel Ga'afar Nimieri, eastern Sudan flashed in the 1970 news as the Ansar Imam al-Hadi al-Mahdi died "mysteriously" by Nimieri's security officers.

Eastern Sudan was again an observer in the March 1972 Addis Ababa peace accords that reached a settlement between Sudanese government and Southern leaders of the Anya-Nya by recognizing regional autonomy. However, at this time, the intensity of the neighboring war in Eritrea was more of a distraction, and Khartoum gave tacit support to the Eritrean Liberation Front (ELF) guerrillas just prior to the civil war in Eritrea between the ELF and Eritrean Peoples' Liberation Front (EPLF), while both were trying to fight against the Ethiopian forces of Haile Sellasie. Regional events in 1973 such as the "6th of October" and the Yom Kippur War between Israel and Egypt brought the control of the Suez Canal back to Egypt, and by 1974, this was functioning once again, with advantage to commerce on the Red Sea. Later that year, many agreements were announced with other Arab countries to help finance projects in Sudanese agriculture and industry. By January 1976, a $700-million plan for agricultural development was announced, involving more than sixty projects in the next decade. In October, continuing Sudanese–Saudi Arabian cooperation was affirmed during a state visit to Sudan by King Khalid of Saudi Arabia. These agreements were to have a very serious negative effect in eastern Sudan, since this was the location of many extensive mechanized agricultural schemes that further impoverished the people of the region. This much-stirred political pot was further agitated in January 1977 with the continuing crisis over Sudanese-Ethiopian territorial incursions that were only made worse when President Nimieri announced his support for Eritrean independence.

Worse, on 5 June 1983, amid stalled Southern governments, Nimieri issued Republican Order No. 1 that abrogated the 1972 Addis Ababa Accords and self-government for the South. This act embittered relations in eastern Sudan and was soon to launch a new decades-long war in the South, not to mention, ultimately, the overthrow of Nimieri himself and his 28 September 1983 unilateral imposition of harsh measures of Islamic law and the suspension of the secular legal system that had prevailed. In response, the SPLM was founded on 31 July 1983 by Colonel John Garang after he joined the Southern revolt he was supposed to suppress. The SPLM/SPLA resumed military activity against the government of al-Mahdi. In Nimieri's remaining years, he managed to execute Mahmoud Mohammad Taha at Kober prison on 18 January 1985 for a charge of apostasy, causing still more widespread outcry. The architect of the Islamization,Hassan al-Turabi, resigned as assistant to President Nimieri on 8 February. The political bubble was ready to burst; on 6 April 1985, while Nimieri was in the United States, General Suwar al-Dahab seized power in coup for "an interim period." Hundreds of thousands celebrated in the streets of Khartoum. Prison doors were forced open, and on 30 December 1985, the Attorney General, 'Abd al-Ati, amended the penal code to nullify the "September Laws," but he still adhered to the principles of Shari'a that remained a critical issue for many years still to come.

Now, with a fresh war in the South, a new military ruler, and many grave issues unaddressed, a fresh start was very much needed to put Sudan on a road to peace and development. In 1986, just such an initiative was formulated in the creation of the IGADD, which provided a significant forum for cease-fires and peace negotiations in Sudan while trying to get belligerents together on more modest and less complicated issues like Guinea-worm eradication. Meanwhile, on 5 March 1983, SPLA troops captured Rumbek and forced the closure of the Juba airport. On 24 March 2008, the Koka Dam Declaration was signed in Ethiopia by major Sudanese parties (excluding the NIF), proposing a peace framework.

This fresh start was boosted with the peaceful departure of General Suwar al-Dahab and, finally, the multiparty democratic election on 6 May of a coalition government with Sadiq al-Mahdi as the prime minister. But whatever was intentions, the new prime minister could not solve the Islamic law issue, so the war in the South dragged on for its third year. Likewise, the prime minister sent militias in the South to continue his military presence there, and on 28–29 March 1987, as many as a thousand Southerners were reported massacred by Northern militias at al-Da'ien in southern Darfur. This was reported by Khartoum human-rights activists to the annoyance of the al-Mahdi regime. The initial optimism was fading, but by April, former U.S. President Carter got the IGADD talks between North and South in motion to bring the Sudanese conflict to an end. By 24 August 1987, a new Addis Ababa forum was held on "The Struggle for Peace and Democracy"; by 8 September, a Peace Communiqué was issued by the Sudan African Parties and the SPLM/SPLA supporting the Koka Dam Declaration. A year later, the SPLM/SPLA met in Addis Ababa with a DUP delegation that had important links to eastern Sudan through the Al-Mirghaniya *tariqa*. Still, the central issues were more power-sharing, less marginalization, and dealing with the persistent presence of the controversial Shari'a laws that the al-Mahdi government was not able to suspend and abandon indeed, by 19 September 1988, the non-Muslim African parties left the Constituent Assembly to protest the introduction of new Shari'a codes. Distrust of the al-Mahdi regime was increasing, but since it adhered to democratic principles, there was still a bit of hope remaining. DUP leader Muhammad al-Mirghani met SPLA commander John Garang in Addis Ababa on 13 November to sign a framework to end the civil war, now into its fifth year. The NIF refused to sign this joint DUP-SPLA agreement that brought thousands of NIF supporters and Southerners to street battles in Khartoum. By mid-December, Prime Minister al-Mahdi finally agreed to support the DUP-SPLA agreement and requested the authorization of the Constituent Assembly to implement the agreement, which was, sadly, rejected. Amid this legislative struggle, economic issues of price rises had made al-Mahdi steadily less popular.

As the year turned, Hassan al-Turabi, former Nimieri advisor, was appointed Deputy Prime Minister on 31 January 1989. In the political background, on 21 February, an Armed Forces commander and 150 officers asked Prime Minister al-Mahdi for action on economic deterioration, a balanced foreign policy, and an end to the civil war that was dragging the country down. Al-Mahdi did not need more bad or problematic news, but on 26 February, the SPLA captured Torit, near Juba. While in Khartoum, the Constituent Assembly introduced emergency preventive detention for up to ten days. By 3 March, the SPLA captured Nimule near the Ugandan border. The steadily more isolated prime minister was in virtual gridlock, and on 4 March, the leaders of all major parties (except the NIF), associations, and trade unions signed a seven-point program, the "National Declaration for Peace." Two days later, the DUP, labor unions, and trade associations called for the resignation of the Prime Minister. Far to the south, the SPLA shelled a besieged Juba and controlled most of Equatoria. With pressures mounting daily, by 10 March, a broad political coalition issued an ultimatum that Prime Minister al-Mahdi should submit his government's resignation within twenty-four hours; in two days, the State Council accepted the resignation of the cabinet, but the prime minister did not resign and the crisis deepened. On 11 April 1989, the SPLA captured Akoba in Upper Nile, just over the border from Ethiopia, and the al-Mahdi government ended three-day talks with SPLA representatives in Addis Ababa. In desperation, on 7 May, the prime minister announced a new experiment in the application of Shari'a law that would preserve the rights of non-Muslims. On 1 June, the now very strong leader of the SPLA, John Garang, announced his three conditions for peace: (1) freezing Shari'a laws, (2) cancellation of emergency laws, and (3) ending all defense agreements with Egypt and Libya. By this time, al-Mahdi had run out of political maneuvering room, and the problems were crushing him. How, or if, he might have solved these will not be known, because on 30 June 1989, the al-Mahdi government was overthrown, toppled in a military coup led by Brigadier General Hassan Omer Ahmed al-Beshir and his fifteen-member Revolutionary Command Council (RCC) that dismissed senior commanders and placed government officials under arrest. Al-Beshir moved quickly to ban all trade unions and political parties; property owned by political parties was confiscated. Foreign currency could no longer be held by private citizens. It is widely understood that Islamist intellectual and lawyer Hassan al-Turabi and his NIF played the "kingmaker" role and provided the ideological underpinnings of the government. By 2 July, the new government closed all trade unions, political parties, and associations, ending Sudan's third period of democracy; most former high-ranking government officials were arrested.

During this early structuring of the latest Khartoum military elite, the East was again neglected, as the government was sharply focused on regime security itself and the continuing battle in, and over, the South. Al-Beshir was not prepared to give in on many, or any, points, and John Garang and his SPLA, fresh from more battlefield successes, were in a parallel mood. By October 1989, full-scale fighting had resumed in the South after about a seven-month cease-fire. With little hope for flexibility in Khartoum, the Charter for Democracy was signed by the NDA, meeting in Eritrea, and in November, the (Northern) Sudanese militias (*murahileen*) were renamed the Popular Defense Force (PDF), and cross-border raids into the South were back in force. Also, on 17 November, there was the first sign of accommodation when former Prime Minister al-Mahdi, DUP leader Muhammad 'Uthman al-Mirghani, and NIF leader Hassan al-Turabi were all freed from prison and put under house arrest. Reading between the lines, the Umma Party and the DUP were put on warning to undertake no political actions, while the NIF was steadily brought closer into the ruling circles. With this analysis, the NDA called for further resistance and the expansion of a united front to topple the regime. Khartoum politics had literally gone full circle, with much motion and no direction.

Contemporary Responses to Underdevelopment in Eastern Sudan

As time passed, the regime used every sort of repressive means to preserve itself. The NDA opposition, weak and disorganized, turned to underground meetings and small-scale actions, and life in exile. The DUP was pushed aside, and the only person with deep roots to the East was Hassan al-Turabi, who was increasingly the source of the problem. What kept the East connected to the core was the main hard-surfaced Highway 21 from Khartoum to Wad Medani to Gedaref to the border town of Qallabat on the road to Gondar, Ethiopia, which the Khalifa had tried to use a century earlier. The other, more important, highway led to the Red Sea coast and passed through the Nubian resettlement area of Khasm al-Qirba and its reservoir, on through the much-disputed town of Kassala, and across the Red Sea Hills, down to deserted Suakin and to the growing city of Port Sudan. Private cars and heavy trucks went back and forth, but there was little change in the East. Compounding this were more large-scale mechanized agricultural schemes built around private foreign and domestic investors, and the privatization of local land. For the "typical" Eastern peoples, this all meant that they could easily see what was going on, but they were in virtually no position to do much about it as wealth passed through the Eastern roads and more land and product were lost to their control. The local commercial economy could not thrive, and smuggling and support of local armed groups seemed to be a "reasonable" alternative.

In this context, the relations between Sudan, Eritrea, and Ethiopia could only sour into distrust and tension. This evolved into two armed groups frustrated with these circumstances: the Rashaidya Free Lions and the Beja Congress. The Beja are one part of several ancient populations (Beni Amer, Hadendowa, Bisharin, and Amarar) in eastern Sudan, ranging north to southern Egypt and south to northern Eritrea. Their Afro hair style earned them the pejorative nickname of "fuzzy-wuzzies" from writer Rudyard Kipling; they were skilled and effective in fighting against the British during the Mahdiya. Although they are Muslims, their syncretic Islam has unique features, and the preservation of their own traditional language, Tu-Bedawi, also set them apart from Nile Valley Arabs, for whom they had little respect (and vice versa). As nomadic populations, they were reluctant to settle, and as they did so to become agriculturalists, their territories were challenged by outsiders to the east or west, especially by forces allied with Khartoum. In this marginal position, the Beja Congress was formed in 1957 by Dr. Taha Osman Bileya, and it expanded in the 1960s to address their many grievances and state their objectives of democratic federalism. With electoral options open after the 1964 popular revolt, the Beja Congress competed in national elections, with several candidates winning seats in the Constituent Assembly that functioned from 1965 to 1969. The military coup of Ga'afar Nimieri on 25 May 1969 brought the Beja Congress into suspension, but with underground recruitment and organization until the Nimieri years were brought to a close on 6 April 1985. This coincided with the 1984–1985 drought that severely affected eastern Sudan, but with democracy (and rainfall) restored, they could again compete for public office, at least until 1989, when military rule retuned to Sudan. They turned to small-scale armed struggle in the 1990s after the 'Umar Beshir government seized power in 1989. In order to broaden their support, the Beja Congress joined the NDA and signed the 1995 Asmara Declaration seeking to restore democracy to Sudan. Some internal divisions about radical Islam and mutual respect for religion damaged their unity, but they still maintain strength in the borderland region between Hamashkoreib and Garaoura. In early May 2000, it was apparently members of the Beja Congress, with perhaps five hundred armed forces, affiliated with the Sudan Allied Forces, the military wing of the NDA, who sabotaged the oil pipeline, but with no lasting effect, even though this was the third effort to damage this critical export since 1999. Through the early 2000s, repeated small-scale attacks took place on police posts and military targets, with some loss of life but no real defensible gains. In a communiqué from their office in Asmara, they claimed a 14 October 2003 attack on a Tandalai camp near Kassala, but after very bloody fighting, the Khartoum forces rather quickly retook the city. By late 2004 or 2005, the Beja Congress recruited the Free Lions to join them and form the more extensive Eastern Front.

In order to strengthen the Beja Congress, the Eritrea government sought to unify them with the Rashaidya "Free Lions." Although the Rashaidya are culturally Arabs, and relatively recent nineteenth-century migrants to eastern Sudan from Saudi Arabia, with ongoing family ties to Kuwait, they have suffered from much of the same discrimination and marginalization suffered by the various Beja peoples. In November 1999, Mabrouk Mubarak Salim pulled these Rashaidya together in a program similar to that of the Beja Congress that had been formed more than forty years earlier. Perhaps more interesting, with Eritrea having its own interests and tensions with Khartoum after the war in Darfur expanded, since the February 2003 attacks on Sudanese military targets in Darfur, this was an opportunity to link both conflicts, with members of one wing of the Darfuri SLA and the Beja Congress to make a joint, double flank attack on Khartoum from the two peripheries, the far east and far west of the country. The struggle to end marginalization and to achieve federalism, and decentralized sharing of the wealth within a united and democratic Sudan, was their joint objective. Neither considered their goals secessionist, but they were linked in their common struggle to rid Khartoum of the military government.

At last, and most recently, in October 2006, the Eastern Front, with its two major component groups, concluded a peace agreement with the Khartoum government termed simply the "Eastern Sudan Peace Agreement" (ESPA). This was modeled after the CPA (9 January 2005) and DPA (May 2006), but it was simpler in terms of lacking many external parties being involved. Essentially, this agreement has held since then, despite slow motion from Khartoum and heightened expectations from the Eastern Front. In this relatively happy outcome, the voices of the marginalized were heard, and there was a positive response from overburdened Khartoum.

Strategic Trends in Eastern Sudan

In this review of Sudanese history looking out from the East, we found those ancient Blemmyes and Medjay as spectators and facilitators of the regional powers, especially from Egyptians who came as traders on the Red Sea and in need of border guards along the Nile. This seemed to offer reasonable alternatives to the Eastern people as long as they managed to keep their autonomy for the pastoral nomadic economy. In the Greco-Roman period, little changed in this strategic relationship. Trading routes passing through the Butana down to the coast gave some economic stability, and the only real threat to their local autonomy was from the ancient state of Meroë. Occasional raids and counterraids kept the relationship in some sense of balance. The first sense of disequilibrium occurred with the campaign of Ezana, sweeping down from the Ethiopian plateau to crush Meroë, but even then, he did not stay, and between Butana and the Atbara River was just a more trampled corridor, not a staying place. With Meroë gone from power, the East settled back to local self-reliance and did not seek to create a state power for itself. Mutual nonaggression and relative isolation worked from an Eastern point of view. Even with Christianity in Sudan for a thousand years, none of the three Christian kingdoms (Nobatia, Mukurra, and Alwa) ever consolidated power in eastern Sudan. Small-scale trade to the coast and relative isolation still functioned well. The same story prevailed during the Funj Sultanates (1504–1821 CE), when the slave and ivory trade from the South passed through eastern Sudan down to the coast for export. The Easterners were still left with relative regional autonomy at the edge of empires.

The first substantive shift in this pattern took place with the brief Turco-Egyptian imperial rule (1821–1885 CE). This time, the aim was territorial conquest and resource extraction. Eastern Sudan had never been incorporated in a state, and they were willing traders, but not very willing subjects for those interested in taxes, slaves, gold, grain, and livestock.

They were familiar with resistance when required; the Turks were resisted, often passively, by crossing the border to Eritrea and Ethiopia and by long-distance smuggling. The resistance took a much more active form during the Mahdist insurgency, when the famed Suakin slave trader and Mahdist military tactician 'Uthman Digna "broke the British square" with his "fuzzy-wuzzies." Mahdist forces were able to seize Kassala in the east in 1885, and they maintained control of that town and region until 19 July 1894, when Italian forces were able to take it back from the Mahdists for just two years, until the British pushed on toward Khartoum and the Italians were driven back to Eritrea. After successes in Sinkat and Tokar, and wide-ranging attacks by his Beja Ansar troops, Digna was essentially never defeated, but by 1898, there was no more point in fighting any longer. Even when he died in exile in the North, his remains were exhumed and he was later reburied in Erkowit in his beloved Red Sea Hills. Easterners knew how to fight when necessary. This new strategic relationship from the eastern periphery to the Nile Valley core challenged Eastern peoples with being incorporated in a state that they did not want, and it gave them the self-confidence of effective resistance. When colonialism was over in 1956, they found themselves back in the periphery but essentially left alone, until the Arab agricultural development schemes began the assault on their dignity, property, and sovereignty. It was time to resist once again; welcome the Beja Congress and the Rashaidya "Free Lions." Finding more allies in the NDA, the Eastern folk fought on but did not overreach their political or territorial demands; with the signing of the ESPA, there was a truce again between the Nile core and the Eastern periphery.

Now, for eastern Sudan, there were some very fundamental changes—indeed, imbalances—that had not been seen at any previous time. The apparently eternal equation was recalibrated. The balanced relationship of marginalized periphery and weak core that was built on mutual disinterest or mutual respect started to give way in the Turco-Egyptian and colonial periods, but erosion of this relationship was accelerated in the postcolonial period, in which the colonial boundaries inherited from the Berlin Congress (1884–1885) gave the impression that the million square miles of Sudan really was a functional unitary state, when in reality it was not, and essentially never had been.

THE CASE OF THE NUBIAN NORTH

Reflections on Historical Northern Security Dynamics

Ancient and medieval northern Sudan has gone by various names, covering changing territorial domains. They have ranged from *Ta-Nehesi* ("land of Nubians") to *Ta-Seti* ("the land of the bow people") to *Kerma*, *Kush*, *Meroë*, and the three Christian kingdoms (*Nobatia*, *Mukurra*, and *Alwa*), not to mention the Islamic lands of the *'Abdallab* and the *Funj Sultanates*, or, most simply, just *Nubia*, "the land of gold." Today, Nubia stretches from northernmost Sudan from Dongola north to Aswan in southern Egypt. Already, a number of passing references to these states and lands have inevitably been noticed in the commentary on eastern Sudan, with which Nubia long interacted. There is no need to repeat this information; but, as above, some general strategic relationships emerge that are worth recognizing. First, the security threats to any of these configurations were generally not with the Nilotic Southern peripheries, nor much to the East, as long as mutual trade routes were kept open and thriving. Far to the west, the contemporary peoples of Kordofan and Darfur were largely left alone. It was from the north, from Egypt, that the serious security threat to Nubian states and kingdoms emerged. But it is too simple to summarize Egyptian-Nubian interactions with this bald statement, since the relationship

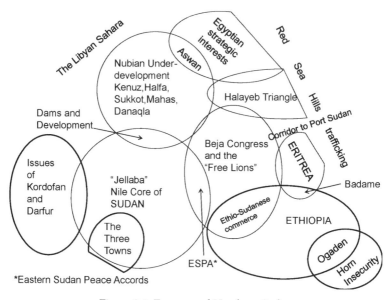

Figure 3.1 Eastern and Northern Sudan

between Egypt and Nubia was one of many innuendos and nuances. It was a love-hate relationship. There were cases of mutual defense, and there were times of mutual aggression. It was, at times, a tempestuous and suspicious relationship, and it was a loving and attractive relationship. There were times of colonial occupation and military counterattack. There were dimensions of jealousy and brotherly love; it was, in short, a rivalry. There was mutual admiration and mutual suspicion. It was such a relationship that one of the world's longest treaties (the *baqt*) managed to endure for more than six centuries. Married as neighbors for five thousand years, one could probably not expect otherwise.

So, in such complex respects, the strategic relations with Nubia (northern Sudan) and Egypt have been among the most complicated in all of Sudanese history. For much of the time, central and southern Sudan was distant, remote, and far removed from this dominant preoccupation. Relationships ranged from raids and counterattacks for millennia between Upper Egyptians during the thousand-year epoch of the Kerma (2500–1500 BCE) civilization in Nubia, including a Kerma effort to trap Egyptians in Upper Egypt by aligning themselves politically and militarily with the Hyksos, who had taken over the Egyptian delta in the Second Intermediate Period (1782–1570 BCE). Nubians took over Egyptian forts in the Middle Kingdom, and brought trophies and captured loot back to their capital at Kerma. Getting their revenge, the Egyptians drove out the Hyksos (possible ancestors of the Jewish Exodus?) and then turned south to establish five centuries of Egyptian colonial occupation of Nubia during the Egyptian New

Kingdom (ca. 1500–1000 BCE), during which a score of huge, strategically placed mud bricks forts secured the Egyptian frontier, and an Egyptian viceroy of Kush (Nubia) was maintained full-time to produce gold, slaves, ivory, and taxes, along with military security in Nubia. After a "Dark Age" (1000–800 BCE) recovery, Egypt found itself under foreign attack and occupation from southwest Asia, while Nubians recovered sufficiently to achieve a century of Nubian occupation of Egypt in Dynasty XXV.

Egypt finally and utterly lost its sovereignty, falling under invasions from Assyrians, Persians, Greeks, and Romans, who arrived as polytheists and departed as Byzantine Christians, leaving the Monophysite Egyptians in a theological dispute in the fourth century CE that is unresolved until today. This was followed by a succession of Muslim invaders. Meanwhile, Nubia generally kept its independence, with the episodic border attack, during these very long periods. The great Egypt was humiliated by foreign occupation, while the "upstart" and "renegade" Nubians kept their autonomy in the empires of Napata, Meroë, and the Christian kingdoms of Nubia that blocked the southward spread of Islam for some six hundred years. Even when Islam took hold in central Sudan with the Funj Sultans (1504–1821 CE), it was a Sudanese state with its own mixture of people and beliefs, even though Nubian teachers did their best to set them on the correct Islamic protocols. Then came the Turco-Egyptians conspiring (1821–1885 CE) to take over Nubia and much of Sudan in their quest for slaves, ivory, gold, and conscripted soldiers for their ambitions as close as the Suez Canal and as far away as Mexico in the New World. There was a Sudanese response led by the Nubian al-Mahdi and his successor to drive these same people out and recover Sudan (1885–1898 CE) in the name of Islam. As noted earlier, the Khalifa also tried and failed to expand his Islamic *jihad* into Egypt at the 1889 battle at Toshka, Nubia, where this ambition was curbed. And, in this eternally unfinished business, this was followed by the Egyptian ruling class and England conspiring to retake Sudan to control the Nile and procure cotton for textile mills in Manchester and Lancashire. To see anything but an eternal back-and-forth in these many contexts would be to miss the strategic relationship whereby the border between Egypt and Nubia mainly tended to oscillate between the first and second cataract on the Nile until the early twentieth century.

In modern postcolonial times, northern Sudan, or Nubia, was similar to the situation of the East, at least in terms of becoming marginal to the politics of the core, but with the great difference that Nubia had been a series of city-states or even empire-states, quite unlike eastern Sudan. The Nubian fall from historical significance to marginality was a greater blow, one imagines, than for eastern Sudan never to have had such glories at all. Northern history is also very different in other respects besides the ancient state tradition, since Nubia and Nubians were perceived as potential threats to the two nation-states in which they were then located. The ruling elites in Cairo and Khartoum agreed that the small, colonial

Low Dam at Aswan was inadequate for the hydroelectric and irrigation needs that they had by the 1960s, so they determined to build a new and much grander High Dam at Aswan. The catch was that traditional Nubia, with its roads, towns, cities, cemeteries, palm trees, houses, ancient landmarks, and immeasurable antiquities of world status, would all be subject to submersion and eternal loss. Nubia would be no more; especially this was the case in Egyptian Nubia, where the inhabitants would be relocated to new sites such as Kom Ombo. The Sudanese side of the equation was parallel, especially for Wadi Halfa and the adjacent parts of Upper Nubia (north Sudan) that were affected by this vast inundation.

Sudanese Nubians (Muslims but not Arabs) had only a few "choices": relocate to Khasm al-Girba and New Halfa in eastern Sudan, where they had no previous connections; move independently to a Khartoum or Cairo Nubian diaspora; or stay approximately where they were but on new sites on higher ground. All the alternatives were terrible from a Nubian perspective. While Easterners had typically been at the periphery, Nubians had been at the core of ancient and medieval Sudanese states. This was a grave blow to their cultural identity. Now, a half-century later, Nubians still feel fundamentally wronged by the High Aswan Dam flood. As if this were not enough to wound pride and history, a new dam project was conceived and is now mainly built at the fourth cataract, the Hamdab Dam, in a region of Sudan rich with Nubian history. The population of Nubians, Arabized Nubians, and others in the Manasir region have again been displaced to make way for vast roadways, a hydroelectric dam, and agricultural schemes, mostly built by Chinese capital and labor. This was another body blow to Nubian identity and territory, while the far North was falling into permanent economic decline, with many homes emptied of young, and marginally employed people finding nothing useful to do in their natal lands, or sent to the far South in the seemingly endless war between Southern aspirations for autonomy and Northern (Islamist) religious ambitions.

Then, it became still worse from their view. Still another dam, at Kajbar at the third cataract, was forecast, and plans were started to trap more water and displace more people in traditional Nubia. There were more protests and more resistance, some put down in violence, as the Khartoum authority and Chinese backers stayed fixed on their development goals. No profound disruption of this magnitude and this duration ever took place in eastern Sudan.

Trends and Conclusions from the Northern Sudan

The age-old strategic interests of preserving territory, maintaining economic relations of mutual interest, and securing control of valued natural resources were all lost to the central authority in Khartoum and its allies in a land where mainly it is the water of the Nile and adjoining lands that give value. The strategic interests of modern Nubians have been reduced, shrunken down, to cultural and linguistic survival in museums, books, and excavations, and expanded development of the towns and new roads that are above the ever-spreading flood plains. So, the issues of development and underdevelopment in the Nubian North have been narrowed to survival, with the old and new dams, seeking jobs, and struggling for a sense of their own ethnic identity within the dominant paradigm of Islamic and Arab national unity. While there is talk of intensifying resistance, it is no wonder that Nubia, so seriously damaged, is at present too weak and Nubians too dispersed to do more than cry foul and buttress themselves to be protected from still deeper falls from their once-glorious history. Only a model of multiethnic, regional diversity, federalism, and national democracy can save Nubia from further decline.

Strategic Observations of the Sudanese State from These Two Peripheries to the Core, and from the Core to the Northern and Eastern Peripheries

For those modern native inhabitants of northern or eastern Sudan, there is a powerful sense of being neglected and marginalized by Khartoum. The perception is that the more power and economic resources that are consolidated in the "three towns," the more they are reduced in their regions. Or, in the case of regional development projects in the East or North, the more the local residents lose consultative decision-making and representation in critical decisions. In these developments, foreign or powerful Sudanese interests move into position, at the expense of the local residents. And the more that relative poverty increases in the North or East, the more that traditional livelihoods become impossible and rural-to-urban relocation to towns becomes the main avenue to economic security, which, in turn, sends their regions into further economic decline. Viewed from the commanding heights of the Sudanese core, they are doing their best to develop these regions with new agricultural schemes, distribution of national resources, and local economic development. If only the peripheral people would be more patient, with fewer disruptive protests, demonstrations, and resistance in various forms, the whole nation would be more peaceful and would advance toward common goals. The lack of articulation of these two views is likely a main result of ineffective local consultation, unresponsive governance, and overly centralized administration that is substantially diverted by the conflict in Darfur and with issues spilling over from the North-South accord. Thus, the powerful engine of development in Khartoum is placed on a weak national framework, with adequate fuel but with the tires of this 'vehicle for change' in serious need of pressure-checks before taking this long journey. On the other hand, the political volatility and even cases of political violence in the capital are rather rarely seen or directly felt in the periphery, so they remain relatively calm, albeit impoverished, areas. The managerial strategy of Khartoum applies "trickle-down" approaches with periodic repression; the peripheral response is one of periodic revolt and protest, expecting repression but ultimately partial accommodation. This sort of *ad hoc* reciprocity means that Khartoum officially never gives up any of its nonconsultative authority in decision-making, and it formally maintains its political, economic, and military hegemony, but there is a sufficient escape valve that spontaneously releases local pressures and tensions until a new status quo can be reached. For a predictable or stable model of governance, this leaves something to be desired, but the value of "unquestioned authority" is so great that its monopoly is placed over other modes of more democratic governance. However bumpy and rough this approach may be, it does, after a fashion, work over long periods of time for these regions. Elsewhere in Sudan, where other variables come into play, this "Eastern/Northern" governance model has failed significantly, perhaps because the stakes are higher and sustained violence is "normal." Also mollifying the core/periphery tensions in the Eastern and Northern regions are a radically improved all-weather road system and reasonable cell phone connections. The much-improved road and airport system means the rapid deployment of police, militia, and military forces in case local conflicts appear to need such measures. The violent suppression of a demonstration in Nubia and the short military work to retake Kassala in the East makes these points clear to local, internal, and external observers. Even the very brief NDA insurgent occupation of Kassala in November 2000 was possible largely because of then-deteriorated relations with Eritrea that allowed insurgents to make a move from this rear area. Once state-to-state relations were restored, there have been no serious repeat attacks or needs for suppressive intervention.

There is still frustrated despair with privatized and mechanized agricultural schemes in the East and loss of irrigated land with new dams in Nubia, but resistance has largely been crushed, displaced, replaced, or bought out to address these issues. The relative lack of foreign interest in these regions has also helped Khartoum to simplify conflict resolution on one hand, and has given the people of the East and the North fewer potential allies from whom they might seek support. Finally, while there are cultural and linguistic distinctions, and political differences about ideological issues, the peoples of eastern, northern, and central Sudan are all practicing and relatively tolerant Sunni Muslims, so this at least is not a very contentious point at the general level.

This chapter has shown that eastern Sudan has rarely been the main focus of regional powers in Eritrea, Ethiopia, or Sudan, whether colonial or national, but eastern Sudan has been worth a tactical fight over wider strategic objectives. So, Kassala has been a frontier "trample town," and it has exchanged rulers multiple times as regional rivals sought access to the main objectives in the Abyssinian plateau or in the Nile Valley. Such patterns were true in the Greco-Roman, medieval Christian, Turco-Egyptian, Mahdist, British colonial, and postcolonial periods. Eastern Sudan in general was worth fighting over, not for its inherent value, but because it controls maritime access from the Rea Sea ports of Sudan to the interior. One of the rare cases in which Ethiopians (Axumites) actually entered Sudan through the Atbara (Asta Boras) River and reached all the way to Meroë was because Meroë was already in very serious decline and very weak. It is equally notable that the Axumites conquered Meroë but left rather promptly, attesting to this peripheral relationship to their own territorial interests.

On the other hand, northern Sudan in general and Nubia in particular has been a most ancient and modern corridor to Africa and to the Sudanese heartland. At many points in Sudanese history, Nubia was the heartland, especially considering the central positions of Kerma, Napata, and Meroë in ancient Sudanese states. Massive and numerous ancient Egyptian defensive forts were built to protect them from Nubian attack. When they finally broke through after 1,500 years of trying, the Egyptians created the New Kingdom by entering Sudan through Nubia to establish a colonial presence for five centuries. At one point, when Egyptian territorial unity was wavering, Nubia conquered and ruled all of Egypt for almost a century in Dynasty XXV. For Persians, Greeks, and Romans entering through Egypt with ambitions toward Nubian gold and slaves, they were typically compelled to curb their ambitions and settle for a territory most often bounded at Aswan or northern Nubia. When Muslims entered Egypt in 640 CE, they tried and failed for six hundred years to break to military defense of Nubian Christianity. In later epochs, such as the Turco-Egyptian times, the armies of Khedive Muhammad 'Ali entered through Nubia, but in a mere six decades (1821–1885), the Nubian al-Mahdi was able to drive them out to recover Sudanese autonomy. Even when the British and Egyptians renewed their effort to control Sudan and its resources in 1989, they entered by ship and rail through Nubia, but the Sudanese did not welcome them, and in even less time (1898–1956), they were also driven away in defeat. One can conclude that the powers in Cairo and Khartoum must take Nubia seriously for strategic reasons of access, transit, and control, even more so than eastern Sudan. Such observations also provided reminders of the mosaic nature of Sudan, in which the various territorial parts are all needed for control of the center but each part has its unique features.

Finally, and by extension, the peripheral and frontier aspects of the East and North can mean that these are avenues for anti-state or non-state activities, such as anti-regime movements in Egypt like *Jama'a Islamiya*, which can and has infiltrated over the (Sudan-Egypt) Nubian border, as well as arms-smuggling along the Red Sea coast, reported in January 2009 with an apparent attack by an Israeli fighter jet (or perhaps drones) on arms being trucked from Port Sudan that were destined to relieve the people of Gaza during the Israeli incursion there. That neither of these events became major suggests both that marginal activities happen in ungoverned or poorly governed spaces and also that they do not directly present existential threats to the regime; however, neglecting such activities will finally put the state at existential risk.

SOURCES

Collins, Robert O. *Eastern African History* (Princeton, NJ: Markus Wiener, 1997).
Lobban, Richard A., Carolyn Fluehr-Lobban, and Robert Kramer. *Historical Dictionary of the Sudan* (Lanham, MD: Scarecrow Press, 2002).
Sidahmed, Abdel Salam and Alsir Sidahmed. *Sudan* (New York: Routledge Curzon, 2005).

CHAPTER 4

Darfur

To understand the present conflict in Darfur, it is necessary to look at its earlier origins and the historical context of the grievances that launched the present round of violence. Only then can one begin to comprehend why this was so difficult to resolve. Without this clear understanding, it is unlikely that it will be possible to formulate practical and effective steps toward the management of the conflict or Sudanese governance at large. Equally important in understanding Darfur is its strategic location. For the majority of its history, Darfur was an autonomous region, and until the nineteenth century was ruled by insiders. Key trade routes passed through Kobbé or al-Fasher. On these routes, trade was conducted in basic foodstuffs, handicrafts, and livestock. After the arrival of Islam in the Western Sahel, the tracks through Darfur were significant Muslim pilgrimage routes from West Africa to the eastern Sudan port of Suakin and on to Mecca and Medina. Control of this transit trade was the essential point of dispute as various Darfur dynasties rose and fell from power. A second trade route was from the southern parts of Darfur, such as "Dar Fertit" and Hofrat an-Nahas, from which slaves were captured and marched to al-Fasher for use by the ruling elites in domestic service or as an export commodity. A third route went further northward to Libya and Egypt from the center of Darfur along the famed Darb al-Arba'ien, or "40-days road," through the desert and the Kharga Oasis to Middle Egypt. The fourth strategic position occupied by Darfur in more modern times was when it became the western terminus of the railway. Regionally speaking, Darfur straddles three major climatic zones, ranging from open desert in the north, to extensive sandy grasslands, to light forests in the south. Amid this broad variation are microclimatic zones due to the high elevations of the central *massif* of Jebel Marra, where there is more rainfall and substantially different ecosystems that support different modes of production. In brief, the physical geography of Darfur, not to mention its large size (equal to France), needs to be put into the equation.

Turning to the basic chronology of Darfur, one may set the stage for some of the modern dynamics and conflicts by dividing its history into four periods.

I. Periods of Sovereignty and Independence
    A. The ancient period, known mainly from archaeological records
    B. The medieval period of rival Sultanate formation
II. Periods of Annexation
    A. The Turco-Egyptian Conquest (1821–1885)
    B. The Sudanese Mahdist Annexation (1885–1898)
III. Restoration of the Keira Sultanate (1898–1916) and Anglo-Egyptian Colonial Conquest (1898–1956)
IV. The Postcolonial Sudanese Regimes (1956–present)

INDEPENDENT STATE FORMATION IN DARFUR

There is a limited archaeological record in Darfur. There are some recent surface surveys and some excavations before 2003 of various ancient and medieval strata, but chronology and pottery typologies are still being refined. Connections with the Egyptian and Sudanese Nile Valley as well as the deeper Sahara are clearly established. People who were essentially ancestors to the present populations have certainly populated the region for many millennia. The main exceptions were the Arab intrusions that are much more recent. Also, there are passing textual references from ancient Egypt from as early as the Old Kingdom in the documented travels to Sudan/Nubia/Kush by Harkuf and other *hekaib* (governors of Aswan). This travel took place along the 40-days road from Middle Egypt to the Selima Oasis and then on to tributary donkey and (later camel) routes into Darfur and Kordofan on the *Wadi al-Milk*. Darfur also straddled east-west trade and migration routes along the Sahel. The control of the established export trade from Darfur was of importance from the start of the historical record.

MEDIEVAL PERIOD OF SULTANATE FORMATION

Precisely who was ruling Darfur in these earliest times is not yet clear, but it certainly was part of the process of the Islamization of the broad Sahelian region in medieval times. Islam arrived in Darfur as part of legitimacy for the small Darfur kingdoms in about the thirteenth century; in a few cases, there may have been Muslims there before the collapse of the Christian kingdoms of Nubia. Medieval Christian Nubian references indicate that there was steady trade from Darfur along the "40-days road" through the Selima and Kharga oases and on to Egypt.

Out of this foggy past, the first names of some thirteen to twenty-one regional rulers are drawn from the Daju Sultans. It is offered that either Sultan Gita or Kosber were the founders of this line of non-Muslim and non-Arab trader kings, and that the last of these eastern Sudanic Daju leaders was Sultan Kuroma (Nachtigal 1971, 272–274). The Daju Sultans controlled the trade on the southern flanks of the Marra Plateau, and to a lesser extent, the eastern sides and to the west up to the Masalit. They also controlled the east-west trade to the Nile.

Gradually, as trade (and conflict) increased, the Daju dominance in Darfur receded and was replaced by the Tunjur Sultans, who ruled from the northern slopes of Jebel Marra and in the Zaghawa areas of the dry savanna in a thirteen-king dynasty (Nachtigal 1971, 272). The Tunjur Dynasty was the successor to the Daju in the fourteen century. They accepted Islam to a degree that syncretically accommodated their traditional beliefs as well. The last sultan of the Tunjur dynasty after 1600 was Ahmad al-Maqur, the "wise stranger." The Tunjur sometimes claimed territory to Wadai in Chad and as far west as Kanem in northeastern Nigeria and western Chad, having no correspondence to the boundaries imposed by colonialism in the nineteenth century. Al-Maqur provided for the peaceful transfer of power to the Keira dynasty by marriage into the ruling circles. He had critical commercial and political links to the surrounding Arab people, both camel-herders to the north and cattle-herders to the south. Variant forms of syncretic Islam were already present during the time of the Tunjur rulers, before the sixteenth century. Controlling the slave trade from Kobbé on to the 40-days road was also an element of their economy, before the intrusive colonial boundaries with little local impact.

The next Darfur sovereigns were the Keira Sultans, who were even more expansive than the Daju and Tunjur insofar as they controlled, at times, greater swathes of Darfur as well as controlling major parts of Kordofan to the east. Within this historical tradition, at least one Darfur rebel group staged military attacks on civilian targets in modern Kordofan and Omdurman. The Keira Sultans claim links to an Arab pedigree, and Islam was their legitimating faith, yet some traces of pre-Islamic matrilineal ties linger on. Typically, the historiography of the Keira dynasty starts with Sultan Kuru, who was the father of the more important Sulayman Solong, who ruled from about 1650 to 1680 (according to O'Fahey). His son Musa carried on from 1680 to 1700, although these dates differ in the works of Nachtigal. This line continued with Ahmed Bakr ibn Musa, 1700–1720; Muhammad Dawra ibn Ahmad Bakr, 1720–1730; 'Umar in Muhammad Dawra ("Lele") 1730–1739; Abu al-Qasim ibn Ahmad Bakr, 1739–1752; Muhammad Tayrab ibn Ahmad Bakr, 1752–1785/6; 'Abd al-Rahman al-Rashid ibn Ahmad Bakr, 1785/6–1799?; Muhammad al-Fadl ibn 'abd al-Rahman, 1799?–1838/9. The dates and leaders are mentioned to demonstrate that for much of two centuries, the Keira Sultans ruled continuously as an independent state larger than modern Darfur.

TURCO-EGYPTIAN CONQUEST

Even when the Turks managed to seize control of central Sudan and Kordofan, two sovereign sultans continued to rule Darfur for many decades: Sultan Muhammad Hussein ibn Muhammad Fadl, from 1838/9 to 1873, and then Sultan Ibrahim ibn Muhammad Hussein in 1873. When the Turks forced the creation of shadow Sultans of Darfur in Turco-Egyptian times, they still had to rule though the Keira dynasty with Sultan Hasab Allah ibn Muhammad Fadl and Bosh ibn Muhammad Fadl ruling in 1874, then with the notorious slave trader Zubayr Pasha Rahma Mansur from1874 to 1875; Sultan Muhammad Harun Sayf al-Rashid ibn Bosh, 1875–1880; and 'Abdallah Dud Banja ibn Bakr, 1880–1884. In the last case, the Fur still resisted the Turco-Egyptians until 1881. Only when Mahdist forces finally defeated William Hicks Pasha at the famous Sheikan battle in December 1883 did Mahdist rule fully replace the Turco-Egyptians or Keira sultans.

THE SUDANESE MAHDIST ANNEXATION

After Khartoum fell on 25 January 1885 with the death of General George "Chinese" Gordon, the non-Arab rulers of Darfur did not deeply accept the Mahdists, who had a Baggara (Ta'isha) Arab base in Darfur and Kordofan that mobilized military forces under the Khalifa 'Abdullahi. Sultan Yusuf ibn Sultan Ibrahim ruled from 1884 to 1886, and in 1886, Sultan Muhammad Khalid actually took his military force to the east to try to overthrow Khalifa 'Abdullahi after the sudden death of the Mahdi in 1885. These relationships reveal patterns from history of core-periphery tensions as well as internal Darfur struggles that are echoed today. At last, Mahdist control of the center was ruthlessly inserted into Darfur with Sultan Uthman Adam violently suppressing revolts of the Keira and Dar-Tama people. Even when Mahdist strength was at its height, it was weak and distracted elsewhere, so they appointed rulers: Abu al-Khayrat ibn Ibrahim (1889 to the 1890s) and Mahmoud Ahmed, the last Mahdist-appointed governor. In 1896, his troops were recalled to the Nile valley, where they tried but failed to stop the Anglo-Egyptian advance that ended Mahdist control in 1898 and began British colonial occupation until 1956.

RESTORATION OF THE KEIRA SULTANATE (1898–1916) AND ANGLO-EGYPTIAN COLONIAL CONQUEST (1916–1956)

Remote from the Nile Valley fighting, the Keira (Fur) Sultanate of Darfur was recreated in the power vacuum that resulted from the overthrow of the Mahdist state. In this context, Sultan 'Ali Dinar ibn Zakariya ibn Muhammad Fadl was again sovereign from1898 to 1916, until the British wished to expand their cotton-producing colony westward from the Nile Valley. Once again, the core of Nile Valley Sudan had its own history, and Darfur went its own way.

Once the Anglo-Egyptians conquered Sudan in 1898, it still took some months to hunt down and kill the Khalifa 'Abdullahi and his few remaining supporters at Umm Dibaykarat, and to sort out rival French claims to the Upper Nile at Fashoda. However, this Darfur rival to English power could not be tolerated forever, so in 1916, the British sent Hubert Huddleston (1880–1950) to suppress the Sultanate, during which time his forces assassinated the last sultan, 'Ali Dinar, and two of his sons on 16 November. During the Anglo-Egyptian condominium colonial period in Darfur, from 1916 to 1956, there were sporadic revolts and frequent interethnic clashes in Darfur, most notably the Masalit Revolt of 1922. Wanting to settle this region down long after the Berlin Congress of 1884–1885, the French and English drew the border that separated Darfur from Wadai in 1924, the same year as the assassination of Lee Stack and the White Flag uprising in Khartoum. Following the lead of Lord Lugard's system of indirect colonial rule formulated in Nigeria, the British experimented with Darfur puppets from 1924 to 1929. This policy was abandoned after the attempt to resurrect a puppet emir, Muhammad Fadl ibn 'Abd al-Hamid ibn Sultan Ibrahim, from 1929 to 1936.

As a conservative colonial military officer, Huddleston also crushed the 1924 White Flag Society revolt and suppressed the Workers' Affairs Association, the nascent Graduates Congress, and even the 1944 protests against colonialism in Tuti Island in Khartoum. Rewarded for this military successes in Sudan, Huddleston was appointed Governor-General from 1940 to 1947. Recalling such memories of British colonial practices in Darfur and elsewhere in Sudan makes modern Sudanese extremely reluctant to have British forces returning to the region. One can understand why the Sudanese are suspicious that any European powers would try to play one region against the other, as was their past practice.

POSTCOLONIAL SUDANESE REGIMES AND DARFUR (1956–PRESENT)

Yet postcolonial administrations of Sudan and in Africa, whether democratic or military, have generally pursued colonial-like policies of strong centralization of power in the capital. Peripheral regions such as Darfur are typically neglected unless there are revolts, which are usually met with military repression. Viewed with this historical lens, the current situation (2003–2005) in Darfur is overwhelmingly more typical than exceptional.

Before moving on to the modern conflicts in Darfur, other factors must be considered, including traditional economic rivalries over various resources. These are especially conflicts over land and water, including systems of land use and land tenure that have long been contested and ambiguous. There are exacerbating factors of ecology, global climate change, irregular and sparse rainfall in the Sahel, desertification, and marginalization. None of these concerns are easily solved, nor is a single person or group easily blamed if the conflicts are to be managed. At the macro-level, not much has changed in Darfur. One's membership of specific ethnic groups in Darfur meant which degree to which you had more, or less access to power and resources. Ethnic cleavages can be found (1) among the traditional Darfur groups, (2) between Darfur groups and "Arabs," (3) between the Darfur periphery and the Nile Valley core elites, and (4) between various rebel groups and with the *janjaweed* in present conflicts. Each force mobilizes resources to the fullest extent possible to achieve its political ambitions.

With this retrospective view, one should not be surprised to find significant divisions present inside Darfur among the modern rebel groups that vary in ethnic composition, ideologies, and political objectives, including (1) contests over models of governance, (2) the role and relationship of religion and the state, and (3) interpersonal contests for leadership of a subsequent political configuration of Darfur. In a parallel fashion, political debates and struggles in Khartoum have taken place (1) between the NPC and NIF, (2) among the NPC, SPLA, and GNU, (3) between the models of military and democratic governance, and (4) regarding the timing and modalities of the elections in 2010 and the later referendum on unity, all of which reverberate in Darfur. Putting this together, there are the persistent issues in Darfur that relate to marginalization and underdevelopment vis-à-vis Khartoum politics and, at present, the counterinsurgency and insurgency activities that are played out amid other judicial and humanitarian concerns. In short, the tactical and strategic stances of the various players are extremely complex and dynamic, but are deeply founded in the regional history.

The first step to understand and analyze the intersecting conflicts in Darfur has been taken with the historical overview to see what is "normal" in conflict-generation in past centuries. This approach has exposed the more recent precipitating causes that elevated the conflict in 2003 to the higher level of violence from 2003 to 2005–2006 as well as the "postconflict" period that may be unfolding in 2009–2010. Among the many *precipitating* causes are (1) the removal of traditional mechanisms of conflict resolution, (2) the growth of political polarization from Khartoum, (3) the lack of democratic forums and negotiation, (4) the relative importance of global climate change and desertification in Darfur, (5) broad-based political marginalization and class formation between the Khartoum "core" and the Darfur "periphery," (6) demographic increase without a corresponding increase in employment or resources, and (7) the widespread proliferation of small arms.

With the Darfur conflict still ongoing and not managed for much of this writing until the 2009–2010 period, there is also need to look more carefully at other *exacerbating* causes, which include (1) widespread internationalization of the conflict, with many more governmental and nongovernmental stakeholders (compared to the ESPA) more parallel to the long conflicts in the southern Sudan;

(2) the "genocide" issue, more civilian displacement, and the judicial charges from ICC, which have complicated the Darfur conflict considerably; (3) the use of sanctions against Khartoum over Darfur while calling for support of Khartoum relative to the CPA in the South and collaboration about the Global War on Terrorism (GWOT), which has sent very confusing messages that give Khartoum opportunities for manipulation of the issues; (4) the Darfur conflict taking the form of proxy wars between Chad and Sudan, only worsening the problems, culminating with serious military attacks by opposing guerillas forces against the respective capital towns of the two neighbor nations; and, finally, (5) the failure of unification of rebels at Abuja and after, for various understandable reasons, making it difficult to impossible for honest brokers to determine who represents whom and which diplomatic approach for unity or isolation should be employed in this changing context.

DEEPER DRILLING INTO THE SOCIO-POLITICAL BEDROCK OF DARFUR

In the early (1969–1971) "socialist" phase of the Nimieri government, the spirits of Arab nationalism and secularism were strong. A comprehensive effort was made to terminate the traditional parties (especially DUP and Umma) and to "reform" or transform governance at the provincial and local level in a spirit of modernization and nationalism. As an employee of that government, then working as a journalist in the Ministry of Southern Affairs, this author could see that this was initially and broadly appreciated among youth and intellectuals, but broadly resisted by the traditional forces it set out to destroy. Whether that was good politics or bad at that time remains debatable, but from the perspective of rural and provincial communities, their traditional governance was seriously undermined and there was nothing substantial left in its place when this approach was terminated. The previous model was with negotiations held by the *Mejlis ash-Shayukh* (council of elders, or *sharati*, in the tradition of Darfur) that could determine compensation (*diya*) in the context of grievances. For centuries, this worked rather smoothly to resolve *shaklat* (troubles) within and between the ethnic corporate groups such as *fariiqs* (lineages) that structured each social segment to be functionally autonomous, thereby tending to lower-level conflict resolution either with payment of *diya* or with a *sulh* (treaty) to avoid conflicts at a larger scale. This worked even when conflicts were interethnic in Darfur and its borderlands, mostly over issues of trespass, insult, water rights, livestock theft, and such, even with loss of life. The leaders of the various groups of Arabs (camel-herders and cattle-herders) and non-Arabs (farmers and herders) could meet and assess the damages and negotiate the compensation. The record of minor conflicts in Darfur is long, but rarely did they get more out of hand than that. Sometimes, neutral government officials provided a positive setting and enforced the peace of the negotiation meetings with the presence of a modest constabulary. This is far from saying that peace and paradise prevailed, but with a functioning local mechanism of conflict resolution and a relatively neutral central government, most conflicts were resolved with negotiation of the conflicting parties or some limited police action. Under the secular nationalist government of the first phase of Nimieri, this began to change, with the withdrawal or undermining of the traditional authorities. However, the damage to this mechanism would not be recognized, or the threat not especially noted, until Darfur issues rose to a higher level of contestation that could not be accommodated. As a precipitating set of factors, population growth and economic marginalization compounded with a decline in rainfall. Prunier (2005, 49) presents rainfall data in Darfur from 1976 to 1986 that show a decline by a quarter to a third. So, the conflicts tended to reach higher-scale group involvement than in previous times, except for times of interdynastic shifts. Again, these changes did not make a noticeable difference until circumstances pushed tensions to unmanageable levels. The final stage of the degradation of conflict-resolution capacity for Darfur took place in the years after the 1989 coup of al-Beshir and the NIF. In this last instance, the government side was no longer neutral, and it sided with the Arab militias (*janjaweed*) as an instrument of its police action, as part of its ideological mission, and as an instrument of counter-insurgency once the Darfur insurgency escalated and assets and personnel of the Sudanese state were attacked directly. It was the "perfect storm," with multiple triangulation of intersecting negative forces that has led to seven years of military strife and massive population dislocation.

While these historical, political, and economic factors are at the foundation of the conflict in Darfur, it has taken place in a region that has substantial ethnic and linguistic diversity, as well as rivalries among Darfur rebel groups that must be considered in the equation of the marginalized people. While ethnic membership is not the primary cause or objective of the conflict, ethnicity became a clear artifact once the armed forces of all sides became engaged in both recruitment and offensive actions. Actually, soldiers from Darfur often made up a large part of the enlisted men in the regular Sudanese military, despite the fact that the rebel insurgency is now based in these same populations, such as the Fur, Masalit, and Zaghawa. With demonization and prejudicial attitudes about the enemy, common to warfare anywhere, this became a self-actualizing dimension of the conflict in Darfur by both sides. To the degree to which the Western concept of "race" has any meaning in the Sudanese conflict, racial/ethnic distinctions can be, and are certainly, made in Sudan, particularly as the conflict goes on without resolution. Despite the charges of "genocide," refugees from the conflict zones sought protection in internally displaced people (IDP) camps in Darfur, and thousands also moved to relative safety in the capital cities. Clearly, such havens were *not* sought by other populations facing genocide in other instances in the nineteenth or twentieth centuries.

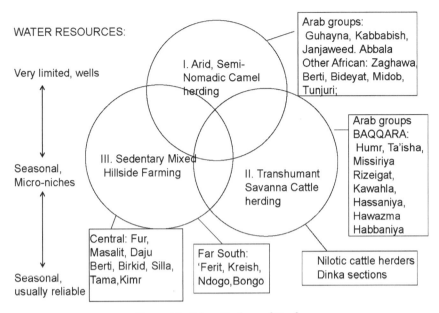

WATER RESOURCES:

Very limited, wells

Seasonal,
Micro-niches

Seasonal,
usually reliable

Arab groups:
  Guhayna, Kabbabish,
  Janjaweed. Abbala
  Other African: Zaghawa,
  Berti, Bideyat, Midob,
  Tunjuri;

I. Arid, Semi-
Nomadic Camel
herding

III. Sedentary Mixed
Hillside Farming

II. Transhumant
Savanna Cattle
herding

Arab groups
BAQQARA:
  Humr, Ta'isha,
  Missiriya
  Rizeigat,
  Kawahla,
  Hassaniya,
  Hawazma
  Habbaniya

Central: Fur,
Masalit, Daju
Berti, Birkid, Silla,
Tama,Kimr

Far South:
'Ferit, Kreish,
Ndogo,Bongo

Nilotic cattle herders
Dinka sections

Figure 4.1 Ethno-Ecology of Darfur

Since Clausewitz informed us that "war is politics by another means," the polarizing and propagandizing on this point has been a strong feature of the struggles in Darfur. Equally so, the manipulation of and either inflation or minimization of the gross estimates of the numbers of dead, injured, and dislocated has become a part of propaganda warfare and is not genuinely focused on the logistical and humanitarian support for the needy people whom the rebels and government both claim to be representing and fighting for. With the world's largest refugee population, Africa has, sadly, become accustomed to such miseries; as it is said, "when elephants fight, it is the grass that is trampled"—or, even more patronizingly, colonialists could speculate on, "how should White people, save Black people."

Far beyond the rebel and government positions and statements, the manipulation and diversion of broad anti-Arab and anti-Muslim sentiments, and the international posturing about "genocide" to put pressure on Khartoum, have actually been counterproductive to conflict resolution, as they have cut off effective pressure points and a spirit of compromise to pave the way to peace-making. This effort is principally mobilized by activists and nations that have very problematic relations with the Arab world, with policies that have collectively caused far more death, destruction, and displacement than has occurred in Darfur, while also ignoring other great conflicts in Africa, such as in the eastern Congo. It is hard not to conclude that the special interest in Darfur became a cause in its own right. This leads to another facet of Darfur, namely the high degree of inter-nationalization of interested groups and agencies that are involved and become stakeholders in one way or another. Broad international engagement was notably absent in the conflict in eastern Sudan, in which an agreement was reached, signed, and is relatively healthy.

As a related effect of the high degree of international prominence of Darfur in certain Western nations, there has been a reluctance to understand, gather, or dis-seminate cultural and political intelligence about the now highly fractured rebel groups. Khartoum, perhaps quite rightly, has been demonized to the extent that the relative lack of press and public information about the rebels and their objec-tives has generally defaulted to their being more angelic. More often than not, the minimal journalistic accounts lump them homogeneously as "victims" along with the greatest victims of all, the noncombatant women, children, and elderly. One is left with the conclusion that their marginalized position apparently justi-fied them to make the first major escalation on February 2003, which has now run out of control and management. Truly, no Sudanist or Sudanese should be surprised by this outcome, with the very predictable counterinsurgency response of the various governments of Sudan and *janjaweed* or *murahileen* militias, which parallels what took place in the South for almost forty years, where parallel charges of "genocide" were rarely heard.

The high degree of international interest and engagement in Darfur resulted in a rush to reach the Darfur Peace Accord (DPA) in Abuja and the (failed) Sirte conference in Libya. So desperately and sincerely was peace being sought that it was tactically concluded that an imperfect peace would be better than none at all. Then, presumably, the parties that were marginalized by nonsignature would splinter, disappear, or otherwise regret the lost opportunity. However, the lack of rebel unity and the pursuit of the noninclusive approach were partially respon-sible for the protracted situation, since it did not incorporate other parties in a Darfur/Darfur dialogue. This includes the *janjaweed*, who, however much feared or despised, *are* part of local politics. In retrospect, slower progress would have been better, and perhaps (taking into consideration the ESPA) more internal bro-kering and less external pressure could have reached a more inclusive result. Moreover, since Darfur is presently in a period of state annexation, despite the revolt, it can only be understood by also looking at the past and present politics of the wider national actors, including the SPLA, ESPA, CPA, GoS, GoSS, and Sudanese opposition groups. All neighbors of Sudan, but especially Chad, Libya, Uganda, and Eritrea, all have stakes in the outcome of the dispute and have played positive or negative roles, depending on one's perspective.

Finally, the international prominence of Darfur in some nations and lack of concern for Darfur in others has resulted in a lack of political will and focus by the United Nations, United States, European Union, and African Union on Darfur priorities has meant slow motion in logistical and financial resources to support effective policing and separation of all of the conflicting parties. Indeed, although Khartoum finally agreed on various diplomatic protocols of the United Nations and African Union that allowed increased troop strength and other logistical support, the participating nations have not yet met these ceiling limits to date. Since 2008 was an active presidential campaign year in the United States, the various candidates did make platform statements about the situation in Darfur that included plans for ICC prosecution (Senator John McCain), plans for putting troops on the ground (Senator Joseph Biden), and plans for a no-fly zone (Senator Barak Obama). It remained to be seen in 2009, with the new Obama/Biden administration, which plans might be operational and to what extent and result. These positions are now largely abandoned or changed, and the ICC has no police powers. The stress on the U.S. military and economy, then or now, suggested even then that Darfur would not, in fact, be a high priority even if the interest is genuine.

From a logistical point of view, it is hard to see precisely what a no-fly zone would interdict and how it would be adequately financed in vast and remote Darfur. In addition, the national interest of the United States—aside from human rights, and humanitarian and security concerns—is, in fact, slight, since the few products and resources available from Darfur to the United States are either excluded from sanctions (gum arabic) or available from other sources (sesame). The United States does not get other resources (e.g., copper, oil, and livestock) from Darfur. The principle concern was a Darfur-destabilized Sudan in a region in which stability and security were in short supply, and anxieties about Somalia, Uganda, Kenya, Eritrea, and Congo were continuing to rise.

By the start of 2010, the electoral rhetoric of the Republicans and Democrats on Darfur had been shelved. The Republicans have been quiet because they lost, and some Democrats have been grumbling and quarreling because they won and had to actually do something practical about Darfur. U.S. Air Force General and African-born Scott Gration was appointed by President Obama as his Special Envoy to Sudan to address the many issues there, ranging from Darfur, the South, China, ICC charges, the LRA, regime stability and security, oil, and so forth. He had previously escorted Senator Obama to Chad. At first, it was anticipated from recent history that the election campaigns would most likely be more of the same. Perhaps there would be inadequate political resolve or inadequate peacekeepers, as if military action would truly address the multiple political concerns circling in Darfur. Even multilateral military action could be recommended in a peacekeeping postconflict phase that may, only now, have been reached, and a number of AU "peacekeepers" have tragically lost their lives in rebel hijackings of humanitarian supplies and vehicles. The "sticks" of the ICC charges, CPA calendar, the 2010 elections, the 2011 referendum, and the various sanctions, and the "carrots" of engagement with Khartoum as well as peacekeeping separation forces, were turned on in mid-2009; by early 2010, the picture in Darfur was beginning to be "postconflict."

By 2010, most of the main parties in Darfur have signed accords with Khartoum, so the number of attacks has reached a very low level for Darfur, especially in comparison with the apparently rising levels of violence in the South.

DEEPER CAUSES FOR THE CONFLICT IN DARFUR

As seen in the above historical review, there is much Darfur history that needs serious consideration in viewing the patterns of local rivalries and of the core-periphery relations of the past and present. In the current journalistic or movie-star "coverage" of the Darfur conflict, many historical factors are rarely discussed or even known. Indeed, one Hollywood office contacted this author and asked for "all the information about Darfur," and was quickly dismayed to learn that it was much too complicated. They preferred to carry on with their activist mission, preferring not to be "diverted by too many facts." Alternatively, which facts could be marshaled to demonstrate the victimization of the "rebels" and the "evil" and "genocidal" nature of Khartoum? While the mobilization of facts to serve causes often has positive effects, the present work tries to look deeper and beyond, and prefers that "the facts" are used more objectively.

As sketched above, at various periods, Darfur has been a sovereign state or Sultanate; it was tenuously conquered in the Mahdist times, and recovered its independence from 1898 to 1916. Then, it was again conquered by the central Nile power at that time, British colonialism. If the British intervened now, when already bogged down in Afghanistan and Iraq, they would hardly be seen in a favorable light by Sudanese. Likewise, the use of militias or mercenaries by the Khartoum government has a parallel with the tens of thousands of formal and informal forces employed by the British or the United States in Middle Eastern wars. Dangers of perceiving a short-term gain of intervention should be considered very carefully in terms of engaging and supplying such forces, not to mention a clear exit strategy, to draw upon the forgotten Powell doctrine for military engagements. Perhaps this explained something of the international reluctance to call this "genocide" or "ethnic cleansing," since that would compel them to act in some way in accordance with the Geneva Accords of 1948. Yet in this world of political schizophrenia and hypocrisy, there may still need to be some engagement with the Darfur problem, if only to distract attention from the miseries elsewhere and salvage the positive achievement of the North-South CPA, assisted by Senator Danforth. A deteriorated situation in Darfur would only jeopardize the Naivasha Accords, which were never popular among Khartoum hardliners.

There are broad economic factors whereby material burdens of Sudan fall heavily against the people of Darfur and the distribution of wealth from manufacture, agriculture, and expanding petroleum production only very slowly reaches this province. Clearly, there are many long-standing economic grievances that precipitated the SLA's and JEM's initiation of this round of fighting, and the disruption caused by the *janjaweed* may even have helped the Darfuri armed insurgent groups to recruit more members, if the relative lack of men in the refugee camps can be interpreted in this way.

It is painfully apparent that the overarching dimension of the conflict in Darfur is political. There are many overlapping and intersecting political variables. There are the domestic issues in Sudan. There is a grave and chronic political crisis in Sudan whereby usual options for dissent, debate, elections, and democracy are foreclosed. The pariah nature of the Sudanese regime has made normal diplomatic measures and negotiations difficult to apply in a broad atmosphere of distrust. As an aspect of this, the secretly published "Black Book" on the political economy of Sudan showed the deep pattern of marginalization of the peripheral regions and dominance by central Nile peoples, whether under democratic or military regimes. This problem is echoed in the East, Nubian North, and very painfully in the South, as explored in other chapters. The once-pronounced role of extreme Islamist governance has only made this worse.

Another complexity of the military equation is that disproportionate numbers of the Sudanese soldiers are from Darfur, while the officer ranks are much more likely to be recruited from the central Nile "Jellaba." Class dimensions of the conflict need to be incorporated, as the bulk of the rebel force are essentially rural subsistence peasants, while the Khartoum government is essentially a military-commercial elite that seeks to maintain its asymmetrical position in a core-periphery dynamic that is being challenged as the central issue of the conflict, that is, economic and political justice and representation. The downward skew of class relations in Darfur simply adds to the general regional marginalization.

There are also a number of regional politico-strategic concerns. These include those internal Sudanese forces that seek to destabilize the regime, which can range from liberal, left, and democratic opposition to rightist forces such as the NIF. Rumors circulate that Hassan al-Turabi, former ally of al-Beshir, but now marginalized, had encouraged the Darfur revolt to weaken al-Beshir. The validity of this claim is hard to ascertain. Equally, to the east, Eritrea and the Beja Congress had their reasons to destabilize Khartoum simply because Khartoum sometimes threatens to do the same in Asmara. The case of Chad is not less complicated; several of the ethnic groups of Darfur range into Chad, either as war refugees or habitual nomads. Amid all of this, the only slightly patched-together Naivasha agreement between the government of Sudan and the SPLA is at risk of collapse if the conflict in Darfur cannot be managed. In fact, few of the neighboring regimes had positive, working ties with Khartoum through 2008 and 2009.

Geo-strategic dimensions of the Darfur conflict at its height could be characterized as close to international paralysis of action, from the delayed, stick-waving trips by Colin Powell and Kofi Annan, to the resource-strapped and diverted AU folks, including the West African Economic Community Monitoring Group (ECOMOG) forces that were preoccupied with policing in Liberia, Sierra Leone, and the Ivory Coast. The Arab League and Libya showed some interest in Darfur, but made no serious inroads and engagement with the problem. Then there are the cash-strapped nations that are fighting AIDS and trying to educate their populations. This is not an attractive short-term conflict with lots of glamour or heroism, but rather mostly poor people trapped in a conflict with few heroes and no major resources to fight over. Who wants it?

Yet there has clearly been a great deal of journalistic interest in Darfur in the course of its recent history. There are very important legal concerns about the Geneva Accords, human rights, and especially genocide. But the weak mobilization of interventionist forces reveals that the EU or U.S. presidential candidates are prepared to expend only a small amount of time, energy, or resources on the conflict. Indeed, the Darfur situation has been used to some extent as a diversion from the wars in Iraq, Afghanistan, and Palestine, and as an easy expression to concerned constituencies who are anti-Arab or anti-Muslim in general or anti-Khartoum in particular. The interest of Israel or pro-Israeli groups in Darfur in this respect is notable, especially when the Palestinian conflict continues on its very bloody and confused course. It is much easier to point fingers at Darfur. One suggestion was floated that Turks should become Darfur peacekeepers, forgetting that the Turks had colonized Sudan just before the English. Perhaps non-Sudanese forgot this history; the Sudanese did not. From a Sudanese perspective, the concern about Darfur expressed by the United States, Great Britain, and Israel in particular is viewed as hypocritical, since those three nations have very little political capital in the Arab-Islamic world, with their military engagements in Iraq, Afghanistan, Gaza, and the West Bank of Palestine. The United States does not have ambassadorial presence at present in Sudan, and Sudan has never given diplomatic recognition of Israel, which periodically supported Southern rebels and one of the Darfur rebel groups.

The ever-increasing hypothetical numbers (200,000 to 400,000) by supposed "observers" of purported deaths was expressed in a range as big as the actual number may ever have been. United Nations reports now show that the greatest numbers of deaths, however great they were, were from disease and dislocation. Even preconflict, the health situation in Darfur was not exactly good. Yet the logistical support provided to the AU force by U.S. firms such as Dyncorp Corporation and the Pacific Architects and Engineers (PAE) group gives rise to substantial anxiety, as these two firms have opaque links to the U.S. military and intelligence communities, as well as non-bid and overcharging controversies in their previous service to the State Department. The formation of the new U.S. Combatant Command, AFRICOM, has also caused a certain degree of anxiety in Africa and the Middle East. The Darfur playing field is not level.

It is clear that this conflict emerged, in part, in the context of the persistent ecological crisis of increased desertification, lack of production, and limited grazing lands among the pastoral and agricultural peoples. It is not just that rainfall declined repeatedly and irregularly in the last decades; the entire ecosystem is so very fragile and precariously balanced that with population pressures, a small difference in rainfall can make a big difference in the regional stress. As important as it is to resist simple-minded unilateral causes that drought causes conflict, it is equally important not to overlook the obvious in climatological data and in oral reports from the inhabitants. Land rivalry and trespass are not new issues in this region. Animal wealth is certainly a factor in the current conflict, which frequently sees cattle and camels seized by the *janjaweed* from local rural populations in scorched-earth practices similar to those employed in the southern Sudan in earlier years. As a result, there are probably hundreds of thousands of IDPs and external refugees, especially to camps in eastern Chad. It is worth noting that the bulk of the external refugees are women and children, with men staying as combatants with the SLA/SLM or JEM, or having already been killed by the *janjaweed*. This dynamic finds women especially victimized and vulnerable.

Some commentators on Darfur are reluctant to consider ecological factors, preferring to simplify the origins of the conflicts, apparently believing that looking at the fragile ecological context would divert the focus of political blame from Khartoum or perhaps even the rebels. Others want to focus on desertification, global climate change, and the recent (2000–2003) decline of regional rainfall as a simplistic or mechanistic source of the problem. In fact, there can be no denying that the weak and unreliable rainfall and fragile water sources certainly have been aggravating factors causing drought and intensified land competition. Had ameliorating measures been taken, this could have been less precarious. The absence of these measures and poor or undermined traditional governance then moved the water-resource dimension into a more critical zone. Thus, water access in Darfur is definitely a factor, but it must be viewed contextually and relatively. To simply ignore this dimension of ecological vulnerability or to maximize water access as monocausal will ultimately not shed light on the problems of marginalization and conflict generation in Darfur. The persistence of cases of trespass and competition for land and water competition cannot be overlooked. The "perfect storm" of the present gridlock in the Darfur conflict includes multivariate factors already noted, as well as those listed below.

Amid the ecological and economic variables, the production of natural resources, mostly subsistence production and small-scale trade, represents the limits of cash exports from Darfur. While it is true that there is little production from southern Darfur, the oil is there, and it is close to road and rail links whenever production might be expanded. Moreover, southern Sudanese oil still buys weapons for Khartoum. Oil attracts foreigners, ranging from China and India to Malaysia. Oil may be worth fighting for at some point, but so far most of the conflict is in the northern and central regions of Darfur, but the oil factor should not be excluded if only as a critical revenue stream for Khartoum.

There are many purely military factors in this situation, which pits the irregular SLA, led by 'Abd al-Wahid Mohamed Nur, and JEM, led by Khalil Ibrahim, against formal elements of the Sudan military, led by General Omer al-Beshir, and the irregular militia, called locally the *janjaweed*, camel- and horse-riding raiders led by Musa Hilal, among several others. Divisions, rivalries, and communication problems within the SLA and JEM, not to mention the *janjaweed*, result in unresponsive and unpredictable activities on the part of most of these groups. Essentially, the SLA and JEM see themselves as part of the armed resistance against the military government of Sudan in Khartoum, but not for the same reasons. The *janjaweed*, especially Baggara nomads, are threatened by both Darfuri groups and have been informally permitted and probably encouraged to function as militias to take matters in their own hands for Khartoum.

Thus, on one hand, the conflict can be characterized as a rural revolt versus a force of irregular militias, but the GoS clearly is backing these militias, and the Darfur rebels also have a base of support, locally and internationally. On the other hand, the Sudanese national army has a disproportionate number of soldiers from Darfur in its rank-and-file, so the conflict in Darfur also provides an internal security issue for the regular army of Sudan. The war continues with sometimes coordinated military and irregular military attacks against rebels very similar to what was well-known in the two decades of North-South conflict. The use of simple Antonov bombers and some helicopters has also been reported, in addition to destruction of some military aircraft from ground fire or airfield attacks. While the SLA and JEM are not formally linked to the SPLA, the conflict has much military, strategic and tactical, and technical similarity.

Other dimensions of the conflict are the cultural and linguistic factors. Central Sudanese are broadly Arabic speakers; in Darfur, Arabic is more likely a second language, rather than the primary language at home. The skilled use of Arabic is emblematic of higher social position; the awkward use of the language can be twisted to imply people of a lesser degree of social status. Related to this is that the ethnography of Darfur contrasts markedly with that of the central Nile. While the identity crisis for northern Sudanese is itself a problematic and much-denied national issue, certainly the vast majority of Darfuris belong to such groups as the Fur, Zaghawa, Masalit, Berti, Bongo, Banda, Tama, Daju, Birked, Kimr, Sila, Ndogo, Tunjur, Kreish, Fertit, and Kanuric. With substantially different cultures in remote locations, it is very easy to have deep misunderstandings.

Not unrelated to culture and language are the racial/ethnic dimensions that are simplistically polarized as "Arabs versus Africans." Buried in this topic is the painful question of racial and ethnic prejudice. Despite the fact that all Sudanese could be perceived as "Black" in the simplistic racial system of America, it is clear that important differences of racial perception in Sudan are powerful and sensitive in terms of alliances, enemies, and the very structure of society. The journalistic gloss of "Arabs" versus "Black Africans" hardly illuminates this central and important topic that is foundational in the present conflict. Race is a dimension in the conflict, but it does not abide by Western conceptualizations or applications of

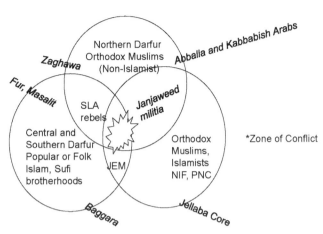

Figure 4.2 Religion and Politics in Darfur

the term. The impressions from the "Black Book" certainly have foundation. There is a lack of serious engagement or discourse on the topic of race and identity in the Nile Valley. Without full press freedoms, public debate, and political opposition, this discussion cannot take place except by violent and destructive means. The potential prejudices of race and ethnicity were used in the Darfur case to mobilize for acts of violence, in particular by the *janjaweed*.

The dimension of religion cannot be excluded, even though the majority of combatants on all sides of this conflict are Sunni Muslims; this commonality has not curbed the bloodshed. Yet religion is still a factor, as the Khartoum government exalts in its rigorous and politicized orthodoxy of Islam. The prejudicial view from Khartoum elites is that the fellow Muslims from Darfur might not be "good Muslims" when viewed through the prism of Islamic politicized orthodoxy in Khartoum versus the syncretic and folk Islam practiced in Darfur.

Another factor is gender and the social order. So far, most victims are refugee women and girls who are intimidated and systematically terrorized by rape, reported by many independent accounts. As long as sexism and gender prejudice are deeply rooted, it is easy to overlook gender abuse worsening the conflicts on the planet. As hard as it is to discuss class and race in Sudan and elsewhere, it is equally difficult to frame a debate or undertake negotiations about reconstructing gender relations.

RECENT CHRONOLOGY AND CONTEXT IN THE DARFUR REVOLT

While the Darfur revolt is commonly dated to 26 February 2003, with the Darfur Liberation Front (DLF)/SLA attack at Golo in western Darfur, it was the 24–25 April 2003 attack on the airport at al-Fasher that ratcheted the war to a higher escalation. At least seven Sudanese military planes were destroyed on the ground and a senior Air Force officer was captured, along with other losses in personnel and material. But this obscures the fact that there had been a decades-long history of small-scale conflicts, violence, trespass, and protest. That these did not reach the bloody and explosive level of 2003 was a complex function of better climates, less droughts, better conflict management, traditional leadership, less population, and fewer arms. The situation in Darfur in the 1990s had not been all that good. At the same time, the Sudanese political climate was producing ever more positive directions in finally "solving" the twenty additional years of the North-South conflict, and shifts in the political actors in Khartoum were clearly heading toward what finally became the January 2005 Comprehensive Peace Accord. The last thing that Khartoum needed was another civil conflict.

Seeing these changes in the political winds in the capital and the region, and perhaps imagining that the world was much diverted with the "shock and awe" of the unilateral military invasion of Iraq starting on 20 March 2003 by mainly U.S. and British forces, the frustrated people of Darfur had a different view. Not wanting to miss their chance at power or reducing their marginalization, the two main segments of the Darfur rebellion, the SLA and JEM, determined to strike during these months, perhaps naively hoping that Khartoum was sufficiently distracted and diverted, and that this would be "rewarded" with rapid political capitulation. This was a tragic miscalculation, in hindsight, and if the deaths and destruction that were to follow for the next seven years had then been perceived on their strategic horizon, they might have rethought this tactical move.

From 2003 to 2005, the worst possible violent outcome resulted among the combatants and civilians in Darfur. On 8 April 2004, representatives of the SLA and JEM did agree to a cease-fire with the government of Sudan, but this did not stick. In September 2004, matters were intensified, with U.S. President George W. Bush and Secretary of State Colin Powell starting to use "the G-word": *genocide*. Then, with the passage of UN Resolution 1564 on 18 September calling for action in Darfur, there was little place to hide. The United States and Great Britain had been bogged down in the Iraq insurgency since 2004, which also gave the Darfur activists something to divert public attention, since they rarely protested the unfolding wars in Afghanistan or Iraq. But no sooner did the attention of the world start to return to Darfur than the catastrophic Asian/Indian Ocean tsunami struck on 26 December 2004, and Darfur was pushed off the front page. In this period, many of the principals on the Darfur rebel side met in 2005 at Haskanita in eastern Darfur, wishing to piece together sufficient rebel unity to offer integrated military resistance to Khartoum and regain their military tempo. This wish did not materialize, and ground attacks by the rebels, air attacks by Khartoum, and more *janjaweed* counterattacks were the sad result. Worse still was that Khartoum concluded that the safe rear areas of the rebels were in eastern Chad, so in the world of "the enemy of my enemy is my friend," Khartoum supported anti-Deby forces in Darfur to the extent that in April 2006, President Deby was almost toppled by heavily armed guerrillas in N'Djamena.

Now even more desperate for peace in this atmosphere of escalation and internationalization, all diplomatic efforts were turned to still more talks in Abuja, Nigeria. While the motivation was timely, the circumstances pressing, and the negotiators passionately committed, the patience required for an Afro-Arab–style consultative *sulh* was not adequate, so on 5 May 2006, when the DPA was signed, it was *only* by Minni Minnawi representing his faction of the SLA/SLM. The *janjaweed*, who had their own grievances against Khartoum and against the rebels, were left out of the DPA-Abuja. More important, this precipitated the steady flood of additional Darfur factionalism that was to make further efforts at peace and unity in Arusha and Sirte even more elusive. 'Abd al-Wahed, for one, stated on 7 June 2006 that the DPA was an unacceptable "quick fix," and JEM carried on with more attacks and counterattacks. Elsewhere in eastern Sudan, covered more in Chapter 3, the combatants did reach an accord on 14 October 2006 when the ESPA was signed, which showed the Darfur rebels that the clock of their own hopes was also ticking. The clock was ticking down for the captured former president of Iraq; he was hanged by Iraqi-U.S. authorities on 30 December 2006. This point was probably well-noted by President Omer al-Beshir. Visiting Khartoum at that time, this author could say that many were very distressed by the circumstances of this execution. But instead of catapulting the rebels to unity, this context seems to have caused a more ambitious struggle for power and position that by February 2007 resulted in the National Redemption Front (NRF) meeting in eastern Chad and the 4–6 August 2007 Arusha meeting in Tanzania. The combined NRF and "Group of 19" (G-19) rebels mounted attacks against the Sudanese regular army at Um Sidr and Kariayri, north of Fasher. Back at the United Nations, Luis Moreno-Ocampo continued his effort to seek ICC charges against al-Beshir for war crimes and "genocide," which were submitted on 14 July 2008. On 4 March 2009, the Sudanese president was formerly charged with being responsible for war crimes. Darfur rebels and human-rights activists were broadly thrilled, Africans and Arabs either puzzled or annoyed by the apparent hypocrisy in which Western interventionist wars were acceptable, while this particular Sudanese war was not. Needless to say, the Khartoum regime was put into panic mode. And so it went, with the situation moderated only by the increasing presence and capacity of United Nations/African Union Hybrid Mission in Darfur (UNAMID) peacekeepers until 2009.

SPLINTERED LEADERSHIP IN THE DARFUR REVOLT

Other chapters have examined the evolution of the rulers of Sudan, so here is it appropriate to take a closer look at the main rebel groups and what keeps them more or less together, as well as the issues and decisions that divided them. Although there is a previous history of the DLF and efforts to protest the marginalization, either by working within the political framework or peacefully protesting outside of it, this was essentially in a former generation, with relatively few of those more senior or traditional leaders retaining leadership positions in the insurgency that erupted in early 2003, or, more accurately, substantially expanded the various unresolved conflicts that were already underway in the previous years.

As minor attacks rapidly evolved to attacks on police and military targets, there was a very brief period in which the SLA was unified with JEM in common armed protest against the Khartoum government over various configurations of the above issues that can be glossed broadly as political marginalization. At an earlier moment, the heads of the SLA were 'Abd al-Wahed Muhammad Ahmed al-Nur and the Secretary General of the SLA, Minni Arkou Minnawi, while the head of JEM was Khalil Ibrahim Muhammad. There can be no question that the different personalities, objectives, alliances, and tactics of the Darfur rebels have substantially complicated this conflict. Aside from the operational difficulty in coordinating their military operations and local opportunistic warlords, the rebels lost the military initiative and often failed to take political opportunities. The first proof of this was the especially bloody first two years of war (2003–2005) in which casualties, especially of civilians, were so terribly high. What gains and promises that had been aired were already in a very sad balance. Few of the Darfur rebels had sophisticated military training, with many leaders coming from education or law backgrounds. The next proof was that when opportunity for conflict resolution was at hand in the DPA in Abuja in 2006, in Arusha in 2007, and elsewhere, it was not seized.

The various rebel forces, by then about eighteen, could not speak with one voice. Among the principle figures in Darfur was Zaghawa Minni Arkou Minnawi, an accommodating and secularist former schoolteacher from northern Darfur. For the period in which the SLA was unified, he was its Secretary General, but as the sole signatory for his faction among the Darfur rebels, he is now officially a member "Advisor" of the GoS. The rest of the rebels were nonsignatories of the DPA. For some time, Dr. Sharif Harir, the Zaghawa anthropologist, was working with Minnawi, but in later periods, he was associated with the Sudan Federal Democratic Alliance (SFDA) and the NRF that largely lingered on as the G-19 after being founded on 30 June 2006 in Asmara, where a numbers of Darfur groups had offices at various points. In turn, the NRF has factions of JEM, parts of the SLA, and parts of the SFDA, and was led by Darfur stalwart Ahmed Ibrahim Diraige, founder of the earliest DLF and later founder of the SFDA and NRF. Diraige was a former governor of Darfur and was known for his democratic and secularist goals. All of these factions refused to sign the Abuja accord that became known as the DPA. Essentially, this was a coalition of the Abuja nonsignatories, without the main JEM leaders and, naturally, without Minni Minnawi, who was the sole signatory of the Abuja DPA. The NRF did manage an attack on the Sudanese Armed Forces at Hamarat Sheik in Kordofan on 3 July 2006.

Mention also needs to be made of the humanitarian Suleiman Jamous, a Zaghawa SLA supporter who was sidelined for this period under hospital arrest in Kadugli, Kordofan. Under these conditions, he did not attend the 2007 Arusha meetings. An ephemeral group, the Alliance of Revolutionary Forces of Western Sudan (ARFWS), existed for about one year, in 2006, and then vanished.

The faction of the SLA led by lawyer 'Abd al-Wahid Muhammad Ahmed al-Nur was more constructed around the Fur people of central Darfur. He was a nonsignatory of the DPA and did not attend the Arusha meetings, and was long an ideological opponent of the Khartoum regime. His independent streak also meant that he would cooperate neither with the SFDA nor the NRF. This caused fellow Fur Ahmed Shafie Yagoub Baasi, his former supporter, to turn to the NRF, where he linked with Adam Bakhit, a Wagi Zaghawa, who was then affiliated with G-19, which had begun as another post-Abuja spin-off from the Minnawi SLA in 2005. Typical of this tumultuous period was the case of Abul Qasim Imam al-Haj, who signed the DPA along with Minni Minnawi but later realigned with 'Abd al-Wahed, with Abul Qasim's strength in southern Darfur measured in 4×4 vehicles and combatant recruitment. Complicating this factionalism and rapidly shifting alliances was the fact that Adam Bakhit needed the secure rear areas of Chad to have support and supply. Since relations with Chad and Sudan were then much embittered, and Chad President Idris Deby was of Bideyat (the Bideyat being neighbors of the Zaghawa), it was easy and normal to make this alliance. He could also move among some of the Arab groups such as the Misseriya, Humr, and Ma'aliya, who did not generally support the *janjaweed*.

Other members of G-19, besides Adam Bakhit, were Adam 'Ali Shogar, a Wagi Zaghawa who was a tactical Deby supporter since he needed security in eastern Chad for his rear area. Both Bakhit and Shogar attended a critical meeting of G-19 in Abeché, a strategic border town that is the fourth largest in easternmost Chad. Other examples of G-19 members include Jar al-Naby 'Abd al-Karim, also a Zaghawa from North Darfur (Kutum). He was a former biology teacher trained in Libya. He attended the Darfur peace meeting in Arusha, Tanzania in August 2007. On the other hand, Khamis 'Abdullah al-Bakr, a G-19 founder, was of Masalit origin and formerly served as a deputy of 'Abd al-Wahed's faction of the SLA, and did represent a faction of the SLA at Sirte, Libya. At times, he was tactically aided by Chad to strengthen the proxy fight against anti-Deby forces backed by Khartoum. Once the SLA began splintering, it split into numerous mercurial factions, ranging from the SLM "Free Will" and "G-10," "G-17," and "G-19" to "SLA Unity," just described. This was itself a spin-off from the SLA-'Abd al-Wahed group and notably included Jar al-Naby, Adam 'Ali Shogar, Adam Bakhit, Khamis 'Abdullah al-Bakr, Saleh Adem Isaac, Mahjoub Hussein, Suleiman Marajan, and Abdallah Yahia, who mostly attended the Arusha meeting to try to cobble together a common position, but failed. Still struggling to present a unified military command, the United Front for the Liberation of Darfur (UFLD) was formed in 2007 as an umbrella group of various field commanders of the SLA, or the "32 Commanders," led by Furawi Ahmed al-Shafei after he broke with the SLA/SLM faction still headed by 'Abd al-Wahed and apparently backed by France. The SLA "Free Will" and JEM "Peace Wing" almost became signatories of the DPA, but in the end were not able to put ink to paper, and factionalism continued to go into free-fall, sometimes degenerating even to the point of local warlords preying upon relief agencies and equipment for survival.

Despite these dynamic complexities, this is barely half of the story of Darfur factionalism. There were also opponents of Deby in the volatile political mixture, as well as those with an Islamist agenda that was much opposed to democratic secular empowerment. In this respect, Khalil Ibrahim Muhammad, a Kobe branch Zaghawa lawyer, was the founder of JEM, and some of the JEM factions remerged with the NRF. Other factions stuck with Khalil Ibrahim while he boycotted the Arusha meeting; still other JEM members attended it. Most problematic was that he had been a pro-al-Turabi supporter of the NIF, and he was certainly not opposed to an Islamic state, wanting to restore al-Turabi to power against al-Beshir. The baggage brought to the Darfur rebel "coalition" is that Khalil Ibrahim also fought in the *jihad* against the South, so the secularists do not find much in common, to say the least. On the other hand, his supposed authorship of the "Black Book" on Darfur clearly demonstrated the problem of marginalization in Darfur. Other members of JEM, such as Nourein 'Abd al-Kafi, were part of the JEM military leadership, and having allegedly attacked AMIS, peacekeepers in Darfur might face some problems with the ICC. Other JEM members, such as Mohammad Salih Harba and Mohammad Anwar Nur, could likely face the same allegations, but both were killed in the audacious but strategically improbable and legally problematic attack on Omdurman on 10 May 2008. Then we have Idris Ibrahim Azraq, a Meidobi, who led the "JEM-Azraq" split after serving as the JEM representative in Holland. Also problematic in Darfur politics is that he was formerly linked to the Sudanese Ministry of Interior.

The complexities in JEM can be further extended to Nourene Manawi Bartcham, who was also a JEM member while serving as the second-in-command of the National Movement for Reformation and Development (NMRD), having been a former member of the Chadian army. The NMRD had quickly broken from JEM proper in May 2004 and, of course, did not sign the DPA, but had a representative at the October 2007 Sirte meetings. Jibril 'Abd al-Karim Bari "Tek," a Kabka or Kobera Zaghawa, the founder of the NMRD who had served as a colonel in the Chadian Republican Guard, also attacked AU frontier peacekeepers in his pro-Khartoum, anti-Deby efforts. For this, he has been charged by the ICC. Other NMRD members such as Hassan Abdulla Bargo or Mahamat Ismail Chaibo are both Kabka Zaghawa. Bargo had been a member of the Sudanese NIF, and Chaibo worked for Chad's military intelligence. Perhaps this is also the place to mention Mahamat Nour 'Abd al-Karim, a Tama member of the United Front for

Democratic Change (*Front Uni pour le Changement*, or FUC), another anti-Deby Chadian group that was sometimes weakly linked to the NMRD and essentially served as a proxy for Khartoum from bases in western Darfur. Two other ephemeral and probably pro-Khartoum Arab groups were the Revolutionary United Movement (RUM), also known as the URFF, led by Al-Hadi Agabeldour, and the Arab-based Revolutionary Democratic Forces Front (RDFF), led by Salah 'Abd al-Rahman Abu Surrah; they were at Sirte, but since that meeting seemed to lead to little, they have apparently vanished from the political scene. No wonder that Sirte made little progress; the main section of JEM, under Khalil Ibrahim, was missing, along with 'Abd al-Wahed's part of the SLA, SLA-Unity, and the *janjaweed*.

The *Socle pour le Changement, l'Unité et la Democratie* (SCUD) was constructed from the Bideyat Zaghawa and, as the French name suggests, were pro-Deby Chadians of the same ethnic stock, thus divided from the anti-Deby Zaghawa. A minor regional player was also the francophone *Union des Forces pour la Democratie et le Developpment* (UFDD), made up of Arab-dominated Daju and Tunjur who were generally poorly armed and capable, at best, of only local self-defense.

Congratulations are due if the reader has been able to follow these complex acronyms, personalities, and shifting alliances, but if not, the takeaway point is simple. The many grievances and circumstances of the marginalized people of Darfur are very sympathetically understandable, but the uptick of violence in February 2003 was at their hands, and the response of Khartoum was, sadly, highly predictable. Moreover, the multiple divisions, objectives, proxy interests, and political affiliations meant that any unity of position was destined to fail. The heavy price was paid by the protracted combatants themselves and, most tragically, by the civilian women and children noncombatants, and struggling peacekeepers from Africa and around the world.

WHAT TO DO

First, this situation has possibly crossed the threshold of the "G-word"—*genocide*—at least for some people and some incidents, but this determination is made in a highly political and complex legal context. At least, we should not debate that this is an urgent matter for self-evident humanitarian and human-rights concerns, especially for women, children, and other noncombatants and with regard to the pressing horrors of the noncombatant refugees.

Second, all measures and manners need to lead to rapid negotiations for a cease-fire and political stabilization. The resumption of sincere and productive peace negotiations needs all endorsement and support to make it hold. Third, the intervention by a non-European, AU separation force and international monitoring force should be marshaled without further delay. An African intervention force should be assisted in creative logistics, but this is also more complicated than it seems. The Arab League could start to take this much more seriously. Fourth, keep in mind the dozen factors already mentioned. This is not a simple conflict, and the effort to make it simpler will not lead to a lasting resolution.

WHAT NOT TO DO

Sanctions and the threat of sanctions did not work very well in the short and urgent term, although the record of sanctions in Sudan is better over the longer term, as one can see in the history of pressures on Sudan generated by UN Resolutions in Appendix C. Steady escalation in the application of UN resolutions and war fatigue has finally converged with some sense of optimism that there is a road to peace in Darfur. At least civilian casualties were reduced in this process. The world does not have enough leverage to apply to all of the conflicts in the world today. On the other hand, this approach, up to and including the introducing of peacekeeping forces, balanced by sovereignty issues, should not be forgotten or neglected. Even in very serious cases like Darfur or southern Sudan, foreign military intervention in this Afro-Arab country should be well-considered, especially by U.S. or British interests, who will not be perceived as evenhanded. Efforts to curb Sudanese arms acquisition had some notable blowback by making them even more self-sufficient in arms manufacture, from small arms to heavy armor and light spotter planes, and by making Sudan turn to "pariah nations" for arms support.

In a few words, there is no single cause of the conflict in Darfur. It is very complex in historical, anthropological, moral, climatological, political, religious, and economic terms. Simplistic and reductionist observations shed more shadows than light. Moreover, the more internationalized the conflict, the more stakeholders need to be brought into negotiations over peace-making and peacekeeping. Some perhaps well-motivated but misguided international actors have done little to get a common position among the fractious rebels, or motivate Khartoum to move beyond military "solutions" for this conflict and humanitarian crisis that continued for seven years.

SOME GENERAL CONCLUSIONS

1. The crisis in Darfur is multifaceted and needs serious reflection on cultural, historical, ecological, religious, political, and racial/ethnic variables.

2. Foreign intervention has both positive and negative features, but the best (although not simplest) hope lies in constructive intervention (if not too little and too late) with the UNAMID force. Perhaps this will ultimately lead to increased capacity for regional military interventions in African conflicts by African forces with some role for logistical support from other nations.

3. This crisis situation is still serious, but is, in 2010, likely getting better, with more factions laying down their arms in mutual fatigue, more peace treaties signed, and an increase in the capacity and deployment of the UNAMID forces. In human dimensions, the chance for anyone to control the levers of power in Darfur is slowly improving.

4. The rebel movements, the *janjaweed*, and Sudanese political players all have substantial complexity relative to their own orientations and objectives. They appear to be essentially retired from the Darfur theater of proxy operations for political, legal, and practical purposes.

5. There is broad domestic and regional linkage of this conflict to other issues, and political players inside (and especially outside) Sudan, in the use and degree of concern for the Darfur crisis. The apparent rapprochement between N'Djamena and Khartoum is an encouraging sign worthy of cautious optimism.

6. From the ambiguous start of this conflict without a programmatic strategy, to the ambiguous practices put in practice by all sides, to the ambiguous "genocide" noted by Gerard Prunier, to the ambiguous end of the violence, the question remains: Was this all worth it?

SOURCES

Africa Confidential, 47(10), 12 May 2006, Khartoum politics; 47(11), 26 May 2006, S. Sudan, Uganda, and the LRA; 47(15), 21 July 2006, South Sudan and the LRA; 47(16), 4 August 2006, Darfur mess post-DPA; 47(17), 25 August 2006, New factions in Darfur; 47(19), 22 September 2006, Islamists in Khartoum; 47(22), 3 November 2006, Darfur conflict spreading to Chad; 47(25), 15 December 2006, Fighting in south Sudan; 48(2), 19 January 2007, Parties and peace-keepers in Darfur; 48(4), 16 February 2007, Biographies of leading figures.

Ahmed, Abdel Ghaffar M. and Leif Manger. *Understanding the Crisis in Darfur: Listening to Sudanese Voices* (Bergen, Norway: University of Bergen, 2006).

'Ali, Hayder Ibrahim. *Darfur Report* (Sudan Studies Center: Khartoum, 2006).

Cox, Philip. "Inside Sudan's Rebel Army." BBC Focus on Africa, 5 April 2004, 12:14 GMT.

De Waal, Alex. *A Famine That Kills: Darfur, Sudan, 1984–1985* (Oxford: Clarendon Press, 1989).

De Waal, Alex. "Tragedy in Darfur." *Boston Review.* November–December 2004.

De Waal, Alex. "Briefing-Darfur, Sudan-Prospects for Peace." *African Affairs*, 104, No. 414, January 2005.

Esam el-Din el-Haj. "Interview with the Sudan Liberation Movement/Army." Gamal Abdelrahim for the Darfur Task Force. 15 February 2006.

Holy, Ladislav. *Neighbors and Kinsmen.* (New York: St. Martin's Press, 1974), 63–65, 117.

Iyob, Ruth and Gilbert M. Khadiagala. *Sudan: The Elusive Quest for Peace* (Boulder, CO: Lynne Rienner, 2006).

McDoom, Opheera. "Darfur Rebel Leaders Urged to Unite in Peace." *News from Africa*, 28 October 2005.

McGregor, Andrew. "Terrorism and Violence in the Sudan: The Islamist Manipulation of Darfur." Part Two. *Terrorism Monitor*, Vol. 3, Issue 13, 1 July 2005.

Nachtigal, Gustav. *Sahara and Sudan, Wadai and Dafur* Vol. 4, translated from the original German with new introduction by Allan G. B. Fisher and Humphrey J. Fisher (London: Hurst Publishers, 1971).

Nkrumah, Gamal. "Winning the West." *Al-Ahram Weekly*, Cairo, 2003, reprinted in DAMANGA: Coalition for Freedom and Democracy, Representatives of the Massaleit Community in Exile.

Peoples Daily Online. "Darfur Peace Talks in Nigeria Drag on as Peacekeepers Killed." *Xinhua*, 10 October 2005.

Plaut, Martin. "Who Are Sudan's Darfur Rebels?" BBC Africa broadcast, 30 September 2004, 08:27 GMT 09:27 UK.

Prunier, Gerard. *Darfur: The Ambiguous Genocide*. (Ithaca, NY: Cornell University Press, 2005).

Respini-Irwin, Cyrena. "Geointelligence Informs Darfur Policy." *Geointelligence Magazine*, 1 September 2005.

Segar, Derk. "Sudan: UN Official Urges Darfur Rebel Leaders to Unite." *Sudaneseonline/IRIN*, 9 November 2005.

Sudan Liberation Movement/Sudan Liberation Army, *Press Release and Political Declaration*, 14 March 2003.

Theobald, A. B. *'Ali Dinar, Last Sultan of Darfur, 1898–1916*. (London: Longmans, 1965).

United Nations. Daily Press Review, 16 March 2003. Information Center, Khartoum.

United Nations High Commissioner for Refugees. *The State of the World's Refugees: Human Displacement in the New Millennium* (Oxford: Oxford University Press, 2006).

United Nations Mission in Sudan. "UNMIS Media Monitoring Report," 29 January 2006, Khartoum.

United Nations Security Council Resolutions 1706, 1679, 1665, 1663, 1593, 1591, 1590, 1574, 1564, and 1556.

Young, Helen, et al. *Darfur: Livelihoods under Siege*. (Al Fasher: Feinstein International Famine Center, Tufts and Afhad Universities and the Darfur Development Service, 2005) [especially pages 35–36 on SLA and JEM].

CHAPTER 5

The Political Economy
of Sudanese Oil

This chapter focuses on the history, political economy, strategic value, and military significance of, as well as violent conflicts over, petroleum in the contemporary Sudan. A whole chapter is devoted to this topic because of its increasing and timely importance. World consumption or "addiction" to oil is increasing, despite major efforts to reduce consumption of, locate new sources of, and address ecological issues linked to petroleum as a primary energy source. Competition and consumption increases as world populations grow and, for some, their standards of living improve. Some major producing nations have domestic instability, unpopularity, or political "pariah" status; thus, the world dilemma of being a "hostage to oil" is steadily aggravated. It is painfully apparent that oil has such significance that nations will go to war to have access to it. Sudan is a case study of these critical points.

African nations, often heavily in debt, try to market their agricultural goods on a world market (without a "level playing field") and are tempted to think of the "blessing" of oil to grow their economies and achieve fiscal security. As oil prices rose dramatically in recent years, the world dream of "salvation by oil" was infectious, particularly in Africa. All too often, this blessing becomes a "curse" of distorted development, of corruption rather than transparency, of ecological degradation, and of other issues that divide populations rather than unifying them. The "megabucks" of oil often go to support military budgets more than health, education, infrastructure, and employment needs. Even for creating jobs, oil needs highly trained specialists; once production is underway, the "trickle-down" theory of development becomes another frustrating illusion.

HISTORY OF OIL IN SUDAN UNTIL THE 2005 COMPREHENSIVE
PEACE AGREEMENT (CPA)

The first steps in seismic exploration and drilling into the geological petroleum traps of Sudan took place shortly after independence along the Red Sea littoral with the Italian firm Agip and the French firm Total, along with several American companies (Occidental, Chevron, Texas Eastern, and Union Texas). Agip drilling in the Suakin area gave some hope, but it was the Chevron explorations of 1975 and 1976 that were more promising, especially for gas. During the same period, Shell/BP explored northwest Sudan. Over the years, other firms from Germany and France did more geological documentation, but no production resulted.

The interior regions of Sudan drew more interest. The first oil production was at Abu Gabra in southern Darfur as early as 1979. For Standard Oil of California Company (which became Chevron), this was a time of excitement, but substantial production was still decades away; in 1983, the North-South war resumed, and prospecting became impossible without full-scale seismic work. Judging only from geological formations and river basin systems, it was imagined that there might be a modest total reserve of 700 to 800 million barrels. The reserves sought by Chevron were in the South, precisely where the war was intensifying.

Denying Northern access to the Bentiu fields became a goal of the newly created SPLA. In February 1984, guerrilla units attacked the Chevron drilling site at Bentiu, and its oil workers were withdrawn. By June 1984, Chevron improved its security by clearing the Nuer and Dinka people concentrated in the oil battle field to resume development. Even when President Nimieri was overthrown in 1985, the war continued under the Sadiq al-Mahdi government, with intense fighting in the borderlands from Bentiu to Abyei. The SPLA tried to block oil production and prevent slave raids by Northern militias (*murahileen*) backed by the al-Mahdi government. Even when the al-Mahdi government was toppled in 1989, the war intensified as an Islamist *jihad* to further the political ambitions of Dr. Hassan al-Turabi, then backing Osama bin Laden. The military pressures of the SPLA and splinter Southern groups finally brought Chevron's efforts to an end on 15 June 1992. There was too much risk and too little return.

The new military government (the fourth in Sudanese history) faced all the same problems that the previous administrations had. Al-Turabi continued to hope that oil would fuel his ambitious plans of regional *jihad*. The more the quest for oil intensified, the more the SPLA sought to block it. This vicious circle was ramped up steadily because the oil resources were in the South, and thus, the Northern Islamist forces wanted to seize them. After establishing stronger security measures, the GoS created the Greater Nile Petroleum Operating Company (GNPOC) on 22 February 1998. This move would finance a $600 million agreement with companies from China, Canada, Argentina, and the United Kingdom to build a 1,600-kilometer pipeline from southern Sudan to the

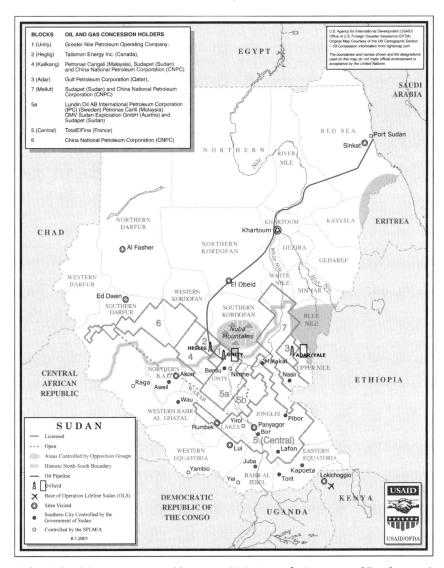

Sudan: Oil and Gas Concession Holders, 2001. (U.S. Agency for International Development.)

Red Sea. In particular, the Talisman Company was to come under intense criticism by Western activists because it had a New York office; other nations outside of the USA were not so easily targeted.

By August 1999, the tenth anniversary of the Islamist government, more backers had been won over, including Austria, Croatia, France, Germany, Malaysia, Qatar, Romania, and Spain. When it finally functioned, it pumped 185,000 barrels per day (bpd). This is trivial on a world scale, but its four huge pumps were designed to reach a future capacity of 450,000 bpd. The more this production increased, the more the SPLA saw it as a tempting political and military target. Those working with Khartoum became the targets. These included Chinese companies such as China National Petroleum Company (CNPC) and China Petroleum Technology and Development Corporation (CPTDC), the Canadian Talisman Energy Company (investing $1.4 billion), and the GNPOC oil production at Hegleig and Unity (*Wahida*) oil fields in Blocks 1 and 2 in the Muglad Basin. The SPLA attacked in 1999 at Leer in Block 5A (Thar Jath) in Unity State and were opposed by the *mujahidin* militias ("Protectors of the Oil Brigades"). Sudanese conscripts were sent to defend the pipelines and oil fields against further attacks in May 1999. Twenty-three Chinese oil workers were seized at Bentiu (not far from the Unity field) on 8 May by local residents opposed to their presence. By June 2000, GNPOC shareholders were 40 percent China National Petroleum Corporation, 30 percent Petronas of Malaysia, Talisman Energy of Canada with 25 percent, and Sudan National Petroleum Corporation (Sudapet) with only 5 percent interest. Considering that the estimated reserves of Hegleig alone were about 800 million barrels, with vast areas of southern Sudan not surveyed seismically, the lure of still greater oil discoveries and production spread excitedly.

As this struggle intensified, another dimension emerged, with divisions within the SPLA as Nuer opposition rose against the Dinka leadership of John Garang. Local, personal, and political ambitions of the Nuer were coupled with a divide-and-rule strategy from Khartoum that meant rapidly changing and violent times in the oil fields. The United Democratic Salvation Front (USDF, and its Southern Sudan Defense Forces, SSDF) and its breakaway leader, Riak Machar, claimed that Khartoum had given them authority for security in the region. Needing a local ally, Khartoum patched up this "misunderstanding" of the 1997 Khartoum agreement, but another Nuer rival to Machar was General Paulino Matip, who was also brought back into the Khartoum security plan. Amidst the overall North-South conflict, there was also Nuer-Dinka competition as well as Nuer-Nuer rivalry and Talisman trying to figure a way to drill for oil. Such factors complicated the now perilous struggle for oil. Another political casualty of the turbulent oil disputes was the sidelining of al-Turabi, now perceived as a threat to the NCP and to the legitimacy of al-Beshir himself. On 14 December, the Parliament was dissolved and a state of emergency was declared. Al-Beshir's strong ties to the military were sufficient to keep his hold on power. These acts were deemed "unconstitutional" by al-Turabi, although he had ridden to power twice before in unconstitutional military coups. So it was that the 1997–1999 struggles for the oil fields became a war of all-against-all.

During these multifaceted battles, the Wunlit Nuer-Dinka Reconciliation Process on the west bank of the Nile agreed to make peace for that part of the South-South conflict that had gone on since 1991. The agreement called for an end to cattle raids, destruction of villages, abductions of women and children, and use of armed forces to escalate disputes. Their various traditional and modern leaders agreed to endorse and support this agreement. This fresh start brought some peace, but the value of the oil fields did not mean that Khartoum's "divide-and-displace" strategy with Southern accomplices was abandoned. By October 1998, Talisman went ahead with its investment in the GNPOC concession, and it bought out the Arakis Oil Company. In May, the GNPOC pipeline started carrying oil from Blocks 1 and 2 all the way to the Red Sea. The situation looked good, even optimistic, with conflicts ebbing and oil generating the promised wealth. By June 1999, the relatively small oil refinery at *al-Shajara*, south of Khartoum, owned by Sudanese company Concorp, was completed by the Chinese company CNPC. This private oil refinery in Sudan cost US$15 million and was projected to refine 10,000 barrels of crude oil per day from the GoS share of crude from the GNPOC oil fields and pipeline, which would meet Sudanese domestic fuel needs. On 30 August 1999, Sudan exported its first crude oil as the International Monetary Fund (IMF) lifted its decade-long suspension of Sudan. IGAD peace talks limped on inconclusively.

The momentary excitement returned to reality when, in September 1999, armed units (Sudan Allied Forces and the Umma Liberation Army) of the National Democratic Alliance blew up a small section of the GNPOC oil pipeline in an rural area 14 kilometers east of Atbara (northeast of Khartoum). This was followed by more sabotage attacks in October and November 1999, and in January and May 2000. Khartoum took note of this "message," but quickly repaired the damage. Meanwhile, the world price of crude oil began to rise until it more than doubled. Talisman continued to locate and drill new wells in its concession, resulting in more GoS revenue. Elsewhere, in early 1999, the dispute between the GoS and its Ministry of Defense, and Riak Machar and his ex-rebel SSDF, came to a critical point in determining who would defend Block 5A oil fields prospected by the Swedish oil company Lundin AB. Machar opposed any army presence, saying that he brought Block 5A to the GoS in 1997 under the Khartoum Peace Agreement. His military forces would and could protect Lundin's concession, naturally to his benefit. Not trusting Khartoum in "his" area, he did not want to be shoved aside.

Everything was contentious at this crucial time, and on 11 March 1999, the GoS mobilized its "volunteer" *mujahidin*, termed the "Manifest Victory (*al-Fatih al-Mubin*) Brigade," along with is regular army. Islamist militias were recruited in the cities and colleges to create the PDF so that it could protect the valuable oil fields in the concession areas of GNPOC and Lundin.

By mid-May 1999, the Sudanese military initiated an offensive of several weeks at Ruweng (Panaru) County on the eastern side of Block 1; this region had long suffered from military displacement of the extensive Dinka communities. Despite this situation, many thousands remained. Following their standard counterinsurgency tactics, the government started with aerial bombardment, with follow-up by militia troops who were free to loot and destroy. The SPLA was not able to marshal more than token resistance. The result was that still more thousands of Dinka residents were again displaced. While some people gradually returned, most fled the region for good. This was not the only area to be subjected to this military approach as Talisman's active interests in oil development increased. The more Talisman needed security, the more the SPLA tried to disrupt it and the more the government counterattacked in a spiral of increasing violence. Nonetheless, the pipeline was on schedule, new wells were located, and some were already being drilled (Human Rights Watch [HRW] 2003, 42).

On 30 April 1999, *Agence France-Presse* quoted al-Turabi in the official newspaper *Akhbar al-Yom*, saying that "we are currently building several factories to produce our needs in weapons, and we plan to manufacture tanks and missiles to defend ourselves against conspirators." When this information caused a storm of protest, Khartoum immediately denied the assertion, but arms production continued, including all manner of small arms, tanks, armored personnel carriers (APCs) and, by 2009, even light military spotter planes.

The June 1999 pipeline opening raised interest in linking Block 5A and Block 1 together, since they were *only* 75 to 100 kilometers apart. To beef up security in the area, Major General Paulino Matip's Nuer militia was to accompany the SAF into Block 5A to protect Lundin's exploratory drilling operation at Ryer/Thar Jath. But Riak Machar's SSDF attacked the facility and executed three Sudanese GoS employees, while allowing the rest of the 100-person crew to evacuate. The attack caused little damage to the facility. The SSDF then attempted unsuccessfully to push back the advancing Nuer militia and SAF, which ultimately reached the river at Mayandit. Since the SSDF lacked ammunition to sustain the attack, the battle was brief, enabling the GoS forces to drive out both civilians and the SSDF. Matip's militia remained to protect Leer and Ryer/Thar Jath. The SAF returned to Bentiu and, along the way, its troops abducted and raped women, burned homes, and abducted young boys to carry the plunder (HRW 2003, 141–142).

The complicity of Southern and Northern groups in the struggle for oil was ultimately basis for dismissing a New York legal case against Talisman, which tried to simplify the conflict as a battle of "evil" Northerners versus "innocent" Southerners. Already, it was way more complicated.

The SSDF moved out with the civilians of the Dok, Jikany, and Jagei sections of the Nuer. Some went into Dinka/SPLA territory to the west, which they had avoided before the Wunlit peace agreement was signed. Desperate for ammunition, the SSDF agreed to fight the Sudanese forces along with the SPLA, which gave them more firepower. This rearmed section of the SSDF launched attacks against Matip's and local Commander Peter Gadet's forces at Leer on 3 July to force them into the northern part of Block 5A. With their plans unraveling, the GoS deployed Hind military helicopters and Antonov light bombers to block the SSDF/SPLA drive toward Wangkei. Running out of ammunition, the SSDF retreated to Nyal, a swampy area or *sudd* to the south that provided some protection (HRW 2003, 55). Shifting battle lines marked the next phase when Matip's forces counterattacked the SSDF. Following no rules of war, his military arrested and executed some SSDF/ UDSF civilians, including state ministers, on 11–12 July 1999 in Bentiu town, causing additional civilian displacement from the area. Amid this back-and-forth clashing, the Lundin operation shut down. Consequently, the SPLA "won" this objective, and it won back Machar's forces for the first time since the SPLM/A split in 1991. Even though all SSDF forces did not rejoin the SPLM/A, they stopped being aligned with the GoS, in part because Machar saw how he was being used to divide the South and not strengthen access to "Nuer oil." When Gadet broke from Matip, he easily captured the Mankien base, where he rearmed, putting him into a strategic position to move on to the GNPOC oil fields, where they killed several Sudanese oil workers and government soldiers. By early November 1999, many Nuer commanders made peace, including Gadet and Zone Commanders Tito Biel and Peter Paar Jiek, to create an Upper Nile Provisional United Military Command Council (UMCC). The Western Upper Nile (WUN) group of Gadet's SPLA forces managed to expel the poorly trained and motivated Northern conscript guards from Wells 5, 6, 9, 10, 13, and 16 in the Hegleig fields. During this period, the SPLA spokesman, Dr. Samson Kwaje, stated threateningly that any foreigners working in the oil fields would be a "legitimate military target." On 8 May, twenty-three Chinese oil workers were captured by local Nuer people in the Bentiu area.

In May 2000, the GoS declared that it could end imported high-cost crude oil for the first time in its history. It was now self-sufficient due to the new Chinese-built oil refinery in al-Jaili north of Khartoum that produced fuel (even aviation fuel) and could meet all domestic needs with Sudanese crude oil. The oil business quickly became the impetus behind economic growth. Also in May 2000, the human-rights organization Amnesty International published a book entitled *Sudan: The Human Price of Oil*, which was followed by the Human Rights Watch publication on *Sudan, Oil, and Human Rights* in 2003, pushing pushing the topic of Sudanese oil production into global debate, led by Sudanese diplomats and the pro-Sudan European-Sudanese Public Affairs Council headed by David Hoile. Notwithstanding the military attacks and the political controversies over Sudanese oil, a Turkish tanker departed from Port Sudan on 6 June 2000, with a first load of 20,000 tons of refined gasoline from Sudan. With this shipment to Malta, Sudan entered the club of oil-exporting nations. Lundin transferred its interests at Thar Jath, Block 5A to IPC Sudan before June 2000. These interests were shared with Malaysia's Petronas, Austria's OMV, and the tiny 5 percent Sudanese interest from Sudapet. The Chinese kept exploring Block 6 after the Romanian firm RomPetrol revisited the oil field of Abu Gabra in southern Darfur. Meanwhile, Fosters Resources of Canada was starting its own modest $30 million project in the

Melut Basin along with Qataris to increase its holdings from 25 percent to 83 percent of the Melut Petroleum Company.

The wealth of oil and the hope for peace kept petroleum interest high even as the campaign against vulnerable Talisman was underway. On 12 June 2000 (*Toronto Globe and Mail*), the exiled Southern political leader Bona Malwal, now an al-Beshir advisor, was strongly critical of the presence of Talisman and its president, James Buckee, whom he considered facilitators of the raging war. Adding his voice to the movement against Talisman was American English-professor-turned-activist Dr. Eric Reeves, who launched his own website crusade. Khartoum simply went ahead. Many Sudanese benefitted from lower-cost petroleum products produced by Talisman's $640 million refinery, and the economy grew. By 2000, it produced 50,000 bpd of oil, which was virtually all domestic petroleum. Cooking gas prices went down by half, and the long waiting lines for fuel in Khartoum were over. Sudanese president al-Beshir had something to celebrate in his eleventh year in power, and if Talisman stayed or left, it hardly mattered. There were many others interested.

On 19 June 2000, Buckee spoke openly about pulling out of Sudan, with so many uncertainties in oil production. He worried about Talisman share prices, as well as the endless political attacks by Sudan oil activists, especially by Dr. Reeves, and with many oil interests elsewhere, he did not need the frustrations (*Dow Jones Newswires*). By August 2000, the political campaign had turned Talisman into a pariah company, and the bombing of the U.S. embassies in Kenya and Tanzania, and President Clinton's bombing of Khartoum North, had polarized the situation even more. The October 2000 Sudan Peace Act proposed in the U.S. Congress for more sanctions against Sudan added heat to the controversy. The "great deal" for Sudanese oil was at the wrong time, and U.S. State Department opposition to Sudan made it harder and harder for Talisman to claim neutrality. Allegations of providing logistical support to Khartoum's military and benefiting from regional "genocide" and ethnic removal from the oil fields added to Talisman's miseries of political isolation, with stockholder protests and stock sale declines.

Clearly, all these events had their own stresses and internal conflicts, but the strain was also showing among the Khartoum rulers. Al-Beshir demoted Hassan al-Turabi to a lesser role in the National Congress on 12 December 1999. On 28 February 2000, al-Beshir blocked al-Turabi from speaking at a rally in front of the presidential palace, where he was about to denounce al-Beshir for wandering off the Islamic course outlined by al-Turabi's NIF. By May, al-Turabi was stripped of his position as Secretary General of the National Council after charging that al-Beshir was a military dictator and predicting that he would be toppled in a popular uprising. Evidently, al-Turabi had forgotten about his role in supporting al-Beshir's military coup, thus risking himself by these outspoken statements, which revealed his own ideological extremism that had directed al-Beshir in several failed courses of action, including the SPLA peace talks that had just collapsed. The *jihad* in the South was losing momentum. On 9 May 2000, this power struggle climaxed when the audacious al-Turabi and his supporters decided to "sack" al-Beshir and his deputies. While he had no power to accomplish this, he still called for "the people" to "rise against the al-Beshir regime." Al-Turabi failed in all of these plans to overthrow the NCP. In June, al-Turabi continued his challenge to al-Beshir by forming his own party. The response by al-Beshir was to promise "free and fair" elections in October after multiparty opponents were "officially" allowed to return in 1999. He would stand as the candidate for the NCP.

Seeing only more Islamist squabbling in Khartoum, the SPLA continued its military offensive in southern Blue Nile that had started in April. It claimed scores of Khartoum soldiers killed, with many small arms, mortars, and howitzers seized, and even a T-55 tank was captured. Firm police action squelched a pro-Turabi rally in Khartoum on 9 June 2000. On 13 June, there was more bad news for Khartoum when the SPLA claimed almost two hundred more government troops killed in the southern Blue Nile, while capturing an additional three tanks, heavy trucks, small arms, radios, and ammunition. This fighting finally brought oil production to a halt at Hegleig. The typical fight-back spirit of al-Beshir quickly appeared on 16 June when he proclaimed that Sudan would be self-sufficient in arms production, including heavy APCs, main battle tanks, rocket-propelled grenades (RPGs), Kalashnikov machine guns, mortars, and heavy artillery, and he announced plans on 27 October 2000 to manufacture warplanes and rockets. The oil revenues and Chinese technical expertise at the vehicle-assembly plant on the Wad Medani road made this a reality. The political and military back-and-forth featured another SPLA attack in mid-June at Gogrial, which symbolized the North-South standoff, while "peace" negotiations were continuing quietly on behalf of the IGAD Peace Initiative.

During GNPOC's first full year of oil production in 2000, GoS oil revenues surpassed projections by nearly 122 percent. Instead of projected revenues of 63.6 billion *dinars*, actual income was 140.9 billion *dinars* (US$546.1 million) for the year. In other words, Sudan's oil output had reached 185,000 bpd by the third quarter, whereas it had been only 126,000 bpd at the beginning of the year. Moreover, international oil prices had soared from US$19.8 per barrel in 1999 to US$27.9 per barrel in 2000, a 40 percent increase (HRW 2003, 346). In short, for 2000, the volatile mixture of oil, armies, and politics continued into the nineteenth year of the civil war and an estimated two million deaths. Ironically, the "sanctions" against Sudan gave it more incentive to become arms-independent with Chinese help, and to diversify non-American oil investors. The counterproductive "law of unintended consequences" of the political activists resulted in more Chinese in Sudan, more Sudanese arms, and no oil going into American tankers.

As 2001 opened, the controversies did not abate surrounding Sudanese oil and arms. Block 5A, Bentiu, and Upper Nile and Lundin oil prospecting were especially central concerns of fundamentalist activists and nongovernmental

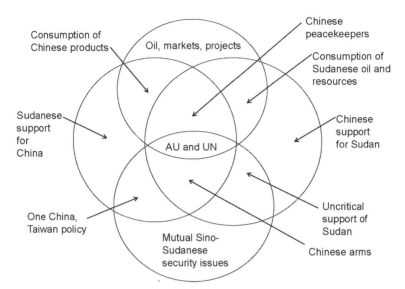

Figure 5.1 China and Sudan

organizations (NGOs) (Safe Harbor International Relief, the Holocaust Museum, Samaritans Purse, Operation Life Line, Catholic Relief Services, Sowing Circle Foundation, Christian Aid, the United States Catholic Conference, Norwegian Church Aid, the Southern African Bishops' Conference, Operation Save Innocent Lives, UNICEF, and *Médicins Sans Frontièrs*), all concerned about southern Sudan and the Khartoum government. The American Anti-Slavery group was busy with its "hot-button" mission of freeing/buying slaves and calling on Fidelity Bank to stop its investment in Talisman. In addition, the SPLA war of John Garang and Peter Gadet continued, along with the Khartoum-backed war of the LRA just over the border in Uganda. The *New York Times* (13 January 2001) climbed aboard with an editorial on the "Oil Wars in Sudan" that criticized the foreign powers supporting Khartoum, without recognizing the United States' support for the SPLA or Clinton's bombing. Meanwhile, the oil companies finished the all-weather road from Bentiu to Ryer/Thar Jath, Leer, and Adok by January 2001.

In February 2001, Gadet's SPLA attacked Machar's forces (and the United Nations') base at Nyal, Western Upper Nile/Unity State in Block 5B. Although this action threatened the 1999 Wunlit peace agreement, an emergency meeting of the peace council prevented further local attacks and reprisals so that the situation settled down greatly by April 2001. At that time, GoS Brigadier General Gatluak Deng, the government's top Nuer army officer, was able to unite the Southern pro-government militias under one command in Juba, but the other rebel movements remained fractured (HRW 2003, 196, 274).

Under domestic pressures, the U.S. Congress passed a resolution 422–2 for measures to pressure the Khartoum government to end the war, bombing, and slavery, and to continue U.S. economic sanctions. Oil companies singled out for criticism were China's CNCP, Qatar's Gulf Petroleum, Sweden's Lundin Oil, Malaysia's *Petroliam Nasional Berhad*, France's TotalFinaElf, and Canada's Talisman. Even after 9/11, Talisman vowed to stay on in Sudan. David Mann, a spokesman for Talisman, noted that even if his firm stopped oil prospecting in Sudan, it would be replaced by others that might be less helpful (*New York Times*, 14 June 2001; 17 June 2001). *Jane's Intelligence Review* (June 2001) estimated that the size of the Sudanese government's regular army was 100,000, and its militia was about 15,000. There can be little question that substantial amounts of the new oil funds were diverted to military needs in weapons and personnel, despite assertions to the contrary that the funds were used for development. The process and accounting was not transparent.

In June 2001, Sudan signed an agreement whereby Ethiopia would import 85 percent of its fuel requirements (gasoline and kerosene) from Sudan beginning in 2002. The general manager of the Ethiopian Petroleum Enterprise added that Ethiopia would save US$7 million a year by importing directly from its neighbor Sudan rather than from greater distances. Kenya was also interested in importing Sudanese oil because it could be imported duty-free pursuant according to the Common Market for Eastern and Southern Africa (COMESA), but domestic political opposition to Sudan raised moral and human-rights objections. In July 2001, Kenyan officials blocked Sudanese oil imports, but Sudan threatened that it would ban high-value Kenyan tea and coffee. Both nations flinched, and the trade war promptly stopped. Sudan was a quick study in the lessons of oil diplomacy.

However, Sudan failed to meet the optimistic 2001 oil revenue projection of 153.2 billion *dinars* (US$593.8 million). Actual 2001 oil revenues were only 140.9 billion *dinars* (US$547.4 million), which was less than projected but still higher than the 2000 oil income. The government did not heed the IMF and made the mistake of assuming that the 2000 high price of crude oil would continue; it dropped in 2001 to US$21.5 per barrel from the previous price of US$27.8.

The oil war, religion, and human rights were gaining center stage in the United States and other world forums. African and Middle Eastern nations were more skeptical of American motivations. Others saw this as outside interference and a thinly veiled attempt to topple the Islamist government of Sudan, which was broadly opposed in the United States after hosting Osama bin Laden for many years, not to mention its ghost houses, and had a pariah status in general, with aerial bombardment and displacement of civilians at Raga in western Bahr al-Ghazal. At the United Nations on 2 November 2001, the Security Council voted 14–0 to lift the sanctions against Sudan. The United States abstained, but extended its own unilateral sanctions that were opposed by Khartoum. The SPLA called for the imposition of a no-fly zone against Khartoum military aircraft. Hope grew to a certain extent with a joint Libyan-Egyptian peace initiative in July, especially since IGAD had been dormant, but the joint initiative did not address self-determination. By November, SPDF leader Riak Machar came out in full opposition, along with leader John Garang, since there were no reasons for SPLA support. While this did not directly yield the CPA, it created a blueprint for peace that emerged four years later with the Comprehensive Peace Agreement. In August, President George W. Bush hesitated to support the Senate version of the Sudan Peace Act since it interfered with the U.S. Securities and Exchange Commission and would not be very effective given the small American investment in Sudan. To engage constructively with Sudan, Bush appointed in September 2001 Republican senator from Missouri and Episcopal Minister John C. Danforth as his Special Envoy to renew the peace-seeking efforts. This appointment was broadly welcomed and was another step toward the CPA in 2005.

In August 2001, Commander Peter Paar's SPDF and SAF forces guarded the road to Lundin's new well at Ryer/Thar Jath in Block 5A. This arrangement served Lundin well until Paar changed sides and reached a truce with Peter Gadet of the SPLA. The situation refused to be stabilized and, in October 2001, in Block 4, thousands of civilians were displaced by a new round of GoS army/helicopter attacks on the local population. GNPOC then wasted no time in beginning drilling and extended the road from Hegleig to the drilling site (HRW 2003, 274).

In November 2001, U.S. peace envoy Senator Danforth arrived in Khartoum for "positive" meetings with al-Beshir, and tours of the West and the SPLA rebel-held South, that resulted in a four-point peace plan. The SPLA staged a major attack at the Hegleig area and killed some hundred Sudanese troops, while also bringing down two helicopters and seizing considerable military equipment. The SPLA renewed its warning that oil regions are legitimate military targets and oil companies should withdraw since oil revenue fueled the Khartoum military. Danforth said he was eager to work toward peace, but he would not work month after month unless the parties were serious, and he had his doubts that they were. Susan Rice, Assistant Secretary of State for African Affairs, shared Danforth's skepticism. On 19 November, *The Oil Daily* noted that the U.S. political climate against Sudan demanded passage of the Sudan Peace Act with its sanctions. Yet Khartoum continued its aerial bombing in Aweil East villages in Bahr al-Ghazal, and the SPLA also continued its attacks on oil facilities, amid recurring reports of Northern slavery. Clearly, Senator Danforth had many reasons for his hesitancy, but as the year closed, the efforts to build a cease-fire resumed during active warfare.

During dry season, from December 2001 to April 2002, fighting continued in Block 5A. After Garang's SPLA and Machar's SPDF united forces attacked GoS convoys in the area, they counterattacked with Antonov bombers, helicopter gunships, Baggara horse-backed militia, pro-GoS Nuer militia, and Sudan Armed Forces (SAF) troops. This drove civilians from the oil road and from the oil fields of Lundin. From 2000 to 2001, GoS defense expenditures leapt from $250.9 million to $345 million, 45 percent higher in just one year. The largest source for these expenditures was oil revenue from total government revenue, which grew from US$799.9 million in 1999 to US$1.415 billion in 2001, an increase of 80 percent! Depending upon the forum, the GoS reported oil statistics that could be celebrated, minimized or denied. To promising investors, higher numbers were circulated. Various regulatory bodies such as the United Nations and the IMF also had to figure out where the reality was among daily fluctuations in production, prices, and petroleum quality. The GoS figures supplied to the IMF projected a production increase from 209,000 to 230,000 bpd for 2002. Yet the GoS agreed to an IMF suggestion to base government expenditures on an assumed constant price of US$20 per barrel. Oil revenue resulting from potentially higher prices could then be deposited in the Bank of Sudan. This action would greatly reduce expenses and allow adjustment when oil prices dropped (HRW 2003, 348). However, instead of declining, the international price of oil increased from US$21.5 per barrel in 2001 to US$23.2 per barrel in 2002. The price per barrel was expected to increase in 2003 to US$24.5. With this added revenue in 2001, Sudan purchased from Russia twenty-two APCs and twelve attack helicopters, both well-suited to the Sudanese counterinsurgency strategy. In 2002, Sudan bought another eight APCs and four more attack helicopters from Russia, plus fourteen large-caliber artillery systems from Belarus. These military hardware acquisitions represented a substantial increase in armament.

In 2002, Riak Machar formally joined what was left of his SPDF forces with the SPLM/A after nearly eleven years of strife between his mainly Nuer soldiers and the heavily Dinka SPLA. Some of Machar's followers joined the government rather than the SPLM/A, but on balance this was a victory for the SPLA and a defeat for the GoS. In reaction to this setback, the GoS initiated another militia recruitment drive and deployed its regular armed forces in the South, especially in the GNPOC area of operation. Infrastructural development continued in Blocks 1 and 4. Oil roads were built to reach drilling sites, and the government planned a bridge across the Bahr al-Ghazal (Nam) River near the Wangkei garrison. These measures were not sufficient to regain Lundin's confidence, so this firm suspended its activity in Block 5A. By this time, the peace initiative was gaining traction (HRW 2003, 383).

In January 2002, the GoS and the SPLM/A signed a six-month cease-fire in the Nuba Mountains, which was to be monitored internationally. They then signed another agreement in March (proposed by Senator Danforth) to cease targeting civilians and related targets. The regional Intergovernmental Authority on Development (IGAD) sponsored additional peace talks, which resulted in the GoS and SPLM/A signing a protocol in Machakos, Kenya on 20 July. The protocol provided a Southern referendum on self-determination and an option for independence after first a six-month pre-interim and then a six-year interim period. Moreover, the protocol stipulated that that South adopt civil law instead of Shari'a (HRW 2003, 505). This critical turning point did not end the war, but provided more of the roadmap for what would be the CPA.

Rosy images of endlessly increasing oil production and of luring an infinite number of investors to Sudan were not realized. Military costs steadily spiraled upward while production snags, lower yields, and price fluctuations did not help. At least one change took place with the reunification of the Nuer leader Machar's SPDF and Dinka Garang's regional SPLA. It was thought that this move toward Southern unity might strengthen their negotiating position vis-à-vis the North to bring the conflict a step closer to peace. This was a concrete result of the efforts of Senator Danforth and former U.S. president Carter's tireless support of the IGAD trust-building initiative on Guinea-worm eradication. There was a fear that if al-Beshir was seen as too conciliatory to the West, it might also "invite" a return of al-Qa'eda to Sudan, where it had numerous supporters. Needless to say, a foreign policy built on this fear would not be constructive, but this persistent concern was part of the political equation as President Bush was considering a renewal of diplomatic relations that were seriously broken over Sudan's previous support and links to al-Qa'eda. Sudan got some credit with the United States when it arrested a man at first thought to be Anas al-Liby, accused of plotting the bombing of the U.S. embassies in East Africa in 1998 and the assassination attempt on Egyptian president Hosni Mubarak in 1995. This state of flux in early 2002 prompted Lundin Petroleum to think it could resume drilling and seismic studies in Block 5A as soon as a cease-fire could be settled. With goodwill still shallow, the SPLA spokesman Samson Kwaje charged in March 2002 that Khartoum was fomenting revolt in CAR to undermine and divert SPLA forces that had expanded in western Bahr al-Ghazal. At the same time, some traditional Northern opposition leaders (such as Sadiq al-Mahdi) lobbied for reopening ties with a "reformed" Khartoum government.

Meanwhile, Talisman continued its explorations in southern Sudan at Diffra West Well in GNPOC Block 4 (*The Oil Daily*, 3 May 2002), raising once again the cries of alarm from humanitarians and activists who feared more displacement and food catastrophes for the local population as long as the SPLA continued to consider the oil fields military targets and as long as Khartoum continued military operations as their counterpoint. By June, Petronas was also announcing additional production in conjunction with CNPC, GNPOC, and Talisman at the Seventh Asia Oil and Gas Conference in Kuala Lumpur. Of interest were reports that Talisman's CEO James Buckee was considering sale of its controversial 25 percent interest of this 230,000 bpd project, which caused Talisman's stock to rise sharply with rumors of its sale to Malaysia or India. The rumors turned to fact on 12 June when Talisman sold its $750 million interest in prospecting blocks in the Muglad Basin to ONG Videsh, Ltd., the state-run oil company of India.

While the activists felt a sense of "achievement" in driving Talisman from the oil fields, they did not have much leverage with the Indian firm, nor did this stop the flow of oil revenue to Khartoum for its military purchases. Even the suspension of oil work by Lundin was temporary according to Sudan's Energy Minister, Ahmed Awad al-Jaz, who expected oil production to reach 500,000 bpd by 2005. While this was a major surge in Sudan oil production, it can be said by way of comparison that tiny Qatar produced 640,000 bpd in May 2002. *Africa Energy Intelligence* reported (26 June 2002) that Romania (RomPetrol), Algeria (Sonatrach), Belarus (Slavneft), and Japan (Japan National Oil Corporation and Impex) were all negotiating for Blocks 8 and 9 south and east of Khartoum, Block 15 on the Red Sea, and Block 12 in northern Darfur. In Block 8, one owner was American Philip Stephenson, a former official of the U.S. Treasury Department and president of the International Equity Partners investment fund. Other news in June was the resignation of Transport and Foreign Minister Lam Akol of Shilluk origins, Presidential Advisor Mekki Ali Balyel from Nuba Mountains, and Deputy Justice Minister Amin Bannani from Darfur, all of whom withdrew because they judged that the ruling National Congress was backtracking on basic freedoms.

Yet on 30 June 2002, the SPLA and Khartoum finally produced a Draft Peace Agreement that was considered another step toward peace, but was far from ready to be signed, not to mention enforced. Nevertheless, the United States stayed engaged with Sudan's counterterrorism measures and with somewhat improved access for humanitarian relief, as well as some steps toward a peace agreement under the auspices of IGAD and General Lazaro Sumbeiywo of Kenya. Finally, the Machakos (Kenya) Protocol was drafted and signed by Dr. Ghazi Salah al-Din Atabani for the GoS and by Commander Salva Kiir Mayardit for the SPLA. Among the provisions of this protocol were agreements for ongoing negotiations for a peaceful settlement of the conflict, respect for religion, and acceptance of a common declaration of principles, as well as provisions for self-determination while seeking unity of Sudan. This did not end the war, but it did lead directly to the CPA of 2005. Governments, parties, and movements in the world breathed some collective but cautious relief that Sudan might be at peace and could finally develop, especially in the South.

The year 2003 started with a genuine sense of optimism, beginning with an agreement in January between Sudan and Ethiopia that Sudan would export 13,000 tons of gasoline per month to Ethiopia, which spent half of its export earnings on imported fuel. The first Sudanese shipments were made on 31 January, but were soon halted by Sudan because of a six-week shutdown of its oil refinery and delays in upgrading the road to Gedarif, which had been affected by the rainy season. Another blow to Sudan's optimism occurred when Ethiopia decided to drop Sudan as a gasoline supplier and signed an agreement with a Kuwaiti company, which also discussed constructing a pipeline between Addis Ababa and Djibouti. Apparently seeking further independence of importing oil products,

Ethiopia also signed an agreement with Petronas to explore and develop oil fields in its Gambella region, considered an extension of the Sudanese Melut Basin (HRW 2003, 359).

Having the Machakos Accord in place added to the optimism, but this also did not last long. Heavy fighting broke out at Leer south of Bentiu. This was a serious breach of the 15 October 2002 Memorandum of Agreement and the Amended Accords of 18 November 2002. An investigation by American Brigadier General (Retired) Herbert J. Lloyd of the Civilian Protection Monitoring Team found that both forces were involved. This military brinksmanship again put human rights, humanitarian concerns, and the future of peace at severe risk. Foreign firms were scurrying around for ownership of Blocks 7 and 8, thinking that the war was soon to be over.

The precarious balance was soon upset, with events in Darfur suddenly erupting into bloody armed conflict that is still ongoing; this was covered in more detail in Chapter 4. This situation will not be recounted here, except to say that to a certain extent, the briefly unified guerilla leaders in Darfur probably struck, thinking that the Machakos Protocol signaled a time for other marginalized peoples to move into negotiating positions of strength. Certainly, the marginalized voices of the Southerners saw some "natural allies" in Darfur. Indeed, some units of the SPLA had sought to spread their territory into the Nuba Mountains of southern Kordofan and southern Darfur. Not only did they miscalculate their political options and military strategy, they also miscalculated Khartoum's very predictable military reaction, which unleashed bloodshed and disruption in Darfur at levels never imagined. As the Darfur battles and crimes overflowed into Chad and ignited world attention, it also served to divert human, financial, and political resources needed to build upon the achievements represented by the Machakos Protocol that did not cover the rapidly deteriorating situation in Darfur. Later, when the CPA was signed, politicians and activists sadly learned that there is more to Sudan than Darfur and that other strategic and political issues there also needed to be considered.

So in 2003, the South was put on the "back burner," and humanitarian relief there became more problematic and contentious. If journalists went to Sudan, it was to cover the events unfolding in Darfur. An SPLA press statement by Dr. Samson Kwaje on 20 March 2003 highlighted the problem of nationalist division as a function of the Islamist "exclusivist project" that sought to "institutionalize the hegemony of a small minority in the center." The SPLA sought to make a "New Sudan" with democracy and equitable power distribution. The SPLA position was that it was in solidarity with the people of Darfur in their struggle for justice and equality for themselves and for all Sudanese, but that the SPLA was not involved in the inception of the war in Darfur, for which the NIF government was accountable.

Remarkably, this turmoil did not derail the second meeting of President Omer al-Beshir and SPLA Chairman John Garang on 2 April 2003, with the invitation of Kenyan President Mwai Kibaki, under the IGAD auspices and pressures of the

U.S. Sudan Peace Act. Joint talks had the goal of signing a final protocol by June if several serious remaining issues could be addressed. These included the topics of military command, Abyei and Upper Blue Nile borders, the implementation of a cease-fire, and transitional period milestones leading to elections and a referendum on separation. Broadening his political base, Garang met with the Umma Party on 15 April, noting that this was a critical time for both at this point in Sudanese history. His hope was for bilateral relations, but not for an Islamist state.

By 16 April 2003, the joint talks snagged on the nature of the armed forces—one army or two?—as the goal of a final signing in June slipped away. Adding to this setback was another new fissure between the SPLA and SPDF. Perhaps talks in early May would bring the discussions on power- and wealth-sharing back on track? As required by the Sudan Peace Act, President George W. Bush certified that the GoS was still making significant progress on the road to peace. This was neither good enough, nor soon enough, for Lundin Petroleum, which finally joined Chevron and Talisman in pulling out of some of its Sudan holdings by selling its 40 percent share in Block 5A in the Melut Basin Thar Jath oil field to Petronas for US$142.5 million with the belief that it had 149 million barrels of crude oil. Lundin determined to keep its 24.5 percent stake in Block 5B, sending Lundin's shares into a threefold increase. With the peace talks drifting off course, U.S. Secretary of State Colin Powell went to Kenya to meet representatives of the GoS and the SPLA and to nudge them along. On 23 October 2003, he said that "this is a moment of opportunity that must not be lost," but the June deadline was now moved to December 2003, and if the work was concluded, there could be a final signing at the White House in Washington.

For most of 2004, the attention of the world and Sudan was diverted to Darfur, which was then facing some of the gravest charges of war crimes, militia attacks, and ethnic displacement, with human-rights violations, arrests, torture, and generally a high level of violence by all armed parties. This culminated on 18 September, with UN Security Council Resolution Number 1564 that took note of these major violations of human rights and war crimes. For the South, this was a time of relative calm and intense behind-the-scenes negotiation that had brought peace ever closer; indeed, some 85,000 refugees were expected to return to the South in 2004.

Later, in 2004 and 2005, Nuer interests sued Talisman, saying that the company was complicit in the displacement that amounted to ethnic cleansing. The case was finally dismissed, largely on the basis that many Nuer were equally engaged in pursing their own oil interests and that the entire region was engulfed in a war that was chiefly aimed at securing that resource rather than specifically targeting Nuer.

OIL IN SUDAN AFTER THE 2005 CPA

The beginning of 2005 was heralded by the hard-fought achievement of the 9 January 2005 signing of the CPA, which *inter alia* indicated that Sudan's oil wealth would be shared 50–50. Living in Khartoum at the time, this author recalls the great sense of excitement that the war was over; when debriefed by U.S. Ambassador Carney, flying just hours before from the historic signing, his enthusiasm was contagious. While criticism has mounted about what the CPA did *not* do and did *not* solve, there has been no sustained fighting since then. But some violent clashes did take place over the still unresolved borders at Abyei, and troop strength and redeployment in Upper Nile Province, not to mention other armed groups (OAGs), South-on-South interethnic clashes as well as the ongoing mayhem caused by the LRA in the Southern borderlands. Despite these significant problems, a new trend was taking shape, at least between Khartoum and Juba. Perhaps the GoS was at a weak moment, with GNPOC production off-target and counting on Block 5A and other new production to return to their goals.

Euphoria was quickly tempered when, on 29 January, police opened fire on a Port Sudan demonstration in which nineteen people were killed; dozens more were wounded, followed by arrests of Beja Congress people as the Eastern region moved on to the ever-complicated Sudanese political agenda. By February, the situation had settled down, and the United Nations announced that it would pay US$1 billion for peacekeeping in southern Sudan, with a robust staff of 10,131 military personnel, 755 police, 1,018 international staff, 2,623 national staff, and 214 UN volunteers. More good news was announced on August 30, 2005 in an agreement between GoS and Petronas for a refinery that was expected to produce 100,000 bpd.

Meanwhile, the war in Darfur plodded bloodily along; then came the totally shocking news on 30 July that southern Sudanese president and SPLA hero John Garang had died in a helicopter crash. Conspiracy theories and suspicions zoomed to the foreground, but subsequent professional investigation by FAA officials confirmed that it was a tragic accident compounded by bad weather. This was a staggering human loss, but the political roadmap of the CPA was sufficiently strong that, while torn, it survived his death, and the bumpy road to peace and development in southern Sudan could be resumed, even as the situation in Darfur deteriorated according to AU press statements in October. A first meeting in November of the Oil Commission with GoS President al-Beshir and Lieutenant General Salva Kiir Mayardit, now vice president of Sudan and president of GoSS, reviewed the political contract, and the two men functioned together rather than fighting each other. In a report on 27 December 2005, the UN Secretary General noted general progress on the CPA, but also noted that there were serious lags in some parts of the implementation. A struggle over the Ministry of Energy, a serious lack of progress of the Abyei Boundary Commission (ABC), and limited demobilization of OAGs were all problems.

Previous bilateral optimism was low but still going forward. Suspicious were high, especially on oil issues and the mandated approach to "make unity appealing" was not going well. At least the UN Mission in Sudan (UNMIS) was still

committed to the principles of the CPA, and the GNU was more or less functioning. The persistence of the LRA insurgency was another problem when peace
overtures were rebuffed by its leader, Joseph Kony. The military redeployments
increased but were behind schedule, especially in the oil field areas, and there
were many, luckily small, security incidents, including internal Southern strife.
The Ceasefire Joint Military Committee was functioning through JIUs,
reconstruction and repatriation was advancing slowly, the rule-of-law project
going forward, along with demining, and work on gender and HIV/AIDS was
on track. Capacity-building in the South was underway, and the two top leaders
of Sudan insisted the peace was indivisible. At year's end, development pledges
for the South reached $4.5 billion. Some 12,000 Dinka and 400,000 cattle
moved back North from refuge in Equatoria to Jonglei in the same period.

On 9 January 2006, on the occasion of the first anniversary of the CPA, Salva
Kiir addressed the citizens of Juba and the people of southern Sudan, Nuba
Mountains, and southern Blue Nile Province, along with President Arap Moi,
IGAD representatives, and, significantly, Major General Paulino Matip Nhial,
Chief of Staff of the SSDF, just after the SSDF and the SPLA had signed a unity
agreement on 8 January, the previous day.Salva Kiir promised improvements in
roads and infrastructure. Some questioned this on 12 January, when the SPLA
publically and summarily executed at least eight people without trial for murder,
revenge killings, and adultery. Juba steadily gained confidence, and repatriation
of displaced people continued as a welcome fruit of the CPA peace. The following day, the UN Secretary General had his own briefing in which he expressed
consternation about the delays, but he continued to note forward progress. He
pointed to the fact that two new constitutions had been adopted, two governments had been formed, and new institutions were established, albeit imperfectly.
About 30 percent of the forces were redeployed, but there was much left to do.
For example, Major General Gordon Kong, another SSDF leader, refused to join
the forces of Paulino Matip. By 25 January, there was deployment of 62 percent
of the UNMIS peacekeepers that reached 5,871 of the allowed 10,000 under
Major General Fazle Akbar. Pakistan, Russia, and Kenya were joining in, and
demining continued, but Aweil was still seriously mined. Work on water and
health resources was going ahead, and the main roads were open. Critical
remarks were echoed on 28 January, when GoSS President Kiir complained
about slow implementation. Funds owed to the South were not paid, and he
wondered if Khartoum had honestly given half of the oil revenues. Khartoum
claimed production of 333,000 bpd, but the SPLA said it was more like
450,000 bpd. At least the military battle field had been replaced with a war of
words and numbers. For the international audience of investors, Khartoum used
high numbers that were complicated by various and changing measures of prob-
able reserves, proven reserves, product refined, product consumed, and product
exported, as well as the daily changes in the price per barrel. Among these many

measures of oil wealth, some confusion was inherent, but suspicious Southerners also assumed more nefarious manipulations when it came time to recover the revenue for "Southern" oil. Such frustrations were augmented by the $4.5 billion in "pledges" that were not more quickly realized.

The tumultuous and contentious complexity of the time is seen in the closing days of January 2006, with South-South clashes in the North over the "unity" between SSDF/SPLA and the SPLA threatening to seek IGAD/UN arbitration over slow implementation of the CPA. Khartoum countered by saying that the UN sanctions did not help the matter; still, tens of thousands of returnees headed back to their original Southern homes, with improvements in health and water delivery, mine-clearing advances, and livestock vaccination making return more attractive. Abyei floundered along with no administration. John Garang's widow, Rebecca Garang, complained on 3 February that the CPA implementation was going slowly. A few days later, on 8 February, President al-Beshir visited the South as more Dinka returned to Bor from Equatoria. Meanwhile, the Rumbek-Wau road reconstruction was advancing. This mixture of good and bad news typifies the post-CPA period; on 22 February, a UNMIS report recorded that five people were killed in an SAF/SPLA clash in the South, and in another incident in Kassala, two were killed. The local Bari were upset with the land policy of the GoSS in Juba, and Salva Kiir said that expelling the LRA should be the joint work of the SSDF and SPLA, which was alleged to received support from the SAF, who totally denied it. With suspicions still high, the SSDF complained on 27 February that the United States had plans to seize oil in southern Sudan. Increasingly, Southerners feared a Sudanese "Kashmir" if Abyei was not resolved. In the February report of UNMIS to the UN Secretary General, extensive travel allowed the observers to report examples of local violence and border conflicts, but that the CPA was working with 6,000 troops in place and with more coming, including Chinese and Russians; however, they maintained that there was still a need for the allowed 10,000. Southerners retained a broad skepticism about receiving a full rebate of oil revenues.

The 1 March 2006 report from UNMIS was not cheerful. There were some al-Qa'eda threats against the United Nations as the AMIS in Darfur shifted to UNMIS; the possibility of NATO forces in Sudan was protested in Khartoum demonstrations. Riak Machar blamed the SADF for foot-dragging and said that there was not enough support for the JIUs. And, responding to GoSS criticism, Oil Minister Awad Ahmed al-Jaz said that oil documents could be viewed by the SPLA. President Salva Kiir thanked Kenya for help in peace negotiations and the CPA, and he wanted them to continue. The UN recovery program for the South progressed with various rehabilitation projects in water, health, schools, sanitation, income projects, and increased local capacity. For the entire Sudan, oil wealth was also fueling the telecoms and Internet sectors, with meteoric growth in Canartel, Sudatel, Areeba, and Mobitel as Sudan became a regional telecom hub. Later, in March, mines exploded in the Malakal area. Fourteen were killed in SAF/SPLA clashes 40 kilometers northeast of volatile Abyei. New oil-prospecting blocks were awarded to the Indian company Oil and Natural Gas Corporation (ONGC).

As 2007 unfolded, the deep distrust between the NCP and SPLA was not healed, and the funding for the census was slow to arrive. Arab militias were reported rearming in southern Kordofan. By 8 October, SPLA recalled its ministers to Juba, where Salva Kiir exhorted all to fight corruption in the South and not to bother Northern traders in the South. He stressed that "we won't return to war," even if the tense, explosive border issues were not solved, and there were important deployment and OAG disarmament issues at hand.

Back in Khartoum, the first Sudanese oil-exploration company was started, as sanctions were proving ineffective and Khartoum elites were prospering. Construction was happening, with Chinese oil money making much difference. Office buildings, bridges, roads, shops, and hotels were appearing. Telecom companies and card dealers were sprouting, and the economy was growing at 13 percent annually. In December 2007, there was time for a diversionary incident over Gillian Gibbons calling her teddy bear "Muhammad."

According to Roger Winter and John Prendergast on 28 January 2008, Abyei could be considered Sudan's Kashmir,and on the South front, the SPLA had ongoing problems when, on 29 January, hundreds of LRA soldiers attacked Equatorian border villages, as they did again on 7 and 17 June. The minister of Equatoria wanted no more talks with them, although Riak Machar still did. Islamic banks in the South were ordered out in early February. It was not only the South that faced insurgent forces. When JEM was alleged to have backed an attack on Ndjamena in Chad, Chad conversely was charged with supporting a JEM attack on Omdurman on 10 May. But this was only a warm-up for Abyei; on 21 May, the SAF's 31st Brigade opened fire with heavy artillery, resulting in the loss of life on both sides. A cease-fire and solution was proposed by the SPLA on 27 May when they suggested demilitarizing the town, with a pullback of troops and fact-finding. At last, some 90,000 civilians were displaced, and Abyei was virtually destroyed. It was time to get serious about this; on 8 June, al-Beshir formed an interim administration of Abyei and sought the return of displaced people. On 9 June, Salva Kiir and his delegation met al-Beshir to sign a plan for Abyei in Friendship Hall that accepted a joint administration to allow the return of displaced people. By 11 June 936 joint forces were deployed, and Abyei settled down once again.

Trying to be proactive, the GoSS organized a conference on Sudan's marginalized people in Kampala on 2 July 2008. Believing that talking was better than fighting, the Southern Sudan Political Parties Alliance was established. Also on the agenda was a message to the Uganda Defense Forces that they should withdraw from southern Sudan. The SPLA would take responsibility for dealing with the LRA.

But the politics of oil continued. On 28 June 2008, the French company Total started drilling for oil in Sudan in their 67,000-square-kilometer Block B holdings after defeating a White Nile claim. Marathon, another American company, pulled out. The GoS and South Korea signed an oil-investment agreement, and Sudanese oil revenues for May 2008 were US$514.51 million. An oil leak reported in February at the Red Sea refinery Bashair II polluted some 9 square kilometers, affecting sea life and mangrove trees.

Ominously, the CPA did not require disarmament or demobilization for either the SAF or SPLA. This was supposed to apply to the OAGs. Accordingly, both sides bought new arms. Khartoum now has twenty-six fighter planes, seventeen fighter bombers, fourteen transport planes, ten attack helicopters, and twenty-eight other helicopters. Sudan might be the third-largest arms producer in Africa. One source (*Oxford Analytica*, 21 October 2008) states that one MiG-29 was shot down in the JEM attack on Omdurman. The SPLA seeks battle tanks—captured, traded from Ethiopia, or bought on the arms market. It is not known how many they have, but southern Sudan is flat "tank country." Open war is not likely, but high levels of military spending with little demobilization expected is a dark cloud hovering over too many unresolved issues. The move to bring ICC charges against members of the GoS and especially its president, as well as certain Darfur rebels, was well-received among activists, but on 27 June 2008, Ambassador Andrew Natsios warned at a forum of the U.S. Institute of Peace that this was also a threat to Sudan's stability. Many African and Arab nations do not respect or favor the ICC charges, fearing Euro-centrism.

As this book goes to press in 2010, a retrospective view is worthwhile. The CPA is still intact, although frustrations abound in the North, in the South, and among peacekeepers. Frustration stays high, with Abyei still very sensitive, but full war has thus far been averted. Oil is still flowing, and more investors are arriving, That is, like it or not, the lifeblood of both the Southern and Northern rulers, but the clock is ticking toward the disputed census, toward delayed elections, and toward the gigantic questions about the 2011 referendum on unity. The weak history of poor and rare elections, the strong history of agreements broken, and the common history of recourse to violence do not augur well.

Other clocks are also ticking. The LRA is on the run, but is still a serious problem. Thoughts of a possible postseparation South incline observers to think of rail, pipeline, or road transport for oil through Uganda to the Indian Ocean. Some investors are already waiting in the wings, such as French and Russian interests, and Americans who have been strategically pushed out by their own sanctions, which certainly in this instance have been counterproductive in blocking development aid and in securing American access. One such firm is Jarch Capital, with offices in New York, for a part of Block B, with links to the financially strapped and renamed AIG Company; Phil Heilberg of Heilberg Management Groups now has a "non-American" office in the British Virgin Islands.

The lure of Block B oil rights has already had many twists and turns; more can be expected.

If separation does occur, it is clear that this would put heavy pressure on Khartoum, and China, India, and Malaysia would have to accommodate in ways not yet seen. South-South violence is a growing, not shrinking, problem in which traditional clashes among pastoralists are on short fuses, and Equatorian worries about Nilotic dominance are already present, along with standard issues of transparency, corruption, and human rights and such. As for the North, the problems in Darfur are still much unresolved in any peace treaty. Khartoum stays preoccupied with regime security, and it has been in power for a very long time compared to other postindependence Sudanese regimes. There are secular and democratic forces knocking on the door, but Khartoum is also very resilient and resistant, and not to be underestimated. This is particularly true relative to the strengths of Islam and the durability of the traditional parties and alliances. Aside from the obvious aspects of oil, Sudan is also being "invested away" by foreign nations seeking agricultural land for livestock and cash crops, and by commercial interests that simultaneously strengthen as well as undermine Sudanese economic autonomy.

Even in the U.S. State Department, there are important groups seeking harsher measures and actions with regard to Darfur. They are tangling with other groups seeing Darfur as only an interconnected part of Sudan in which a preoccupation with Darfur, more or less managed, diverts U.S. interests from oil, Khartoum regime issues, and regional security problems. The ICC charges against President al-Beshir are a case in point. Moral outrage and domestic political activists are pushing one way, while neither Sudan nor the United States is even a signatory of the protocol. African, Middle Eastern, and Chinese resistance to the charges for various reasons is pushing another way, as traction is made difficult on a slippery slope of conflicting interests. Presently, this struggle is intense in Foggy Bottom and the White House. The campaign rhetoric of candidates Barack Obama, Joe Biden, and Hillary Clinton has been suspended when President Obama appointed a new Presidential Envoy, Major General Scott Gration, to try his hand at putting the Sudanese jigsaw pieces back into a recognizable puzzle.

In an article in the 26 March 2009 issue of the *Sudan Tribune*, Sudan was tendering a new offer for 800,000 barrels of Nile Blend "crude sweet" for loading in May 2009. Although this is less than 1 million barrels, this still represents serious oil wealth. In the South, new safety regulations are moving through the legislative branch as more and safer oil products are flowing there. December oil revenues of Khartoum, that is, the GNU, fell by 21 percent to US$274 million amid the global financial crisis, but oil prices have recently been going back up. Oil revenue for October 2008 was over US$600 million. Such is the volatility of oil prices. The March tender for oil was 2.2 million barrels, either to snag higher prices or to meet budget needs in Khartoum. The new Qamari oil field opened in January 2009 and is expected to produce 30,000 bpd. Malaysia announced that it was interested in a new oil refinery project. Sudanese oil products are now being sold to Ethiopia. The Sudanese minister of oil says that the SPLA is interfering with production, but no doubt the SPLA holds the opposite view. White Nile Company, which was shoved aside by Total, is now shifting its oil interests to agriculture. Also very important, the South Sudan has established its own Nile Petroleum Corporation Board, or Nile-Pet. Overall, Sudan Oil's production target was projected to hit 900,000 bpd in 2009, and if oil prices continue to recover, this will be a massive financial windfall for peace and development. Oil in Sudan has turned—or spun around—the nation and opened this chapter; as this chapter closes, the role of Dar Blend and Nile Blend crude oil can only be seen as becoming even more significant, in both positive and negative ways. The Sudanese future is hard to see in the "crystal ball" with petroleum clouding our vision in the future.

CHINA, AFRICA, AND SUDANESE OIL

According to the *Economist* (21 June 2007), China buys about 80 percent of Sudan's oil production, at 480,000 bpd, and 2005 production was about 500,000 bpd. Sudan's Oil Minister al-Jaz said that production would reach 1 million bpd by 2008, but it did not. At the same time, some oil fields are starting to mature, but more are probably to be found. Low-sulfur, light crude sweet "Nile Blend" is the most easily refined, and thus the most valuable, but some new oil is lower-quality; hence lower prices, creating a flurry of new concessions awarded across the nation. Some firms are small with little experience. In short, there are many variables to consider, and some cannot yet be known. China takes about 64 percent of Sudan's exports, most of which is oil, and in 2004, it had about US$1 billion in direct investment. China has sold a great deal to Sudan, ranging from consumer goods to US$100 million of Shenyang fighter planes, including twelve supersonic F-7 jets. In June 2008, Sudan signed economic and agricultural agreements with China, including their construction of bridges, roads, dams, pipelines, and refineries. There are Chinese programs on Sudanese television and Chinese signs in the Khartoum tourist market, as well as a Chinese hotel right along the Nile.

In 2005, Chinese invested US$175 million in African oil exploration. China is now the second-largest consumer nation after the United States, passing Japan. Buying African crude oil for Chinese arms is part of its foreign policy and a security tool in its policy of "noninterference" in domestic affairs, which it considers part of African "sovereignty." Africa had 5.2 percent economic growth in 2005, partially because of Chinese investment. Its projects are low-cost, high-quality, and speedy. In 2004, the Chinese had 1,500 peacekeepers in Africa and canceled US$10 billion of bilateral debt. China might jump-start Africa. From 1955 to

1977, China sold US$142 million of military equipment to Africa. From 1996 to 2003, this was 10 percent of all arms transfers to the continent.

China built the first-ever oil refineries in Chad and Niger. Landlocked Chad found oil in 2003 and now pumps its crude down a 620-mile pipeline to Kribi, Cameroon. China also has a $5 billion deal with Niger and a 2,000-kilometer pipeline, and is building its first import-replacing and hard-currency earning refinery, which is very popular (Reuters, 28 October 2008). Talisman was driven out in 2003, the Swiss Cliveden Group left in 2006, and Marathon American sold its 32.5 percent share of Block B (*CFR Publication 9557*, 26 January 2007). It did not take long for China to fill this void and create ever-expanding needs for its bankers, soldiers, workers, engineers, and merchants.

Harbeson and Rothchild (2009, 65) also state that Chinese-African trade has leapt from a mere US$12 million in the late 1980s to $3 billion in 1995, $10 billion in 2000, $40 billon in 2005, and $55.5 billion in 2006. China is Africa's second-largest trading partner, after only the United States, and it may surpass the United States by 2010 as well as reverse Africa's marginal position in world trade. Eighty-five percent of Africa's trade to China is in primary goods, especially oil, and China is primarily trading with Angola, Sudan, Nigeria, Congo-B, and Equatorial Guinea. Thirty percent of all Chinese oil is from Africa, and Angola alone supplies more oil to China than Saudi Arabia. Sixty-five percent of Sudanese oil production goes to China.

HOW MUCH OIL IS THERE?

According to the *Oil and Gas Journal* (January 2007), Sudan has 5.0 billion barrels of proven reserves of oil. This is strikingly up from 563 million barrels of proven reserves in 2006. The conflict in the South prevented exploration and exploitation, so the peace dividend of the 2005 CPA has changed this dramatically. By October 2005, new contracts were let by the National Petroleum Commission (NPC) and Sudapet, but with limited capital and expertise, and trade sanctions from the West, the main Sudanese partners are notably Chinese (CNPC), Indian (ONGC), and Malaysian (Petronas). The main oil-producing basins are Muglad and Melut. Estimates also project reserves in the Red Sea zone, northwest Sudan, including Darfur, and in other parts of the Blue Nile basin. In principle, the revenue generated to Sudan is to be shared equally by the GoS and GoSS. By 2007, Sudan went from barely being a producer at all to being the fifth-largest producer in Africa after the super resources of Libya (41.5 billion barrels [bbls]), Nigeria (36.2 bbls), Algeria (12.3 bbls), and Angola (8 bbls). Angolan offshore oil reserves were put at an amazing 30 bbls (*US ITA/USGS World Oil*, Vol. 232, 2002).

Clearly, these numbers are large, and every year, the description of the proven reserves seems to mount. From October 1999 to June 2000, Sudan was producing 20,000 bpd (*AFP*, June 13, 2000). Its reserves were put at 403.6 million barrels in 1998; 528 million barrels by 1999; 562.8 million barrels in 2000; and at 725.2 million barrels in 2001. A GoS Minister of Oil told a youth conference that oil reserves explored in Hegleig could reach 1.2 bbls by the end of 1999, and *CFR Publication 9558* states that Sudan now produces 500,000 bpd. In 2008, the proven reserves were put at 1.6 bbls.

In the early 2000s, Sudan was not among the top fifteen oil producers, which include (in million bpd [mbpd]) Saudi Arabia (9.817 mbpd), Russia (8.543 mbpd), and the United States (7.454 mbpd, but none of the U.S. oil imports are from Sudan). Then we have Iran (3.852 mbpd), Mexico (3.789 mbpd), and China (3.396 mbpd, with about 7% of Chinese oil being from Sudan). Sudan is still not on this super-producer list, but the numbers and conditions are favorable for the future. It is not even at the level of Nigeria. The *New Statesman* (14 September 2007) had about 22 percent of U.S. crude imports from Nigeria in the first quarter of 2007 and 25 percent of U.S. crude imports from Saudi Arabia in the same period. Africa is catching up, since 75 percent of the Nigerian economy is oil-related. But with the widespread Movement for the Emancipation of the Niger Delta (MEND) revolt in the Niger Delta and attacks on oil production, some 680,000 bpd is lost through leaks, bunkering, stoppage, and attacks. If Nigeria does not soon address this problem, Sudan will be pushing hard to meet this level of production. If peace can prevail and exploration, refining, and production increase, Sudan is not too far from being on this list.

Oil is not simply the value of production and export; it might have greater value in terms of foreign revenue generation, more wealth for debt reduction, and generating spin-off industries in the service sector and in manufacture and transportation, as long as there are refineries to produce the more expensive finished fuels and refined goods that are otherwise imported. Among the top fifteen oil-consuming nations, Sudan is also absent. The United States is facing a strategic energy crisis in that its consumption of 20.071 mbpd represents almost three times more oil than it produces. Africa is seen as part of the solution to diversify exporting nations while trying to address issues of energy conservation and new energy technologies. China is now a net importer at 5.982 mbpd, and its further growth requires increased imports from Sudan and other nations in Africa. Japan imports 5.451 mbpd and is not remotely self-sufficient in oil, but its economy can afford the imports. Russia consumes much less at 2.503 mbpd, so it retains a strong global position. India, also buying Sudanese oil, has consumption of 2.426 mbpd, but its consumption is rising rapidly along with India's development, and Sudan plays an important role. Finally, the sparsely populated kingdom of Saudi Arabia only consumes 1.437 mbpd, ensuring that it will be a major oil producer for many years to come.

In sum, Sudanese oil production is rising quickly and could reach levels of over a million bpd in a short time. Also notable on this list is that Chinese production falls far short of its own domestic needs, and Sudan plays a critical role in

Table 5.1 Oil Revenue and Military Expenditures, 1999–2002

	1999	2000	2001	2002
Total GoS Revenue	799.9 m US	1.267 b US	1.415 b US	1.798 b US
GoS Oil Revenue	61.1 m US	547.4 m US	572.6 m US	805.1 m US
GoS Oil Revenue as % of Total GoS Revenue	7.64%	43.18%	40.45%	44.76%
GoS Expenditures	227.2 b US	349.9 b US	401.1 b US	503.4 b US
GoS Military Expenditures	242 m	250 m	345 m	312.7 m
GoS Military Expenditures as % of GoS Oil Revenue	27.38%	45.8%	60.25%	38.8%

Source: Sudan Oil Revenue and Military Expenditures, 1999–2002. Human Rights Watch. 2003.

producing oil for China. Moreover, African producers Nigeria and Algeria are already on this select list and are OPEC members. By 2002, South African off-shore oil was producing over $4 billion worth of U.S. imported oil, with Angolan oil imports at $3 billion per year (*US ITA/USGS World Oil*, Vol. 232, 2002). According to the BBC (9 July 2003), about two-thirds of the oil used in the United States is imported, with about 15 percent presently coming from Africa; it is estimated that this will rise to 25 percent in the next decade, and this is one growth area in African economies that helps the oil producers address the balance of payments and debt servicing. The Gulf of Guinea is one of the main production areas, although the revolt in the Niger Delta of Nigeria has severely cut production there. The more African nations to purchase from, the more the United States can reduce its dependence on Middle Eastern oil nations.

THE WIDER CONTEXT OF SUDANESE OIL

To state the obvious, everyone is interested in Sudanese oil, both those who have it and those who want it. It represents a great prize for those who have control and a primary ambition for those who want more, either for the revenue it can bring or for the security and diversity of petroleum resources for outside powers. In this sense, the moral hand played by the United States relative to Sudanese human rights won a certain status and respect, but it lost access to the oil; on the other hand, Chinese foreign and domestic policies are not so high-minded, but they have access to the oil that the West covets. This is not the place to judge this strategy, but it remains to be seen if oil is also be fought over by foreign powers, particularly if the South breaks away from the North. The nineteenth-century struggle between France and Britain over who would control southern Sudan that was "debated" at the Shilluk royal town of Fashoda comes to mind, in which two major powers were ready to clash over a place of no inherent significance, with no valued resource. Will the Fashoda incident of 1898 be repeated in a new format?

The United States' attention to the Middle East and to world oil has long been significant. But after the 9/11 attack in New York, the problematic invasion of Iraq, al-Qa'eda footprints in Sudan, the ongoing war in Afghanistan, the broad decline of the American economy, increased concern with energy supply and related issues, and a new American head of state, the world presents a very different context. On this laundry list of urgent topics, the U.S. Department of Defense has created a wholly new combatant command structure called AFRICOM that took shape in October 2008. For the first time, it unifies virtually all African nations under the military and political gaze of the United States. According to the AFRICOM website, it has a new and fresh approach to Africa, with a limited budget and personnel, and with a strong focus on humanitarian topics, mutual security issues, and capacity-building for African institutions. Only future history will show if this is "too little, too late" and if while overstretched in Afghanistan and Iraq the United States can address African problems with adequate cerebral versus kinetic forces.

Unfortunately, there is not sufficient space here to pursue all strategic matters and political complications of American interests in African oil, except to say that this is a world concern and that Sudan is but one of several major sources of African oil, including Chad; the Gulf of Guinea region, especially Angola, Nigeria, and Equatorial Guinea; Algeria; and Libya, as well as the strategic pipelines present and planned to pump crude oil to the convenient coasts. Had things been "normal," no doubt Sudan would have been brought into the domain of AFRI-COM as it was with "Operation Bright Star," but American-Sudanese relations were far from "normal," with its engagement and hosting of Osama bin Laden, the endless civil war and the CPA, and then, in 2003, the Darfur conflict dramatically expanding and becoming a prominent American domestic issue. Things were far from "normal" between Washington and Khartoum.

SUMMARY REMARKS AND THEMES

One can hope that the past conflicts over petroleum in Sudan are over, and that peace will prevail; however, the deep sense of distrust, along with many unresolved issues and the elections and referendum looming ahead, it would be unrealistic not to fear for the future. The relative poverty of the oil-producing region, coupled with still unmeasured oil reserves that already have produced great wealth, is not a recipe for a conflict-free future. Lacking a crystal ball for predicting the future, one looks for guidance in the recent Sudanese past and in other regional African elections. The CPA, combined with JIU separation forces, provides a framework for conflict negotiation, but unless or until an ungraded commitment by the Sudanese parties and forces takes place, a wider international resolve to support the Sudan at this critical transition is very important but at present it is deficient in important ways. As an Afro-optimist, this author remains hopeful, especially when it is far better to avoid the human costs in violent "solutions" that have rarely produced good outcomes. To conclude on an upbeat note, there is a great potential for win-win scenarios for collaborative relations over petroleum production between North and South, but the past history suggests that this optimism must be very guarded, as the potential for future conflict is clearly at hand.

NOTE

Elizabeth F. Closson contributed to the initial research and writing of this chapter. Frederick F. Fullerton contributed to revising and copyediting the final draft.

SOURCES

Energy Information Administration. "Special Report: Growth expected for global oil demand, production," *Oil and Gas Journal* (vol. 105, no. 3) 2007.

Harbeson, John W. and Donald C. Rothchild (eds.). *Africa in World Politics* (Boulder, CO: Westview, 2009).

Human Rights Watch. *Sudan, Oil, and Human Rights* (New York: Human Rights Watch, 2003).

CHAPTER 6

Contemporary Regional Strategic Issues

THE *MATRUSKA* DOLL OF SUDANESE POLITICS

With a political, economic, cultural, and military situation as dynamic and complex as Sudan's it is not surprising to find a model of a "*matruska* doll" of intersecting and nested strategic concerns of equal complexity. This book has dissected each region's history and dynamics, so by way of conclusion, it is time to put the pieces back together again to see the national, regional, continental, and international strategic dimensions that are at stake in the case of Sudan. Each one of these levels from the national to the international does interface with one another, so they are separated for analytical rather than functional purposes. In another sense, the *matruska* doll is not an apt model; perhaps something of a *yin-yang* symbol or stretchable clay is better. All parts of Sudan are interacting in one way or another, but at every moment, the playing field is changing, with new rules and new players. Such as it in Sudan; this may explain why governments fail, conflicts arise and external observers get it wrong since such actors are always seeing and preparing for things as they were and not as they are, or will shortly become. Strategic planning for Sudan or for Sudan-watchers requires considerable patience and a long-term view.

SUDAN NATIONAL STRATEGY: (SACRED) ISLAMISM OR (SECULAR) NATIONALISM?

Much of the future configuration of Sudanese politics will be a function of who is in control of the ruling heights of the society. We have seen in the past both democratic and military governments. We have seen rather secular and democratic states, socialist and capitalist states, and now an Islamist state. Regimes have lasted only months, and up to two decades. While more of the postcolonial administrations have been military rather than democratic, they have behaved in rather similar manners, aside from the variations in transparent popular input. Most have been coalitions that are balanced in some fashion to achieve a sort of legitimacy relative to their constituencies. Typically, this is an Arab and Muslim elite from the Sudanese Nile Valley, the ruling elite of Sudan who seek to broaden their regional support by diversity in cabinet and ministerial appointments, who rarely are included within the ruling circles. Matters of state security are typically matters of regime security, and in Sudan, systems of domestic repression have tended to be intensified in subsequent regimes. Especially in military regimes, there are counterbalancing instruments of state power, from police, to different military branches and bodies, to intelligence, financial, and judicial bodies. The leadership of most civil-service agencies is highly politicized and cannot take great autonomous initiatives. So, strong centralization maximizes regime security, but minimizes the regime's effectiveness, and there are endless illustrations of political marginalization seen in the previous chapters.

Each ruling elite in Sudan, from 1956 to the present, has sought some sort of legitimacy; the present regime has sought this through Islam. In one sense, this is ironic, since there has never been a president of Sudan since independence who was not a Muslim. There hardly seems to be a need to have an Islamic state if all leaders already follow this faith. Clearly, there is much more to this equation and historical evolution. The tactical expressions of an Islamic identity can range from the uniqueness of tolerant and accommodating Sudanese Islam, stressing the importance of mystical and magical Sufism, to the Mahdist traditions, local *fuqahah* (Muslim saints), and *turuq* (Islamic brotherhoods), along with the *Maliki* school of Muslim jurisprudence in which Shari'a law had worked long and well to coordinate personal-status matters such as marriage, divorce, child custody, and inheritance. Alternatives to this mainstream popular Islam were also present in Sudan. These ranged from some tiny numbers of secular Ba'athists to the much more important *Jamhuriyeen* (Republican Brothers), who gained a substantial following among intellectuals who wanted a thoughtful, reformist, and modern Islam.

When more and more became attracted to the *Jamhuriyeen* movement, along with its allied Republican Sisters, this was perceived as a direct challenge to the Nimieri government in its last, Islamic phase. Rather behind the scenes in this decisive period was the very wily Dr. Sheikh Hassan al-Turabi. As a longtime Muslim Brother leader, he had tactically accepted the secular socialist government of Nimieri in the 1970s and was even a member of the Sudan Socialist Union at one point (Sidahmed 2005, 33). He was appointed Attorney General under Nimieri and was thus captain of the legal ship for the September 1983 adoption of the full *hudud* (measures) of Shari'a law, including *qasas* and *diya* (negotiated retribution and compensation), courts of "speedy justice," flogging, amputations, and execution for specific crimes. These "September Laws" became a hurdle that the subsequent Sadiq al-Mahdi government could not climb; for Southerners, the laws represented everything that made them opposed to the North and encouraged them to fight on in the South.

"Imam" Nimieri, guided by his Attorney General, arrested Mahmoud Mohammed Taha and some of his top associates, and charged them with "apostasy"; he probably thought that an intimidating death sentence would cause them to recant their beliefs and that Nimieri's military Islam would regain its monopoly of interpretation. Two of the followers did recant and were freed, but the elderly Mahmoud refused and was hanged in Kober prison in January 1985. In such historical instances, this caused Mahmoud to be broadly seen as a martyr and probably hastened the April 1985 demise of Nimieri, since broadly tolerant Sudan indicated that the extreme punishment did not fit the "crime." Miraculously, the fall of Nimieri only temporarily moved al-Turabi out of power during the transitional period of military custodianship under the Transitional Military Council (TMC) of Suwar al-Dhahab from 6 April 1985 to 1986, and when the civilian government of Sadiq al-Mahdi took office in May 1986, Hassan al-Turabi (the prime minister's brother-in-law) was ready to make another move toward power. During the military interlude, al-Turabi had busily renamed his Islamic Charter Front (inspired by the Muslim Brotherhood in Egypt) the "National Islamic Front," officially founded in May 1985 to compete as a political party in the forthcoming 1986 elections. Since al-Mahdi's government rested on a coalition between his Umma Party (the Ansar) and the DUP (Khatmiya), that was nothing new in Sudan postcolonial political history. However, the NIF managed to gain a minority position in the new parliament on al-Turabi's way to rehabilitation and reengagement.

By 1988, the NIF managed to become part of the government of Sadiq al-Mahdi, with the implementation of the Shari'a laws being its iconic calling card. Al-Turabi was restored to the position of Attorney General and Minister of Justice (Sidahmed 2005, 52), and also, miraculously, by 31 January 1989 became the Deputy Prime Minister as the Prime Minister desperately tried to find a combination of alliances that would give him political strength in the North while fighting a losing war in the South. The contradictory irony was that the SPLA wanted al-Mahdi to end or limit Shari'a law, while al-Turabi's Northern Muslim coalition insisted that he keep it. Even when the onerous September Laws were transformed to the 1988 Criminal Bill, there was little perceptual change in content. Clearly, another crisis moment was rapidly forming that left little room for accommodation or compromise. The political winds of change were blowing, but the NIF had been preparing itself with youth groups, through infiltration in the universities, and within various branches of the military, while being assisted financially by overseas remittances amid a broadly rising Islamic revivalism across the Arab world.

Fearing that the emblematic Shari'a laws were at risk under these defining times, General Omer al-Beshir struck on 30 June 1989 and overthrew the Sudanese civilian government for the fourth time in its postcolonial epoch. To give cover to a "behind-the-scenes" al-Turabi, he was placed in custody in Kober prison for a short while, and a number of military officers who opposed the coup were promptly executed. The security regime of "ghost houses" was initiated, and when matters were "calmed down," al-Turabi was ready to return to his vaunted political mission, now financed by the entire Sudanese treasury and supported by its military. After the 1989 coup, the NIF essentially became subsumed under the National Congress Party or the National Salvation Movement (*al-Inqaz*). Now at the commanding heights of Sudan, *al-Inqaz* could pursue a policy of *jihad* in the South as the SPLA was steadily gaining more strength and territory. As thousands of Sudanese youth were drafted into the army and *murahileen* (militias), it is not known how many gave their lives in this cause, but it is said that no village in the North was without its fallen *mushahadeen* (martyrs), and the number of displaced, wounded, and killed Southerners equally goes without precise reckoning. After consolidating its rule by March 1991, *al-Inqaz* drafted a "new" penal code with few substantive alterations from the previous forms, except to say that the formal implementation of the harsh measures might have been reduced, while informal punitive measures only increased in "ghost houses" and in extrajudicial proceedings in the field of widening combat.

1991 also saw the creation of the Popular Arabic and Islamic Congress (PAIC), headed by al-Turabi, that expanded the invitation to fellow *jihadists* to Sudan, including, *inter alia*, the prominent al-Qa'eda leader Osama bin Laden, but also Hamas, *Jama'a Islamiya*, *Jihad*, Salafists, *Takfir wal-Hegira*, *an-Nahda*, Abu Nidal, Iranians of various types, and Carlos the Jackal, among others who were attracted to this open-door policy of Islamic extremism. A lack of modesty, never a virtue of al-Turabi, made him steadily more emboldened, but the 1993 first bombing of the World Trade Center and support of other violent worldwide and regional acts also earned him the attention of the world. In August 1993, Sudan was placed on the list of nations supporting world terrorism as well as recognized for having a horrible human rights record. Not to be deterred, the audacious al-Turabi was not slowed down, and by 1996, he became the speaker of the Sudanese National Assembly. Perhaps as a case of classic Greek hubris, al-Turabi felt further inclined to show no restraint, but the military regime, of which he was a part, started to perceived him not only as an insider threat, but also as a global liability. The attempted assassination of Hosni Mubarak in Ethiopia in 1995 and the deteriorating relations with Eritrea in 1994 and 1995 made the political cost of having al-Turabi in the ruling circles greater than the purported advantages he might have brought. On 19 February 1998, al-Turabi reached his last height of political influence when he was elected Secretary-General of the NCP, but a stalled war in the South, increased political isolation by the United Nations and other international bodies, and then the 7 August 1998 dual bombings of the U.S. embassies that had some fingers pointing back at Sudan, his presence was even more of a liability. The angry, probably mistaken, and perhaps diversionary bombing of Khartoum North by President Clinton on 20 August 1998 just put more pressure on Khartoum. By December 1999, it was "show-down" time, and al-Beshir totally ousted his ally and rival, al-Turabi, from the government. Ever the survivor, even following house arrest and more incarceration in Kober prison, the now elderly al-Turabi has formed the new National Popular Congress, and he intends to compete (and is competing) in formal elections. Once again, he returns to being a behind-the-scenes player in eastern Sudan, especially in Darfur, through JEM. He is still a feared and influential factor in Sudanese politics.

As this work heads to press, representatives of the Khartoum government met with JEM officials in Doha for inconclusive meetings. Likewise, Hassan al-Turabi was recently released from prison, again, and the ICC arrest warrant for President al-Beshir has caused a predictable backlash from Khartoum; the Obama government has also increased the political temperature, with calls for a possible no-fly zone and other military threats as well as appointing a top military officer as the U.S. negotiator for Darfur.

The central question for Sudan is whether the Islamic project to achieve national unity as an Islamic state can or will continue, or whether the unilateral focus on this project will make sure that the nation will enter a political centrifuge that refracts the nation into two or more parts with two (or many more) differing ideologies.

RIVAL ARCHITECTS OF IDEOLOGY

So, just as the late Ga'afar Nimieri went through four hegemonic epochs of governance, from secular socialism to capitalism to his closing chapter of Islamism, the twenty years of the Omer al-Beshir government has gone through at least three phases. First is the phase of political consolidation of the "Salvation" government (June 1989 to 1992). Second is the *jihadist* period (1992 to May 1996), with both Osama bin Laden and Hassan al-Turabi in strong leadership positions in Sudan. The third Islamist period (May 1996 to February 2001) was the phase without bin Laden but still with al-Turabi. The fourth phase of military governance was without al-Turabi or Osama bin Laden in political positions in Sudan (February 2001 to March 2009). Perhaps a fifth phase (March 2009 to The Future) should be added: post–ICC warrant for the arrest of Omer al-Beshir. In any case, all phases sought to place Islamism at the center, even to the point of driving the marginalized periphery into a frenzy of armed centrifugal opposition. Perhaps we are about to exhaust these models of Islamism; perhaps we are not.

Despite the different individuals involved, the overall effort was to put Sudan in a leadership position of the "world Islamic movement," making tactical retreats as circumstances dictated. In the context of colonialism, there was Sudanese resistance with the Mahdist movement; in the context of postcolonialism, Islam is projected as the "best" unifying answer for galvanizing the nation against its perceived enemies. The difficulty is that there are multiple practices and attitudes about Islam in the world and in Sudan, and there are those who would prefer to have Islam as a personal belief system and code of personal values and conduct, rather than a state authority; in the South, there are those who prefer a democratic secular state with a firewall between religion and politics. Time will tell, but these are certainly not the only models for Sudanese governance.

MULTIPLE IDENTITIES, MULTIPLE MODELS

It is not just by ideology that multiple models of national and personal identity vary in Sudan. The historical record in the postcolonial period has three epochs of multiparty democracy: from 1956 to 1958, from 1964 to 1969, and from 1985 to 1989. Admittedly, these periods were tumultuous and complex, but they were democratic, and if popular mass action is included, revolutions in October 1964 and April 1985 were able to topple military regimes. Indeed, one military regime (of General Suwar al-Dhahab) relinquished its power to a democratic regime in May 1986. While the current military government is about to complete its second decade and has come to represent Sudan as the "typical" model, it is well worth recalling that there is deep and enduring engagement with democracy. Even in this period, the united front of the NDA has sputtered along, keeping this sentiment alive. However it was in the South, from 1985 to 2005, that democracy was especially alive as an objective. The SPLA movement, led by John Garang, was always aiming at making a democratic and secular national state. He was not seeking separation. Ironically, it was the secessionist Anya-Nya who achieved regional authority for eleven years, while the national integrationists of the SPLA may end up with a separate nation. Populations in the East, in Nubia, and in Darfur are overwhelmingly Muslim, but they have their own interpretations of an Islamic state and a state for Muslims, as well as their own cultural identities of African, Nubian, and Beja, for example. The other irony is that the more a central Sudanese government uses its state instruments of power to attempt unification, the more the opposite result is often the case, and the people who are disenfranchised and in the periphery are usually spun off in revolts and resistance of various sorts.

REFERENDUM AND SEPARATION

According to the terms of the January 2005 CPA, an election was scheduled for 2009 that is designed to pave the way for a return to democracy. Given the fact that the ruling party did not enter governance in this way and that it has not maintained itself in power in transparent governance; that elections in Sudan have often brought more problems than solutions; that there have been incidents of recent and grave postelection violence in some African elections; that substantial areas in Darfur cannot hold elections out of security fears; the serious border tensions between North and South; and the issues of political and military security in and around the South, there is accordingly very considerable anxiety about these 2010 elections being free, fair, and transparent.

Similarly, the slated referendum in 2011 has a similar set of problems, with the implications even bigger. Some in the North are ready to have the South go its own way; some in the North fear separation and war over oil. Some in the South are ready to have another war if needed, and others in the South are trying to hold together the GNU to pave the way for a restructured Sudan. Clearly, many of these models are contradicted by others, and Sudan stays a "graveyard of prophecies." Moreover, it is hard to say which of the original signatories will still be politically viable in 2011 amid such volatility and changeable political terrain. Essentially, this is the key question for Sudan. Will there be two or more Sudans, or a new Sudan?

SUDAN'S MILITARY APPROACHES TO INSURGENCY

When the conflict in Darfur expanded in February 2003, it was clearly a unilateral escalation by rebel groups. Darfur resistance and conflict management did not start on this date, nor did Khartoum's experience in counterinsurgency start at this time. The differences were that this was a briefly coordinated joint Darfur rebel attack on Sudan military assets in al-Fasher and that Khartoum clearly took sides in this conflict. From the insurgent rebel side, this was a strategic provocation, and from the Khartoum side, this was a time to reopen their standard manual of counterinsurgency that had long been applied in southern Sudan in the two decades of war with the SPLA. Critical in the southern Sudan was the use of *murahileen* militias of local Baggara Arabs, who were privileged to loot, kill, and enslave in the South. In Darfur, the militias were known instead as the *janjaweed*, but they were equally privileged to despoil the region and conduct acts that were likely in violation of the rules of war. For the South, the forced displacement was to make a buffer zone between North and South and to remove the Nilotic populations from the development of the borderland oil fields. In Darfur, the military objective was to drive the rural population into refugee camps and across the borders to deny support to the rebel insurgents. Both military objectives were probably not well-thought-out. On the rebel side, it is hard to believe that they imagined that Khartoum would roll over and not respond with serious armed forces, both regular and irregular. On the government side, it is hard to believe that they thought the war in Darfur would not bog down in a sustained, exhausting, and ever more complex military, political, and now judicial struggle. The poor calculations of both parties have already led to seven years of war with tens or hundreds of thousands of deaths and vastly more injured and displaced. As long as the Sudanese government devolves to military solutions for political problems, they will engender military resistance at the periphery, and as long as such measures are an access point to power, with other options closed, the dysfunctional cycle of military instability will be regenerated endlessly. Autocracy will be substituted for democracy; political centralization will resist regional autonomy; and small-arms insurgency will be met with major-arms counterinsurgency.

INSURGENT REBEL MILITARY APPROACHES TO KHARTOUM

It is extremely difficult to characterize the insurgent tactics and methodology, since it is rapidly changing for specific groups, and new splinter groups are emerging; some are strong, some are weak, some are engaged politically, and some engaged militarily. All are endlessly jockeying for power as they create and terminate alliances that seem appropriate for the moment. Because they do not speak with one voice, this then benefitted Khartoum interested in having a good reasons for talks to fail. Because they do not speak with one voice, this also means that the conflict in Darfur is virtually out the control of any single party, however well- or bad-intentioned they might be. At this point, to note the main partisans, there is the Minni Minnawi faction of the SLA that is officially, but very weakly, in the Khartoum government. There is the main 'Abd al-Wahed faction of the SLA negotiating for support in Israel while residing safely in France, and there is the militarily ambitious Khalil Ibrahim faction of JEM that has greater political ambitions and may be closer to al-Turabi than the West prefers. While the times, places, and actors certainly differ, there are notable tactical parallels of earlier Southern factional insurgents with Darfur insurgency and factionalism today. Likewise, the military tactics of Khartoum's counterinsurgency strategy, with militias, population displacement, and divide-and-rule approaches, is similar in Darfur to that used in southern Sudan. Either no one learns from the past, or is willing to try new approaches to grievance or conflict resolution, or it is believed that the old approaches to power are working.

REGIONAL STRATEGIC CONCERNS

The LRA and Relations with Uganda, the DRC, the CAR, and the Wider Region

During the long civil war with the SPLA (1983–2005), various successive Khartoum governments found it expedient to support the LRA, which was centered on Gulu in the Acholi areas of northern Uganda. Nursing his own

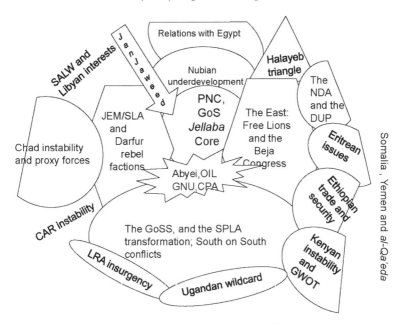

Figure 6.1 Map of Sudanese Conflicts

grievances with the Yoweri Museveni in Kampala, the LRA under the leadership of Joseph Kony had recruited by fear, maintained discipline by terror, and been supplied with women and soldiers by forced capture; yet it has not been defeated after two decades of atrocious behavior that has disgusted the world and put Kony under ICC war-crimes indictment. As long as the SPLA was supported, in part, by Uganda, Kony was equally against the SPLA and the regular Uganda military. Following the slogan "the enemy of my enemy is my friend," Khartoum secretly backed the LRA as long as it would attack the SPLA and Uganda forces. From December 2008 to February 2009, a major joint offensive was undertaken by the SPLA, Uganda, CAR, and DRC forces to bring the LRA to an end. Clearly, the effort did serious damage to the LRA rank-and-file soldiers and perhaps to a number of high-ranking officers, but it failed to kill or bring Kony to justice or capture. Observers wonder what can keep this damaged movement still alive and ready to conduct raids for supplies and slave wives as well as recruits; the finger of accusation has again pointed toward Khartoum, but only with circumstantial evidence. In the most recent instance, the four-way offensive was also enjoined by the new U.S. Combatant Command, AFRICOM, which provided some financing, logistical support, and fuel, as well as a measure of intelligence, surveillance, and reconnaissance (ISR). During this same period, while the Israelis were executing nonstop air strikes against the Hamas-backed Palestinians in Gaza, there were apparently air strikes in eastern Sudan by either

U.S. or Israeli planes or drones (the reports have been very inconsistent and incomplete) against Iranian arms shipments heading to Gaza along the Sudanese coast. In short, these small-scale conflicts throughout the region just give more opportunities or necessities for external forces to become involved. And the more players involved, the more complex peace negotiations become, if they are even possible at all.

Another small and enigmatic piece of this relationship between Khartoum and the South is the Allied Democratic Forces (ADF). The ADF, a small Salafist group following the Tabliq sect, was formed in the early 1990s in the heyday of Hassan al-Turabi, his NIF, and Osama bin Laden when he was in Sudan. This Islamist-armed guerrilla group had some hundreds of members, perhaps more, and was alleged to be backed by both Khartoum, with training in Sudan and in Baghdad (under Saddam) and al-Qa'eda. While documents surfaced in Baghdad from the Saddam era showing communication with the ADF representative in Iraq, Bekkah Abdul Nassir, it is not clear that there was any substance to this relationship. In principle, the ADF was to initiate military actions against the Museveni government, much like the LRA, which was also believed to be backed by Khartoum at this time. The ADF intended to launch their *jihad* in Uganda and other parts of East Africa. The ADF was led by Sheikh Jamil Mukulu. The U.S. embassy bombing in East Africa in 1997 brought renewed interest in the ADF, not to mention the World Trade Center plane crashes in 2001. But after a Uganda offensive in the late 1990s and the high scrutiny in 2001, the ADF seems to have vanished into the ungoverned spaces of the eastern Congo. But by 2005, in taped remarks, the ADF was trying for a comeback. And in March 2007, combat operations were once again conducted by the Ugandan Defense Forces against the ADF, killing Bosco Balam Isiko along the DRC-Uganda border.

Eritrean/Ethiopian Relations

Over many decades, relations among Khartoum, Asmara, and Addis Ababa have had many and considerable fluctuations, from solidarity, to accommodation and collaboration (the Addis Ababa Accords), to hostility (the Mahdist invasion and Khartoum-based assassination attempt of Hosni Mubarak while in Ethiopia). At the present time, relations are rather favorable, because the NDA, backed by Eritrea, has been eclipsed by events and no longer is a threat to Khartoum. Likewise, the support that Ethiopia gave episodically to the SPLA is superseded by the semiautonomous status for southern Sudan. Proxy wars (no more insurgent forces stationed on opposing territory) and refugee streams (from revolutionary events in Ethiopia and "Lost Boys" from southern Sudan) have also abated considerably in the most recent years. To the extent that this present steady state is a function of solid diplomacy and good policy, this shows that the foreign ministers of all three nations have effective application of their approaches. While the headlines on Sudan have predominantly been focused on Darfur, the rather quiet situation on the eastern borders is worth including in this complex mix.

Chad Strategic Relations

The relations between Khartoum and Chad have long been tempestuous. There are some inherent state-to-state security conflicts exacerbated by external forces, especially Libya, which has not only supported various insurgent movements in Chad for many decades, but even when Chad has been calmed, there is a residual spillover of small arms that function as land mines ready to trigger subsidiary conflicts. Even then, the external forces, ranging from European and U.S. and from military to NGOs, tend to pick local favorites to some extent, and this adds to the complexities of Sudan-Chad relations. On top of this are colonial borders that make little concrete sense on the ground, with various ethnic groups such as the Zaghawa and Bideyat transcending the border from Darfur to Wadai. Then, as relations between the two nations deteriorate, it gives both an opportunity for sustained proxy warfare among the various insurgent groups that they are willing to back or those that are in temporary disfavor. This has long been the case, but since the Darfur violence took a turn for the worse in February 2003, the role of the proxy forces only intensified to the extent that Khartoum-backed insurgents narrowly missed taking the capital of N'Djamena, and N'Djamena-backed forces led by JEM carried out a two-day assault on Omdurman across the Nile from Khartoum. Earlier, JEM had sped across Chad to help protect the Idris Deby government. Periodically, Khartoum and N'Djamena call a truce with a flurry of diplomatic actions proclaiming their friendship, with few imagining that there is very much depth to these proclamations under the conditions of the ongoing strife in Darfur.

Egyptian Strategic Relations

Just as Sudan has a millennia-long love-hate relationship with its Nile brother Egypt, the Egyptian view on Sudan ranges from strategic ally to annoying nuisance to a grave concern about access to the vital water resources for Egypt. Added to this list in the last two decades is a major Egyptian concern with domestic terrorism that is believed, or at least said, to have external origins. To the extent that this fear, and the reality, was linked to Egyptian groups and al-Qa'eda, which was once based in Sudan, the Egyptian finger of suspicion is often aimed southward. Since Osama bin Laden arrived in Sudan in 1992 and spent much time there with Dr. Ayman al-Zawahiri from Egypt, it is not a difficult case to make. In late September 1992, *Jama'a Islamiya* warned tourists not to go to Middle Egypt; on 1 October, gunfire was aimed at a tourist boat near Assiut, wounding three Egyptian crew members. In the same month, a tourist bus was ambushed, killing a British woman and making her the first to die in anti-tourist terrorism. This was only the start. In 1993, at least nine more such attacks took place in such places as downtown Cairo, the National Museum, at the pyramids, against tourist boats, in Upper Egypt, and in luxury hotels, resulting in much property damage, at least six dead, many wounded, and a great deal of fear in the tourist industry that is a bedrock element of the Egyptian economy. In 1994, at least twelve more attacks were recorded against tourist buses and river cruisers, killing at least another five and wounding many others, with deeper shocks in the vital tourist industry. In 1995, the situation did improve, with only five reported attacks on tourist trains. Boldest of all was the attempted assassination of President Hosni Mubarak while on a visit to Addis Ababa.

Most of these incidents were blamed again on *Jama'a Islamiya*, which still had ties to Sudan. In 1996, the year that Osama bin Laden was pushed out of Khartoum in May to Jalalabad, Afghanistan, the attacks fell to only two early in the year, including a particularly horrible incident in which seventeen Greeks were killed at a Cairo hotel near the pyramids. As if to make up for a decline in terrorism, these forces regrouped in September, killing nine and wounding nine more directly in front of the National Museum in Central Cairo. But on 18 November, more blood was to be dramatically spilled at the Deir al-Bahri temple in Luxor, in which sixty-two tourists were shot, stabbed, and otherwise butchered. Pushed to this extreme, and with Osama bin Laden and Ayman al-Zawahiri already planning more actions elsewhere, the Egyptian security officials ramped up measures, yielding a seven-year lull in anti-tourist soft targets. This was to end in

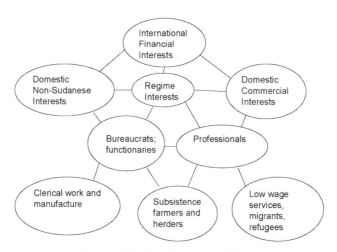

Figure 6.2 Class Aspects of Sudan

October 2004, when major bomb blasts were ignited at Red Sea resorts, killing thirty-four and wounding more than a hundred, mostly Israeli tourists. In 2005, an April attack at Khan al-Khalili, a regular and major tourist destination, killed two more tourists and wounded a score of others. In the same month, more such attacks took place in Old Cairo and near the Egyptian Museum. Clearly, the tourist economy was directly in the sights of the so-called "Islamic Brigades of Pride" and "Abdullah Azzam Brigades." This was to be exceeded in the bloodiest of all incidents to date with three massive explosions at another Red Sea resort center at Sharm-esh-Sheikh—embarrassingly, on Egyptian National Day. These bombs killed at least eighty-eight, if the tally of body parts was correct, and wounded something like two hundred more. The Egyptian security forces were frenzied and highly mobilized, and again a lull was the reward for three more years, until September 2008, in which a group of nineteen travelers in the western desert were abducted. All were freed, and many of the kidnappers were killed, under circumstances that remain shrouded in some confusion. Gradually, tourism was recovering; yet on 22 February, at Khan al-Khalili, the popular tourist market destination was again targeted, killing at least one French tourist and injuring about twenty others. So, it is clear that Egypt has had a problem that they are addressing, but few would say that this is a time for reduced vigilance. To the extent that deep-lying al-Qa'eda supporters may still be in Sudan, it is impossible to know whether (and there is no allegation that) the Sudanese government is behind this, but this is a grave human and economic problem that requires close and harmonious collaboration that sometimes is not so easy to achieve. The critical pivotal position of Egypt in Africa and the Middle East has given it a hybrid position for the U.S. military by placing it simultaneously in Central Command and African Command. The critical relationship it has with the Nile means that Sudan is eternally important despite the preoccupation/diversion it has with Israel. Egypt is one of the three most significant strategic states in Africa by any measure, and it stays very anxious about Sudan possibly dividing, but at the same time, it is hard-pressed to know what to do about it, especially as the Mubarak epoch may be nearing its conclusion.

Kenyan Relations for Southern Sudan

Nominally, Khartoum and the GNU have a formal diplomatic relationship with Nairobi. This was certainly and importantly the case during the Naivasha talks and the final signing of the CPA. But the main Arab-based constituency of the GoS is culturally out of its element in Kenya, while the SPLA is most at home in this fellow brother African nation in terms of shared cultural identities and religious outlook. Despite the rough and bloody postelection events in Kenya in 2007 and 2008, the military kept itself out of the fray. While the struggles and killing were observed on television in Khartoum, they were felt directly in southern Sudan with shipments of food and fuel disrupted, especially to Juba. Kenya Air serves both Khartoum and Juba. Kenyan, Ugandan, and Eritrean businesspeople are found in Juba. One of the more fascinating recent events has been a Ukrainian shipment of thirty-three Soviet-type tanks that was headed to Mombasa. On the way, it was hijacked by Somali pirates and, after a number of months, the ship, crew, and cargo finally reached the port of Mombasa. Kenyan authorities insist that these tanks and a load of small arms as well are for its armed forces, but much speculation suggests that they are truly heading to southern Sudan instead, where they might be joined by some other number of tanks that perhaps arrived through Ethiopia. Although the terms of the CPA do not forbid the acquisition of arms, many observers suggest that the alleged arrival of such weapons could presage regional preparation for separation of the South. Rumors and speculation abound in such an environment, and on this list go thoughts that the South could seize the rich oil field in the South and, with a relatively short pipeline, export oil to Uganda for shipment by rail or tanker to the Kenyan coast. Following this logic, the long-troubled Acholi region around Gulu in northern Uganda needed protection from the insurgent attacks by the LRA. This much-weakened force is now pushed out of Uganda and even out of the Garamba National Park in the DRC, so it now only harasses, kills, loots, kidnaps, rapes, and destroys an ever smaller area, mainly along the DRC and southern Sudan border. The recently created U.S. AFRICOM command saw behind-the-scenes action in logistical, fuel, financial, and communication support to the joint DRC, SPLA, CAR, and Uganda military in "Operation Lightning Thunder," which may have killed or captured one-third of the LRA and several leading officers, but Joseph Kony and Okot Odiambo, who are still at large. In short, as Juba's political sphere of influence and economic orientation may be shifting from Khartoum in the coming years, there is no doubt that the politics, economics, and logistics of Nairobi and Kampala will play a steadily increasing role.

CONTINENTAL STRATEGIC CONCERNS

It may not be surprising that Africa's largest nation, with more bordering nations, refugees streaming in, and great cultural diversity, has many internal and external problems. Sudan has proven to be one of the most dysfunctional of all African nations, which have themselves faced insurgencies, civil wars, decolonization traumas, and the like. But the tragedy of Sudan is that no sooner is one regional crisis resolved or managed than another one springs up. Then, power shifts in Khartoum initiate further rounds of conflict and debate. From the fifty-three years since independence in 1956, only the eleven years from 1972 to 1983 might be termed "peaceful," and even then, the struggles turned to hard-fought political and economic development issues. Therefore, the Organization of African Unity (1963–2002) and its African Union successor

(2002–) spent considerable financial resources and diplomatic time in trying to address the myriad problems of Sudan. Clearly, the expansive size of Darfur complicated the mission of the underfunded, understaffed forces of AMIS. Nonetheless, they did the best they could in protecting internally displaced refugees. They also suffered casualties in this service. When the mission shifted to UN authority and AMIS became UNAMID, the hats were changed from AU green to UN blue. More forces arrived—though probably still not enough—and more logistics were provided by the United States, and more services, weapons, and helicopters arrived to try to quiet this down. Under AU authority, a sincere effort was made to model a Darfur Peace Accord in Abuja, Nigeria, meeting on a similar DoP to that of the CPA. Despite the efforts before, during, and after, the best that could be achieved was an agreement with only one of the Darfur rebel factions, while the others splintered and jockeyed for "better" positions with Khartoum. All African nations have grave anxieties about Europeans (or U.S. forces) coming back to Africa under arms, despite good intentions, and issues of command, control, and authority need special consideration not to be derailed. The Sudanese need no reminders that the last power to invade Darfur and assassinate the Sultan of Darfur was England, and when a proposal to have Muslim troops from Turkey come to patrol in Darfur was made, it was not taken into consideration that the Ottoman Turkish rule of Sudan (1821–1885) was among the harshest and most despised.

As an African subset of actors, the Arab League members of the AU have their own special concerns and perspectives. These include all the North African states and especially Libya, Egypt, and Sudan itself. Not only do they nurse or dwell over the colonial past, but the issues of the Israel-Palestine conflict and Muslim extremism complicate their view of the West in general and the United States in particular. Through this lens, the preoccupation of England and the United States with Darfur and the information/propaganda approach to Darfur by Israel is largely dismissed as diversionary, since these three nations have probably the worst records in recent years in dealing with the Arab world, not to mention causing a large number of Arabs and Muslim casualties because of their own policies and warfare. Thus, from the African perspective, or the supercharged Arab/African perspective, the situation in Darfur is viewed in a substantially different light.

Unfortunately, cynicism in Africa has some rather deep roots in the soil, where colonial authorities carved the continent for whimsical, arbitrary, and greedy purposes, and used brutal punitive campaigns of pacification to do it. Postcolonial Africa was plagued by Cold War polarities, and coups and assassination, and when this era drifted into history, the very uneven economic playing field became one of Africa's new miseries. The preoccupation with some African conflicts (such as Darfur) and the pathetic neglect of others, such as in Rwanda, Liberia, and Eastern Congo, adds to the suspicions. The paralysis and confusion of action in

Somalia and relative passivity in the long battles against settler colonialism and apartheid have shaped the common African view that the West is rarely up to any good, and if it is interested, it is only a cover for some ulterior motive, usually relating to strategic chokepoints or natural resources such as oil, gold, diamonds, uranium, and the like. This is a very deep hole out of which the West needs to climb in order to win sincere African friendships.

INTERNATIONAL STRATEGIC CONCERNS

As seen in the earlier chapter on oil in Sudan, oil is a major factor in the strategic political economy in many ways. Oil has engaged Sudan with China in particular, and China is likewise a defender of Sudan in diplomatic circles. Obviously, it is a major revenue-earner for Sudan, enabling it to pursue development concerns as well as major arms purchases and arms production. The oil aspects of the CPA are equally significant. Perhaps as much as 7 percent of China's oil is from Sudan, and if China's economic growth has been around this level, one could claim that its domestic growth hinges on the balance of acquiring oil in Sudan. While China is not alone in pursuing oil interests in Sudan, since India, Pakistan, Malaysia, and Gulf nations are also there, it is certainly the most important.

While China has turned a blind eye toward some, or most, of Sudan's human-rights issues, it is a major player in Sudan, from vast infrastructure projects to commerce and peacekeeping. The United States' concerns with terrorism and the Darfur situation may be politically correct, but Sudan has many options available to ignore the United Nations and the United States, which is already much diverted with military projects in Iraq and Afghanistan. So far, the United States and China have only had friendly quarrels over Sudanese governance, and these two global powers have collaborated to some extent on Somali piracy, as an example. However, if the United States' tilt toward southern Sudan and the upcoming 2011 referendum unfolds into separation, the southern Sudan might well abrogate the CPA and want all of the oil for itself. To date, there is no practical way to transport the oil, except through the Chinese pipeline to and through the North to Port Sudan, but if this were to change, the U.S.-Chinese relationship to Sudanese oil could be threatened dramatically. This does not necessarily mean a violent clash, but the famed "Fashoda incident" of 1898 suggests a turning point might be reached. In the Fashoda case, a small group of British troops, fresh from their victory over the Khalifa, came down to this village capital of the Shilluk kingdom in southern Sudan to claim it for England. At the other end of this village, a small group of French troops arrived to make the same claim for the French. After a diplomatic *contretemps* and a few more troops, but with no shooting, all of southern Sudan became British rather than French. Perhaps this model would presage the Abyei oil fields, not so far away, changing from Chinese to U.S. domain? Stranger things have happened in Sudan.

These global struggles are also very evident in the ICC charges now laid against President Omer al-Beshir for the bloody affairs in Darfur. Most Arab nations are opposed, as are many African nations, seeing a lopsided application of such war-crime charges as an instrument of a rather hypocritical West against Africa. Chinese, with no colonial history in Africa, will likely block efforts to have the charges stick. It is not clear if the application of these charges was motivated by purely legal or ethical concerns, or if they are being used simply to pressure al-Beshir to bring the Darfur situation to a close; not to say that this is fully in his hands in any case. It is already clear that in the short term, the domestic effect in Sudan as a reaction to the ICC charges has been negative. Not only has he not been apprehended (no one imagined this would happen), but the plight of needy populations in Darfur may have gotten worse. As a tactic, war-crimes charges with arrests are better to seek after someone is out of power, such as with Charles Taylor from Liberia when he was in exile in Nigeria. The case of Joseph Kony of the LRA, also under ICC charge (and perhaps Khartoum backing), has made him more resolute in signing no peace accord whatsoever.

UNITED STATES RELATIONS: NEW PRESIDENT, NEW POLICIES?

Relations between the United States and Sudan have ranged from barely acceptable, to problematic, down to poor for the past twenty years. For much of this time, there has not been ambassadorial exchange. Accusations and hostility have been the principle norm in this period. There have been few acts of collaboration, with the great exception being the relative success of the CPA and the relative failure of the DPA, which has now led to the serious charges of the ICC against the top leadership of Sudan. Ironically, neither the United States nor Sudan is a signatory to the ICC protocols in this respect. Indeed, the application of the word "genocide" to the conflict in Darfur has, at least, in the short run, been counterproductive and contentious, and stands in significant contrast with the U.S. positions on mass killing in Rwanda and Eastern Congo. In short, there has been much more to argue about between Washington and Khartoum than to work together to solve.

At least, this was the case until the November 2008 elections and the creation of AFRICOM, which may have shifted this equation in new linkages of "carrots" and "sticks." During the election campaign, then-Senator Obama spoke about U.S. troops and a no-fly zone for Sudan, but the first act of substance has been to warn Sudan about attacks on Sudan's Red Sea coast to interdict smuggling arms to Gaza and to send an Air Force officer, Scott Gration, as Special Envoy to Sudan to listen and discuss the situation. Divisions within the Department of State between "hardliners" (tough cops) Susan Rice and Jenday Frazier and "softliners" (nice cops) make for interesting domestic policymaking in a political arena notably framed by the Darfur activist community. The high-traffic "figure-eight" crossroads ahead is centered on the political economy of oil, the census, Abyei, the 2010 elections, and the referendum of 2011; all will all be turning points, whatever the outcomes.

Since the coming of the Omer al-Beshir government on 30 June 1989, the United States has played a weak hand rather poorly. It did not seriously or effectively track the implantation of al-Qa'eda in Sudan and the many actions that were undertaken by Osama bin Laden, most notably the first attack on the World Trade Center by Sheikh Omer 'Abd al-Rahman, who got his visa from the U.S. embassy in Khartoum to come to the United States in May 1990. This is the same Sheikh 'Abd al-Rahman who had been jailed for his involvement in the 1981 assassination of Egyptian president Anwar Sadat. Also, the United States did not employ adequate surveillance of Sudanese operatives in the United States, who narrowly missed causing great harm to strategic targets in the New York area. Egyptian Islamic Jihad was housed in Khartoum while they attempted to assassinate President Hosni Mubarak in Addis Ababa in June 1995. This brought the first U.S. sanctions against Sudan. These were essentially in place even though Mubarak later restored diplomatic relations with Khartoum. While Islamic Jihad was pushed underground, it hardly stopped, as we see in the tragic and bloody November 1997 attack on tourists in Deir al-Bahri. Apparently, the attackers received logistical support from Sudanese territory.

President Clinton retaliated against Sudan for al-Qa'eda attacks at U.S. embassies in Kenya and Tanzania in which 258 died and 5,000 were injured on 7 August 1998. But he was much preoccupied with his unfolding impeachment trial in Washington; on 17 August, he made his admission that he had had a "not appropriate relationship" with Monica Lewinsky. And on 20 August, he sent some cruise missiles to a misguided target of the al-Shifa pharmaceutical factory in Khartoum North that was not likely of tactical or strategic value. Indeed, this attack was turned into a propaganda victory for Khartoum and, as some allege, it was not even very diversionary for the contemporary "Monica Case" in Washington.

OIL AND SUDAN

The meteoric rise and great importance of oil in Sudan cannot be overestimated as a bright light for the future, as a source of violent conflict, as a dream for development and personal ambitions, as a source of unity or division, in a scramble for wealth by oil companies, with regard to a realignment of major powers for their own strategic interests, and as a means to achieve peace or rearm for more war. The previous chapter explored this in depth with the focus being on the South, where most of the oil discoveries have been made to date. So whether oil will be, or is, a "curse" or "blessing" will depend on decisions made and the context in the political economy. The African nations where oil tends to be a "curse" are those in which crude oil is directly exported and relatively little is refined for domestic uses. This context favors a lack of transparency, and thus an increase in corruption that creates a strong environment for undemocratic and autocratic rule. From oil field through pipelines to direct export, there is little chance for other economic spin-offs, and this increases the opportunity for low accountability, suspicions, and marginalization. Certainly, the nations of Nigeria, Angola, Gabon, Equatorial Guinea, and Chad are sad cases in point. At first, this was the case for Sudan, and it is in serious danger of continuing.

On the other hand, the first positive spin-off of increased refined product is import substitution, especially for expensive refined petroleum products. For example, to export crude oil and import aviation fuel is an unwelcome irony. The Sudanese case starts to show signs of improvement, and it no longer imports oil or most petroleum products, including its own aviation fuel, and more and larger refineries are being built to cut imports. Sudan is starting to export refined products to Ethiopia, earning foreign currency, and there are more spin-offs in trucking gasoline/petrol pumps. As road traffic increases, there are more roadside "cafeterias," and more areas are opened for development and urbanization. Similarly, road construction, which is a heavy user of petroleum products, expands the now extensive high-speed road network in Sudan that, at the time of independence, had virtually no intercity tarred roads.

EUROPEAN RELATIONS

There is a new, unified Europe on the world stage since the end of the Cold War, with the formation of the European Union with unimagined and new levels of financial, political, and military unification. There are new interests in energy, justice, and ecology, and new needs for markets and natural resources. There is new interest in global and African political stability as well as the special concerns with war crimes and allegations of genocide, with which they are familiar from recent European history. As such, Europeans, through either their own national or collective interests, are very much concerned about stability and peace in Sudan, and have subordinated their police and military to AU and UN missions.

SUMMARY OBSERVATIONS

By way of a conclusion, the final task is to put these strategic pieces together into a bigger picture. Naturally, this is a difficult task given the vast size and complexity of issues, diversity of ethnic groups, presence of multiple armed forces in multiple types of conflicts, and conflicting ideologies. What are the tactics and strategies that are reasonable for Sudan, Africa, and the world to manage this remarkable array of violent conflicts to enhance regional security? First, it seems that a utopian search for common convergence on this goal is far away. Suspicions, manipulations, opportunities, proxy wars, and basic inequalities have paved the way for many small-scale conflicts to come. Rather than dwell on the Afro-pessimist paradigm, it is worth recalling that the days of outright colonialism are over. This primary and major achievement for African nations should never be overlooked. Second, in models of Afro-optimism for Sudan, despite all that is going on inside Sudan and along its borders, overlooking some coup attempts, Sudan has not had any open state-to-state warfare since independence. Yes, there has been much foreign manipulation of proxy forces, many refugees, and severe civilian disruption, but Sudan has simply not gone to full-scale war with any of its nine neighbors since becoming independent. Third, Sudan has witnessed three substantial peace achievements; the Addis Ababa Accords that brought eleven years of peace, the Eastern Sudan Peace Accords, and the Comprehensive Peace Agreement are all holding at this point. Even the incomplete Darfur Peace Accord failed because it was rushed at the end and because the Darfur rebels could not speak with one voice. The dialogue on Sudan is typically so negative and polarized that these three major achievements are overlooked or minimized. On the other hand, the many small conflicts, resistance, and limited wars need serious tactical attention in the general strategy of seeking a stable state and region. One step could be in the direction of reducing marginalization, since it is that status that has kicked off most of the protest that finally erupts in destabilizing wars. Naturally, this is an issue of overall governance and empowerment that challenges the status quo and is hard to change, but the stakes are too high not to try. The other tactical approach relates to efforts to curb the extensive flow of small arms that allow the protests to become conflicts and then wars. Better governance and adjudication, and fewer small arms, would both be steps toward conflict reduction and mitigation. As there may be moves in these directions, this book can end on an optimistic note; otherwise, we should be prepared for more of the tragic waste of human and natural resources.

SOURCES

Sidahmed, Abdel Salam and Alsir Sidahmed. *Sudan* (New York: Routledge Curzon, 2005).

Iyob, Ruth and Gilbert M. Khadiagala. *Sudan: The Elusive Quest for Peace*. International Peace Academy, Occasional Paper (Boulder, CO: Lynne Rienner, 2006).

Lobban, Richard A. and Carolyn Fluehr-Lobban. "The Sudan under the National Islamic Front," *Arab Studies Quarterly*, Vol. 234, No. 2, Spring 2001.

APPENDIX A

Biographies

HASSAN AL-TURABI (1932–)

Al-Turabi was born in Kassala in the eastern Sudan, and he descended from an influential family. His father was a long-standing judge, and al-Turabi seemed to be destined for a career in law after graduating from the University of Khartoum with a law degree in 1955, an M.A. in law from London in 1957, and a Ph.D. from the Sorbonne in 1962. Al-Turabi became a long-standing prominent leader and controversial figure in the Islamic movement in Sudan, especially the Muslim Brotherhood, beginning in his student days, and thus of the NIF, its political wing. As a polyglot gifted speaker, with a lawyer's mind, and a politician at heart, al-Turabi was favored and opposed by various Sudanese governments and was elected to the parliament as a Muslim Brother in 1964 after the October Revolution, but during the early phases of the Nimieri government, he was in and out of jail. He also served as the Dean of the Law Faculty at the University of Khartoum, and after Nimieri's sharp turn from communism to Islamism, al-Turabi was tapped to become his Attorney General from 1979 to 1982. It was in this period and under al-Turabi that the harsh interpretation of Islamic law was introduced to otherwise rather liberal Sudan. So, when Nimieri was toppled in a popular revolt in 1985, the hope and expectation was that the Nimieri/al-Turabi era was over, and he was isolated and stigmatized.

But being out of power was nothing new for al-Turabi, and in this power vacuum, he founded the NIF, which became the third-largest political party in northern Sudanese politics after the traditional Umma Party of Sadiq al-Mahdi and the Democratic Unionist Party of the Khatmiya *tariqa*. This taste of power enticed al-Turabi to greater ambitions and frustrations when his brother-in-law, Sadiq al-Mahdi, came to power in 1986 but excluded the NIF and continued to push for the full introduction of Islamic law as state law. When Sadiq was finally replaced by the coup of Muhammad Omer al-Beshir in 1989, it was believed, but denied, that the NIF and al-Turabi were the instigators. In a short time, it was clear that this was the case, as the new military government sought legitimacy and guidance, which al-Turabi was very pleased to supply. In Sudan or in various international forums, al-Turabi became a lightning rod for opposition to the military regime and to its Islamist projects. But buoyed by his proximity to power, his generous ego, and his charisma and erudition, there was little to make him slow his demands or moderate his purposes. Inevitably, by 2000, in a period of some liberalization, he began to challenge the authority of al-Beshir himself, which reached a critical turning point when he was arrested and held alternately in the Kober prison and under house arrest. At present, he has been marginalized, but he is still a figure who is feared, despised, admired, and criticized.

SADIQ AL-MAHDI (1936–)

Sadiq al-Mahdi is descended from the historic line of Ansar Mahdists; his great-grandfather was Mohammad Ahmed al-Mahdi himself. As such, Sadiq became the leader of the Umma Party. His father was Siddiq al-Mahdi, and his grandfather was Sayyid 'Abd al-Rahman al-Mahdi, the Mahdi's posthumous son. Sadiq was educated at the University of Khartoum and Oxford University, and in the Sudanese parliament, he represented the constituency from Abba Island on the White Nile, which was the traditional stronghold of Mahdism. After Sadiq's father died in 1961, he became the representative of the Umma Party, from which position he was elected prime minister of Sudan in 1966–1967 and for a second term in 1986–1989 after the Nimieri government was toppled. While he was welcomed as a modernizer and democrat, he struggled with his uncle for legitimacy within the Umma Party and quarreled with Nimieri about his role in the future of Sudan. After 1977, when Nimieri was short of domestic allies, he brought Sadiq back to Sudan, but stripped of power. This turbulent era of Sudanese politics saw Nimieri toppled in 1985, and after a caretaker military government under Suwar al-Dahab, Sadiq was elected back to power as prime minister of a coalition government. This period of opportunity for democracy and the promise of much-needed reforms were not seized by Sadiq. The need to negotiate with the mutinous SPLA and to rescind the onerous and harsh aspects of Shari'a law that were introduced by Nimieri was not resolved as he became steadily weaker. Perhaps on the eve of his making a change in these important issues, he was toppled by a military coup led by Mohammad Omer al-Beshir, who was backed by the NIF, led by Hassan al-Turabi, Sadiq's brother-in-law. After 1989, Sadiq was in and out of jail until he escaped in 1996 to temporarily join the NDA, opposing the al-Beshir regime. As the NDA failed to maintain its unity, Sadiq split and returned from exile in 2000 to try to reconcile with the NIF, but in 2001, al-Turabi was himself excluded from power. Sadiq and all traditional political parties rest in a present state of limbo, but he is expected to run in the 2010 elections.

DR. SHEIKH HUSSEIN HAMID HASSAN (25 OCTOBER 1932–)

Hassan was born in Beni Suef, Egypt and received his Ph.D. in Shari'a from Al-Azhar University in 1965 and served as the Attorney General for Egypt from 1969 to 1970. He taught Shari'a law at the University of Cairo and in Libya, and occupied high academic and key advisory posts in Saudi Arabia, United Arab Republics, Pakistan, Kyrgyzstan, and Kazakhstan. He has also received two law degrees from New York University. Hassan is considered the modern "father of Islamic banking" and is a widely sought speaker and consultant on such matters. In this capacity, he worked with the Sudanese government of al-Beshir, especially during the time of Dr. Hassan al-Turabi, who was seeking his "official" word about the legal aspects of Islamic banking. According to Dr. Hassan, "Islamic financing is the most equitable form of financing, since it enables the creation of wealth without fuelling inflation or stoking a financial crisis." At present, he is the Chair of the Fatwa and Shari'a Supervisory Board in the Dubai Islamic Bank, with parallel roles in Bahrain, Sharjah, Jeddah, and Washington. He is proficient in Arabic, English, French, and Russian, and is widely consulted on influential legal and financial matters of Islamic renaissance. He is the author of twenty-one books on Islamic law, Islamic finance, Islamic economics, art, and social studies, as well as over four hundred extensive articles on these subjects.

DR. SHEIKH AJEEL JASSIM AL-NASHMI

Al-Nashmi received his Ph.D. in Islamic jurisprudence from al-Azhar University in 1977 and an M.A. degree in 1995. With these credentials, he became Dean of Shari'a at Kuwait University and a popular and legitimating speaker on his subject area as well as a member of the board or chair of some fifteen Islamic banking concerns, including the influential Shari'a Supervisory Board in the Emirates, on which he is joined by Hussein Hamdi Hassan. In addition, he sits on the Organization of Islamic Financial Institutes and the Kuwait Finance House. Al-Nashmi is thus linked to the Sudanese Sheikh Ahmed Ali Abdulla, General Secretary of the Higher Council of Shari'a Supervisory Boards in Sudan, as well as Sheikh al-Siddiq Muhammad al-Darir, who is a law professor at the University of Khartoum.

HASSAN OMER AHMED AL-BESHIR (1 JANUARY 1944–)

Al-Beshir was born in the Ja'aliyin village Hosh Ben Naqa, then part of the "kingdom" of Egypt and Sudan. He received his primary education there, and his family later moved to Khartoum, where he completed his secondary education. Al-Beshir is married to his cousin, Fatima Khalid. He also has a second wife named Widad Babiker Omer, who had a number of children with her first husband, Ibrahim Shamsaddin, a member of the Revolutionary Command Council for National Salvation, who died in a helicopter crash. Al-Beshir does not have any children of his own. He joined the Sudanese Army in 1960 and studied at the Egyptian Military Academy in Cairo, as well as graduating from the Sudan Military Academy in Khartoum in 1966. He quickly rose through the ranks and became a paratrooper serving in the southern Sudan. Later, al-Beshir served with the Egyptian Army during the October War (Yom Kippur War) of 1973 against Israel. He returned to Sudan as a colonel in the Sudanese Army.

Al-Beshir led a group of army officers in overthrowing the unstable, but democratic, coalition government of Prime Minister Sadiq al-Mahdi in a bloodless military coup on 30 June 1989. Under al-Beshir's leadership, the new military government suspended political parties and reintroduced a strict Islamic legal code on the national level. He then became Chairman of the Revolutionary Command Council for National Salvation (*Inqaz*), to assume the posts of chief of state, prime minister, chief of the armed forces, and minister of defense. Subsequent to al-Beshir's promotion to the Chairman of the Revolutionary Command Council for National Salvation, he allied himself with Hassan al-Turabi, the leader of the NIF, who along with al-Beshir began institutionalizing Shari'a law in the northern part of Sudan. Further on, al-Beshir issued purges and executions in the upper ranks of the army; the banning of associations, political parties, and independent newspapers; and the imprisonment of leading political figures and journalists.

On 16 October 1993, al-Beshir's powers increased further when he appointed himself president of the country, after which he disbanded the Revolutionary Command Council for National Salvation and all other rival political parties. In the early 1990s, al-Beshir's administration introduced a new currency called the Sudanese *dinar* to replace the discredited Sudanese *guinea*. By the mid-1990s, a struggle emerged between al-Beshir and al-Turabi, mostly due to al-Turabi's links to Islamic fundamentalist groups such as al-Qa'eda leader Osama bin Laden. Following the first bombing of the World Trade Center, the United States listed Sudan as a state sponsor of terrorism, and American firms have been barred from doing business in Sudan since 1997. Al-Beshir was later "elected" president (with a five-year term) in the 1996 national election; he was the only legal candidate to run.

In 1998, the Al-Shifa pharmaceutical factory in Khartoum was destroyed by a U.S. cruise missile strike because of its alleged production of chemical weapons and links to al-Qa'eda. In 1998, al-Beshir and the Presidential Committee put into effect a new constitution, allowing limited political opposition to al-Beshir's National Congress Party. After a faction led by al-Turabi, the Popular National Congress Party (PNC), signed an agreement with the SPLA, al-Beshir concluded that they were plotting to overthrow him. On 12 December1999, al-Beshir sent troops and tanks against Parliament and ousted Hassan al-Turabi, the Speaker of Parliament. Despite international criticism regarding internal conflicts, al-Beshir has achieved impressive economic growth in Sudan, mainly due to oil production from southern Sudan. Al-Beshir was re-elected president, receiving 86.5 percent of the vote in the 2000 presidential election and again in 2010.

Al-Turabi's "international Islamist" influence was pushed aside in favor of the "nationalist" or more pragmatic leaders who tried to recover from Sudan's disastrous international isolation and economic damage that had resulted from ideological adventurism. On al-Beshir's orders, al-Turabi was imprisoned based on allegations of conspiracy in 2000 before being released in October 2003. He was again imprisoned in the Kober (Cooper) prison in Khartoum in March 2004. He was released on 28 June 2005, in the height of the peace agreement in the civil war, which had raged between the northern and southern halves of the country for over two decades between the SPLA and al-Beshir's government. International pressure intensified in 2001, however, and leaders from the United Nations called for al-Beshir to make efforts to end the conflict and allow humanitarian and international workers to deliver relief to the southern regions of Sudan. Peace was consolidated in the signing of the CPA on 9 January 2005, granting Southern Sudan autonomy for six years, to be followed by a referendum about independence in 2011. It created a co–vice president position and allowed the North and South to split oil deposits equally, but also left both the North's and South's armies in place. John Garang, the South's peace-agreement-appointed co–vice president, died in a helicopter crash on 1 August 2005, three weeks after being sworn in.

No sooner had the conflict in the south of Sudan begun to subside than a new conflict had already begun in the western province of Darfur in early 2003. The non-Afro-Arab populations rose up in protest of their marginalization while the GoS unleashed its *janjaweed* militia. This conflict has reportedly reached a death toll in the hundreds of thousands, while the Sudanese government has said that the number killed is less than ten thousand. The Sudanese government has been accused of suppressing information by jailing and killing witnesses since 2004, and tampering with evidence, such as covering up graves. Since 2004, the U.S. (George W. Bush) government has described the conflict as "genocide," although the United Nations has not recognized the conflict as such. On 29 June 2004, U.S. Secretary of State Colin Powell met with al-Beshir in Sudan and urged him to make peace with the rebels, end the crisis, and lift restrictions on the delivery of humanitarian aid to Darfur. Kofi Annan met with al-Beshir three days later and demanded that he disarm the *janjaweed*.

After fighting eased in July and August, on 31 August 2006, the UN Security Council approved Resolution 1706, which called for a new 20,600-troop UN peacekeeping force called UNAMID to supplant or supplement a poorly funded and ill-equipped 7,000-troop AMIS peacekeeping force. In March 2007, the UN mission accused Sudan's government of orchestrating and taking part in "gross violations" in Darfur and called for urgent international action to protect civilians there. Sudan strongly objected to the resolution and said that it would see UN forces in the region as foreign invaders. A high-level technical consultation was held in Addis Ababa, Ethiopia on 11–12 June 2007, pursuant to the 4 June 2007 letters of the Secretary-General and the Chairperson of the African Union Commission, which were addressed to al-Beshir.

On 14 July 2008, the Chief Prosecutor of the ICC, Luis Moreno-Ocampo, alleged that al-Beshir bore individual criminal responsibility for genocide, crimes against humanity, and war crimes committed since 2003 in Darfur. The prosecutor accused al-Beshir of having "masterminded and implemented" a plan to destroy the three main ethnic groups, the Fur, Masalit, and Zaghawa, with a campaign of murder, rape, and deportation. The ICC issued an arrest warrant for al-Beshir on 4 March 2009, indicting him on five counts of crimes against humanity (murder, extermination, forcible transfer, torture, and rape) and two counts of war crimes (pillaging and intentionally directing attacks against civilians). The court ruled that there was insufficient evidence to prosecute him for genocide. However, one of the three judges wrote a dissenting opinion arguing that there were "reasonable grounds to believe that al-Beshir has committed the crime of genocide." Al-Beshir is the first sitting head of state ever indicted by the ICC. However, the Arab League and the African Union condemned the warrant. Al-Beshir has since visited Egypt and Qatar. Both countries refused to arrest him and surrender him to the ICC upon arrival. Luis Moreno-Ocampo and Amnesty International claimed that al-Beshir's plane could be intercepted in international airspace. Sudan announced that the presidential plane would always be escorted by fighter jets of the Sudanese Air Force to prevent his arrest.

In other quarters, the charges against President al-Beshir have been strongly rejected. President of Libya and Chairman of the African Union Muammar al-Gadaffi characterized the indictment as a form of terrorism. He also believes that the warrant is an attempt "by [the West] to recolonize their former colonies." Egypt said that it was "greatly disturbed" by the ICC decision and called for an emergency meeting of the UN Security Council to defer the arrest warrant. The Arab League Secretary-General Amr Moussa expressed that the organization emphasizes its solidarity with Sudan. The ICC warrant was condemned for "undermining the unity and stability of Sudan." The Organization of the Islamic Conference denounced the warrant as unwarranted and totally unacceptable. It was argued that the warrant demonstrates selectivity and double standards with regard to war crimes. There have been large demonstrations by Sudanese people supporting President al-Beshir and opposing the ICC charges. Others argue the warrant sets a dangerous precedent in international relations and could hamper efforts to bring peace to Sudan.

Needless to say, al-Beshir has rejected the charges, saying that the Sudan does not recognize the ICC, is not a state party to the Rome Statute, and claims that it does not have to execute the warrant because of this. Amnesty International stated that al-Beshir must turn himself in to face the charges, and that the Sudanese authorities must detain him and turn him over to the ICC if he refuses. This matter stays unresolved in 2010 as the promised Sudanese elections and peace accords in Darfur are taking center stage for the time being.

'ALI OSMAN MOHAMED TAHA (1 JANUARY 1944–)

Taha has been the second vice president of Sudan since August 2005. He held the position of first vice president from 1998 to August 2005. He was the country's Foreign Minister for three years prior to becoming first vice president and is a member of the National Congress Party. Taha is a graduate of the Faculty of Law at the University of Khartoum. He then set up a private law practice before being appointed judge and then entering politics as a member of Sudan's parliament in the 1980s. Taha, along with John Garang, is credited as being the co-architect of Sudan's CPA, which brought Africa's longest civil war to an end on 9 January 2005. The agreement capped an eight-year process to stop the civil war, which since 1983 had taken 2 million lives. Starting in December 2003, Taha and Garang met numerous times to finalize the peace agreement. Taha heads the Sudanese side of the Sudanese Egyptian High Committee, which is headed on the Egyptian side by Prime Minister Ahmed Nazif and includes ministers from both countries and aims to foster cooperation between the two countries. During his address to the UN Assembly in September 2008, Taha called for greater sovereignty in regards to Sudanese governmental management. He was quoted as saying that "Sudan was an environment with enormous resources and that peace in Sudan was a strategic necessity for the stability of the region. Nothing should be done to jeopardize the Government's efforts to bring about peace. The Government must be allowed to carry out national projects for disarmament, demobilization, mine-clearing and reconciliation. The commitments made in Oslo must be honored by the international community to help Sudan deal with the difficulties and obstacles in implementation. Sudan's external debt should be cancelled in harmony with its ability to implement a comprehensive peace." Regarding Darfur, he believes the entire situation should be a "Sudanese initiative" using the views of the people of Sudan as the "yardstick by which resolution will be reached."

NAFIE ALI NAFIE (CA. 1947–)

Nafie, son of a Sudanese sesame farmer, earned his PhD in plant genetics at the University of California, Riverside, USA and served as a professor of agriculture in Sudan. From this simple and academic background he became one of the most powerful and hard-line figures in the al-Beshir government serving as Deputy Chair of the National Congress Party and trusted and surviving Assistant to the President. From 1989 to 1995 he was head of intelligence and security during the bloody period of "ghost houses" noted for their brutality. As the "bad cop" of the Sudanese regime he opposed the presence of UN peacekeepers in Darfur and felt that too much was given away in the CPA accords in 2005. On the David Frost Show in 2008 he dismissed the large alleged number of dead in Darfur as "propaganda" of the west in order to destabilize Sudan and some of the violence in Darfur attributed to "bandits" and not to the "janjaweed" who were in fact under "government control" as members of the Peoples' Defense Forces. He noted that government bombing in Darfur was against rebels and the Sudanese armed forces were entitled to take whatever armed measures they wished. In 2007 he replaced Majzoub al-Khalifa, who died in a car crash, as the chief negotiator for the ongoing Darfur talks. In late 2009, he moderated to the extent that he said the NCP would accept whatever results emerged in the 2011 referendum for possible separation. He predicted chaos after the 2010 elections as a plot to destabilize Sudan. Nafie has represented the Sudan in top diplomatic missions to Egypt, Britain, Japan, and China. While some of his measures and dire predictions have not unfolded he still is within the top leadership in the NCP government.

JOHN GARANG DE MABIOR (1945–2005)

John Garang is a Bor Dinka from the hamlets of Wagkulei. His father died when he was nine, and his mother died when he was eleven, but with family support he continued through primary school in southern Sudan and on to high school in Uganda in the mid-1960s, where he first met Yoweri Museveni, the future president of Uganda. Clearly, he was a self-reliant struggler, and from his Uganda high school, he went on to pursue his education in the United States to earn a B.S. degree from Grinnell College in 1971. Even before this time he had joined the Anya-Nya, a secessionist group in southern Sudan that was active in the early Nimieri years. Once the policy of regional autonomy was determined in 1969 and consummated in the Addis Ababa Accords of 1972, the Anya-Nya guerillas were incorporated into the Sudanese army under Southern general Joseph Lagu. So, at age twenty-six, having served as Lagu's chief aid and with apparently new relations between North and South emerging, Garang entered the Sudanese military with the rank of captain. During this time, Joseph Garang, no relation, was appointed Minister of South Affairs in the new and changed Khartoum government. Moving rapidly in military and academic life, John Garang returned to the United States in 1974 to take a course in military command at Fort Benning, Georgia, and then went on to Iowa State University from 1977 to 1981 to earn his Ph.D. in economics; his primary focus was on the economic development of southern Sudan.

This unusual background brought him back to Sudan to teach at the University of Khartoum and at the Sudan Military College, while the last years of the Nimieri government were growing even more turbulent. Other Southerners were even more impatient for change, and revolts broke out in 1983, led by Kerubino Kwanyin and William Nyuon Bany; Garang was under pressure to join them since he well knew the pressing issues, but his official loyalty was to the lingering Addis Ababa Accords and his military loyalty was to the Khartoum government. By this time, Garang had reached the rank of colonel in the army. In order to crush these revolts, Nimieri sent him to Bor, which was Garang's homeland. This was more than he could take, and instead of putting them down, he joined the revolt that expanded and emerged fully as the SPLA, and he waged war against Khartoum for the next twenty-two years. At first, it looked like this would be a short war, especially when Nimieri was toppled in 1985, but for one year, the transitional military government held power. Garang was insistent upon democracy, and he refused to negotiate with a new group of Northern military leaders. In the interval from 1983 to 1985, the SPLA developed its program of striving for a unitary and democratic Sudan. When they departed and went back to the barracks, this ushered in a brief period of democratic rule under Prime Minister Sadiq al-Mahdi, in whom great hopes were placed for sustained secular democracy and retreat from the harsh Islamic law imposed by Nimieri. The SPLA program also wanted the end of the marginalization of the peripheral regions of Sudan and to move substantively toward national development and integration. This imaginative plan was never adopted by the prime minister, who was trapped in a maze of Northern politics that gave him no maneuvering room. Soon it became moot, and power was seized by Hassan Omer Ahmed al-Beshir, backed by the NIF, which insisted on keeping Islamic laws and barring democracy or secular opposition. Losing this critical moment meant that war in the South was the only route left to Garang and the SPLA. As an effective military leader, he brought most of the rural South under his control and began to make war in the southern parts of the North, in southern Kordofan and southern Darfur. The going was not easy, with reported violations of human rights and the rules of war being charged on both sides, especially by the North, who did not take prisoners. Complicating an already complex situation was the discovery of oil, the overthrow of the Mengistu government in Ethiopia that had supported the SPLA, and Southern revolts, especially in 1991, within the areas controlled by the SPLA (Mainstream). By 1994, Garang finally emerged as the winner in these struggles, and in 1995, the SPLA became the strongest single party of the NDA, aimed

toward the overthrow of the al-Beshir regime and the restoration of secular democracy, and toward regional development. From 1995 to 2005, various behind-the-
scenes efforts in numerous venues were made to negotiate with the Khartoum
government, who periodically thought it might win back the South by military
means. At last, after many setbacks and huge frustrations, the SPLA was able to conclude the CPA in Naivasha, Kenya. The war was apparently over, and a referendum
on Southern unity with the North was set with apparently only a few unresolved
issues to sort out. Garang became the vice president of Sudan in a new government
of national unity. This moment of enthusiastic optimism was eroded as conflict
bubbled in Abyei and Blue Nile, and distrust deepened over various matters. Most
horrible of all was that Garang was suddenly killed in a helicopter crash in the Imatong Mountains in Equatoria in southern Sudan on 30 July 2005, only seven
months after the CPA was signed. As of this writing, the CPA is still extant, but
not well, and Southern and Northern forces are rearming, perhaps to fight again
over oil and sovereignty, especially as the great issues of an Islamic state without
multiparty democracy remained unresolved. No longer will John Garang be present
to see this outcome; instead, it will be his loyal deputy, Salva Kiir Mayardit, who was
appointed as his successor, making him head of the SPLM, vice president of Sudan,
and president of the South. Southern sentiment in favor of separation runs high, so
the first test of Kiir's leadership will be negotiating the rough CPA terrain of separation or unity to keep Garang's lonely mission alive. Already, Shari'a law is withdrawn from the South and from millions of non-Muslims in the North, and the
CPA survives with a new constitution already approved.

SALVA KIIR MAYARDIT (1951–)

Kiir is of Dinka origin and was one of the most persistent and loyal followers
of John Garang, the leader and founder of the SPLA (Mainstream). Kiir has been
involved with the Southern revolt since the 1960s and joined the Nimieri
government after the 1972 Addis Ababa Accords. He has been with the SPLA/
SPLM since its founding, along with his comrade-in-arms, Dr. John Garang.
Amid the many cases of severe discord within the Southern movements, Kiir
and Garang never broke. Officially, Kiir was third in command after Arok Thon
Arok. Prior to Garang's death, Kiir held the rank of Commander and Deputy to
the SPLA council, with a portfolio on foreign and domestic affairs and intelligence. He was also a negotiator in the failed 1994 peace negotiations and ultimately in the successful Naivasha peace negotiations that led to the CPA in
January 2005. However when John Garang tragically and shockingly died on
30 July 2005 in a helicopter crash, the SPLA Council determined that Kiir
should lead the SPLA, and he became the second vice president of the National
Unity government of Sudan as the appointed replacement for his fallen comrade;
he simultaneously became the president of the newly constructed GoSS. His

political tasks ahead could not be much more challenging, as the CPA is not fully implemented, border conflicts at the Blue Nile and Abyei slip out of resolution or control, oil revenues mount, the 2011 referendum on the unity of Sudan draws closer, and both Northern and Southern Sudan are gathering arms for a possible future military engagement or the possibility of a peaceful separation.

'ABD AL-BASIT SABDARAT

Sabdarat was the Minister of Education from 1992 to 1996 in the al-Beshir government. He was then transferred to become the Sudanese Minister of Justice as a loyal member of the NCP from 1996 to 1998. He was shifted to Advisor to the Government on Political and Legal Affairs from 1998 to 2000. From 2001 to 2006, he was Minister of Relations with the National Assembly. From 2006 to 2007, he served as a minister in the federal government until returning to the position of Minister of Justice in 2007 to the present.

MAJOR GENERAL (ARMY) SALAH ABDALLAH GOSH

Gosh was the Director General of the GoS National Security and Intelligence Services. He has been accused of being a key individual in the mobilization of the Khartoum government's counterinsurgency militias (*janjaweed*) in the Darfur conflict. He is listed by a UN Security Council report as one of seventeen Sudanese individuals who were "most responsible for war crimes and impeding the peace process." He is described as the "personal government minder" for Osama bin Laden while the al-Qa'eda leader was in Sudan between 1990 and 1996. The United Nations also accused him of having failed "to take action as Director of NSIS to identify, neutralize, and disarm non-state armed militia groups in Darfur [the *janjaweed*]," and for his command role in "acts of arbitrary detention, harassment, torture, [and] denial of right to fair trial."

On the other hand, because of his key role in Sudanese military intelligence and background with Osama bin Laden, the United States allegedly flew Gosh to Washington, D.C., in April 2005, where he cooperated in discussions related to capture of terror suspects. He was subsequently denied reentry to the United States for medical treatment, but was issued a visa for travel to Britain. During the 2006 attack by anti-president Idris Deby rebels on N'Djamena, the capital of Chad, it was thought that Gosh had a planning role. In April 2008, the Deby government released a telephone conversation between these rebels and Gosh, in which he called for toppling Deby, who had ironically been helped into power by Khartoum in the first place. After the ICC issued an arrest warrant for Sudanese president al-Beshir, Gosh supposedly threatened anyone who tried to assist in his arrest with "amputation of the hands and the slitting of the throats of any person who dares bad-mouth al-Beshir or support" the ICC decision. In May 2009,

Gosh reportedly called for the closure of the Sudanese newspaper *Al-Wifaq* after an editorial called for the death of Yasser Arman, a prominent leader of the SPLA/SPLM. Yet some believed that it was Gosh who may have made the death threat himself.

SALAH ED DIN AHMED IDRIS

Idris is a wealthy businessman who may have been born in Sudan but considers himself a Saudi. He is close to the Sudanese ruling elite through Ghazi Salah Eddin, who connected him to President Omar al-Beshir sometime after 1989. He came to wider attention when he purchased the Al-Shifa pharmaceutical plant in Khartoum North (Bahri). Believing this to be linked to Osama bin Laden and in the wake of the two U.S. embassy bombings in Kenya and Tanzania on 7 August 1998, President Clinton ordered U.S. Navy cruise missiles to attack Al-Shifa on 20 August 1998, essentially destroying the plant and killing one night watchman. Subsequently, Idris sought redress in a U.S. federal appeals court on 27 July 2000. His claim for damages was dismissed on 11 August 2004 as a political issue of a noncitizen. Clearly, he was not pleased with the bombing or this legal failure. He also has had a 75 percent controlling stake in IES Digital Systems, which makes and installs surveillance equipment for the British government, including their army, foreign office, and parliament.

ABD AL-WAHED MUHAMMAD NUR

Nur is a Fur by ethnicity and a lawyer by training. Notably, he was a nonsignatory to the DPA of 2006. In the follow-up effort in Arusha, Tanzania, he also did not participate. From exile in France, he has frequently found reasons not to join his fellow Darfur rebels in reaching a peace accord for this conflict; this is still the case in the Qatar accords of 2010.

MINNI ARKOU MINNAWI (CA. 1972–)

Minnawi is the Zaghawa leader of one of the former largest factions of the SLA, a rebel group in Darfur. As Secretary General of the SLA, this former schoolteacher, his SLA, and JEM launched a coordinated attack in February 2003 on Sudanese Air Force bases in Darfur that proceeded to intensify the violence in Darfur, especially through 2005. As the Abuja Accords evolved, it was only the Minnawi faction that signed the DPA in May 2006. This act brought him officially into the Sudanese government as the fourth ranking member (Senior Assistant) of the Presidency and the Chairman of the Regional Interim Authority of Darfur. The act also gained him an audience with President George W. Bush in July 2006, about the same time that Minnawi's forces were engaged in combat at the town of Korma in northern Darfur.

Despite these titles, he did not wield an effective degree of power. As such, he lost some supporters, and presently he is in limbo between reverting back to guerilla resistance and staying with the Khartoum side. Fighting between SLA-Minnawi and other groups of Darfur rebels has continued sporadically since 2006. He also distinguished his group of the SLA by being willing to accept UN troops as provided for in UN Security Council Resolution 1706. His outlook is broadly secular and democratic, and he is clearly ready to negotiate for peace rather than subject more people from Darfur to further misery.

KHALIL IBRAHIM MUHAMMAD

Muhammad is a Kobe Zaghawa and physician by training with sympathies and support in the past to the NIF. He served the NIF-backed Khartoum regime from 1991 to 1994 as the State Minister for Education in Al Fasher. He also spent four months in 1992 serving as a doctor to the *murahileen*, PDF militias, but he became skeptical of that cause by 1993 and tried to work from within the NIF to reform it and bring it to its noble mission from which it was being diverted. It is believed that he was involved in the secret creation of "The Seekers of Truth and Justice" groups in Khartoum as early as 1994. He served in other medium-level governmental posts in 1997, as State Minister for Social Affairs for Blue Nile and, in 1998, as an advisor to the Governor of Southern Sudan. In December 1999, he was studying for an M.P.H. in the Netherlands. Not being satisfied with his view of these second-rank appointments, Ibrahim's patience was wearing thin, and his frustrations grew. In frustration, he quit his position and formed the "Fighting Poverty" group in August 1998; when his ally Hassan al-Turabi was forced out of the government in December 1999, Ibrahim was actually out of Sudan studying for his M.P.H. degree at Maastricht University. Keeping his link to al-Turabi, Ibrahim backed the Popular Congress Party. At about this time, it is believed that Ibrahim drafted the "Black Book," which was a strong critique of the Arab-dominated government and its policies that marginalized all people of Sudan, especially those from Darfur. This was secretly released in 2000, but by August 2001, still in Holland, Ibrahim announced the formation of JEM, which began joint military operations with the SLA in February 2003 against government targets in Darfur. At the Abuja meeting, JEM refused to come to final terms and did not sign the DPA, but continued military action and split into more factions. Ibrahim, along with other Darfur rebel groups, formed the NRF on 30 June 2006; this was based in Asmara. In a bold, headline-grabbing move, JEM forces drove across Darfur and Kordofan and attacked Omdurman on 10 May 2008. As this book goes to press, his captured soldiers are released and a peace accord is signed in Qatar. Mainly, the Darfur rebel SLA group led by Abd al-Wahed Muhammad Nur remains in the conflict later withdrawing from the Qatar talks.

BRIGADIER MUSA HILAL (1961–)

Hilal is a traditional leader of the Muhamid Arab clan in Darfur who is closely linked to Sudanese military intelligence. During the counterinsurgency against the Darfur rebellion from 2003 to 2010, he was instrumental in clearing the rural populations that supported or shared the grievances with the rebels. He was official Advisor to the Ministry of Federal Affairs in the government, that is, to former Justice Minister 'Abd al-Basit Sabdarat. Darfur and human-rights activists have repeatedly charged him with a central role in the government's counterviolence in Darfur, and he is a likely legal target for ICC charges. Hilal has denied these charges, insisting that he was only a local "tribal leader." He has three wives and thirteen children at last count.

'ABD AL-HAMID MUSA KASHA

Kasha has had numerous assignments in trade and commerce in the NCP government, which include his significant roles as the Minister of Foreign Trade and the Minister of Commerce as well as his appointment as the governor of South Darfur during the period of Darfur conflict. In 2009, he was in office trying to address the soaring prices of meat, sugar, and wheat.

LAM AKOL AJAWIN (1950–)

Akol is of Shilluk origin. He worked as a chemical engineering professor at the University of Khartoum after earning his Ph.D. from the University of London. He joined the SPLA in 1986 after its mutiny from the GoS. Akol, Mansour Khalid, and others represented the SPLA at the failed 1989 Nairobi peace talks. However, he also had criticism of the leadership of the SPLA ("Mainstream"), and he broke from it in April 1991 to join the SPLA-Nasir faction with Riak Machar, which launched a period of civil war in the South in the 1990s. The next phase of this internecine struggle began in April 1992, when Akol was expelled from the SSIM, and he went on to form the Upper Nile–based group termed the "SPLA-United." In January 1997, he split again with that group, and his increased isolation caused him to shift toward the NIF backers of the GoS at that time. However, when John Garang's faction of the SPLA won, Akol sought a new role for himself. After the January 2005 signing of the CPA, he returned to serve as a top official in the SPLA and became the Minister of Foreign Affairs of the GoS in September 2005. During his period in office, he advanced the African Union's African Cultural and Scientific Organization, and also wrote about his involvement in the SPLA negotiations. However, in September 2006, he was charged with being a partner in Sudan's repression in Darfur by the Sudanese journalist Alfred Taban. While he strongly denied this attack, he was also criticized by SPLA leaders for being too close to the regime, and he was replaced by Deng Alor, who had served as Minister of Cabinet Affairs while Akol was demoted and resigned from this lower position in October 2007.

YASIR SAEED ARMAN (1961–)

Born in the Gezira region of Sudan just after independence and raised as a tolerant Sufi Muslim, Arman was a longtime student activist and African National Congress (ANC) supporter in the anti-apartheid struggle. As such, he supported the "radical" cause of a secular and democratic state in Sudan. Under the "progressive" period of the Nimieri regime, he was also arrested. He completed his law degree at the Khartoum branch of Cairo University. He was also a visionary of the "New Sudan," and he joined the SPLA in 1986, a few years after it was founded by John Garang and his comrades. Working with the SPLA in Addis Ababa, he met and married his Ngok Dinka wife, Awour Deng Kuol, and in the spirit of the "New Sudan," they were married in both Muslim and Christian ceremonies. Arman and Pagan Amum were briefly arrested on 6 December 2009 by al-Beshir, but in 2010, he was nominated as the SPLA candidate in the national elections for president of Sudan.

PAGAN AMUM OKICH

Okich is a Shilluk from Malakal who was long engaged in Sudanese activist politics. He gained a law degree in 1982 and immediately joined the SPLA in 1983 as it was founded by John Garang. Early on, he was sent to Cuba for training, and he still speaks Spanish fluently from this time, when the SPLA was backed by the pro-Soviet Ethiopian regime of Mengistu Haile Marium. During the war in the South, Amum served in a variety of military, consultative, and diplomatic positions. In the summer of 1994, Pagan Amum became the official SPLA spokesperson, with the title of Secretary General. In December 2009, he and Yasir Arman were briefly arrested by al-Beshir.

EASTERN FRONT

The Eastern Front in Sudan is a politico-military body composed principally of the Arab Rashaidya "Free Lions" and the Beja Congress. The much older Beja Congress was founded immediately after independence in 1957 by Dr. Taha Osman Bileya. It was, and still is, a loose alliance of the main Muslim groups of the eastern Sudan, such as the Amarar, Bisharin, Beni Amer, and Hadendowa, who have all been continuously in this region for thousands of years. Today, they represent well over two million people. The area that is occupied stretches from northern Eritrea to southeastern Egypt in the Halayeb Triangle. They are traditionally seminomadic people who herd camels, sheep, goats, and cattle, and engage in informal commerce in the region. In the past decades of conflicts in Sudan, they have been, at times, allied with the NDA, SPLA, and JEM as the political winds have fluctuated.

The Rashaidya are very different residents of the region, having only started to enter in the mid-nineteenth to late nineteenth century from western Saudi Arabia. Their women are veiled, and they are famed for their jewelry-making. Their "Free Lions" movement was formed in 1999 by Mabrouk Mubarak Salim, a decade after the Omer al-Beshir government came to power. The general issues of the Beja Congress and Free Lions in their unified ' Eastern Front' have been persistent marginalization and under representation as well as the more pressing issues of increased mechanized and *rentier* agriculture that is undermining their traditional local economy. Both groups are Muslims. On 14 October 2006, these groups reluctantly signed the ESPA, which provided better representation and more power-sharing. There has not been major conflict since that time.

APPENDIX B

Chronology

The following includes important events in Sudan since the coup of Brigadier General Omar Hassan al-Beshir.

30 June 1989	Brigadier General Omar Hassan al-Beshir comes to power by military coup backed by the NIF, led by Hassan al-Turabi. As a result: formation of the NDA.
4 July 1989	One-month cease-fire offered with amnesty. Garang invited to talk.
13 July 1989	Al-Beshir accepts the principle of separation of South.
19 July 1989	Garang sets conditions for talks.
30 July 1989	Al-Beshir says no return to political parties.
14 August 1989	Garang calls for resignation of al-Beshir and the return to a broad government.
30 September 1989	Cease-fire extended.
17 November 1989	NDA announces resistance.
December 1989	President Carter tries to advance negotiations, but sees Shari'a as stumbling block.
March 1990	SPLA joins the NDA. Period of heavy repression and coup attempts.
April 1990	Coup attempt.
June 1990	Coup attempt.
27 December 1990	Al-Beshir goes to Nigeria to talk with Babangida about peace negotiations.
1991–1996	Osama bin Laden based in Sudan.
February 1991	First amputations since Nimieri.

April 1991	Coup attempt. More repression. War intensifies.
May 1991	Mengistu toppled in Ethiopia; crisis for the SPLA since Ethiopia was an important backer.
26 May 1992	First Abuja talks fail. al-Beshir says Saudis support the SPLA. Transitional National Assembly formed.
1993	Beshir becomes President of Sudan.
February 1993	More inconclusive Abuja talks.
26 February 1993	Bombing of the World Trade Center by Sheikh Omar 'Abd al-Rahman.
August 1993	United States charges Sudan with being a state-sponsored terrorist nation.
October 1993	NDA reaffirms self-determination, democracy, and unity.
21 October 1993	Garang and Riak Machar meet in Washington.
December 1993	Umma Party accepts self-determination for South at Chukudum meetings.
1994	Continuing meetings of IGADD.
17 March 1994	First IGADD meeting.
2 May 1994	Second IGADD meeting to form a Declaration of Principles (DoP) with the SPLA.
18–29 July 1994	Third IGADD meeting in Nairobi.
5–7 September 1994	Fourth IGADD meeting.
12 December 1994	Umma Party and the SPLA accept the DoP of IGADD.
1995	Asmara Declaration by NDA.
March 1995	Cease-fire and Guinea-Worm accords of IGADD. Nevertheless, from 1995 to 1999, the war in the South intensifies with many human-rights violations.
1996	"Elections" for president and the National Assembly. Former prime minister Sadiq al-Mahdi escapes from Sudan. Later in the year, Nimieri and Sadiq al-Mahdi return to Sudan.
2000	Arab militias attack Fur villages and civilians without prosecution. The militias are considered to be an informal branch of the government. Amnesty International reports cross-amputation and execution of five in Nyala, Darfur. Repression against university students increases in Sennar, Khartoum, Darfur, and elsewhere.
March 2000	Amputation reported.
June 2000	Eight-eight Rizeigat (ethnic group) members beaten in custody. Tensions rise in Darfur.
November 2000	President Bush "elected" by U.S. Supreme Court.
21–22 February 2001	Turabi arrested.
May 2001	Numerous men hanged in Darfur.
11 September 2001	World Trade Center attacked by al-Qa'eda. U.S. counterattack on Afghanistan.

December 2001	State of emergency continued in Sudan.
February 2002	Woman flogged in Nyala, Darfur.
July 2002	Machakos Accords advance, with peace talks resuming with U.S. Senator Danforth.
October 2002	The Sudan Peace Act is passed in Washington, with sanctions imposed if no good-faith negotiations. There are many cease-fire violations and at least 500,000 IDPs; increased military activity in southern Sudan.
November 2002	Woman flogged in Munwashi, Darfur.
February 2003	Joint Darfur rebel attacks government military assets in Darfur. The Darfur conflict surges to a heightened level of violence.
March 2003	United States invades Iraq. SPLA renews call for separation of church and state as IGAD talks resume on 22 March. IDPs in Khartoum reach 2 million. Sudan Liberation Army (antigovernment Darfur group, former Darfur Liberation Front) is fighting along Chad-Sudan frontier. GoS claims Chadian support. al-Beshir has peace talks in Paris. IGAD talks cover marginalized areas too, e.g., Nuba Mountains, Abyei, and Upper Blue Nile. Other topics incorporated, e.g., power-sharing, constitution, capital, Shari'a, security, wealth, land, Machakos, Turabi, guarantees, etc.; many questions about actual implementation remain, but an agenda is set.
April 2003	Sudan government vows to smash rebels in Darfur. Major refugee exodus takes place from Darfur to Chad amid heavy fighting. The Sudan Peace Act needs further evaluation in this context. Cease-fire continues shakily. Sudan signs military protocol with Egypt and Libya.
August 2003	IGAD talks advance hesitatingly.
September 2003	Sudan Organization Against Torture (SOAT) protests the ongoing confinement of twelve citizens of Darfur without charges.
3 September 2003	GoS delegation to Chad to sign six-week cease-fire with Darfur SLM rebels. 65,000 more refugees cited by UN sources. All prisoners to be released.
4 September 2003	GoS air attacks continue according to the SLA.
5 September 2003	Air attacks continue in Darfur.
14 September 2003	GoS and SPLA continue to negotiate integrated military (3,000 soldiers each) and monitoring of cease-fire between North and South and their contested regions. 90,000 GoS troops still in South. SPLA forces would stay in South. SLM claims the GoS has violated truce in Darfur.
18 September 2003	Northerners claim the SPLA is driving them from the South.
21 September 2003	Cease-fire between SPLA and GoS extended to end of November. Momentum for peace stays strong. Question of how many Northern troops will stay in South, especially to guard the oil wells.

25 September 2003	Agreement signed at Naivasha, Kenya between GoS and SPLA (vice president Ali Osman M. Taha and John Garang) with integrated military force. Date for the creation and deployment not yet determined. Accords agree to merge armies, central command, extend cease-fire to October, and explore power, wealth, and security issues. Joint military command will have 12,000 each for South, 3,000 each for Nuba Mountains, 3,000 each for UBN, 1,500 each for Khartoum province.
26 September 2003	Peace talks adjourned for consultation. Progress hailed by United States and United Nations, but marginal areas not resolved yet.
27 September 2003	United States drops Sudan from terrorism list but keeps Peace Act in place.
30 September 2003	Garang proposes rotating presidency of Sudan for set periods to set relationship of equality. Road to peace declared as irreversible. SPLA plans to keep 80,000 to 120,000 troops in South. Khartoum to withdraw all but 12,000 of its 103,000 troops in South. United States to give $200 million when peace accords are signed and $500 million as peace unfolds.
October 2003	Military tribunal sentences fifteen men to death in Darfur, no appeal. Protested by the Sudan Human Rights Organization.
	Nine Sudanese aid workers for an American agency have been killed in Darfur.
4 October 2003	1,000 men (JEM, then still an ally of SLM?) attack Kulbus in Darfur with armed Toyotas, perhaps coming from Chad.
5 October 2003	Lake Naivasha (Simba Lodge) talks resume 50 miles from Nairobi. Kenyan President Kibaki is represented by General Lazaro Sumbeiyo and United States is represented by Senator Danforth. Sumbeiyo is the official mediator.
6 October 2003	Talks slated to discuss Nuba Mountains and South Blue Nile regions. Omer al-Beshir invites SPLA to join his (Islamist) National Congress Party once there is peace. Or the SPLA could have its own party, he says. Observers note this might be the start of the return to multiparty democracy and that the SPLA military is too strong to be defeated in the field.
7 October 2003	Secretary of State Powell plans a visit to Naivasha.
8 October 2003	Turabi's Popular Congress Party is opposed to agreement. He is still under house arrest. Al-Beshir thanks United States for its role in negotiations.
9 October 2003	United Nations is consulted to play a peacekeeping role conditioned upon signed agreement between SPLA and GoS. Umma Party protests its lack of involvement at Naivasha.
13 October 2003	Naivasha talks continue. SPLA wants self-determination for marginal areas, followed by six-years' interim. Turabi and seven others are released from arrest. Turabi plan is human rights, freedom, and

	democracy. More releases of political detainees expected as wider political freedoms are restored.
14 October 2003	Beja forces skirmish in Eastern Sudan with GoS police. They flee to Eritrea. Beja are linked to the NDA, which has not been included in SPLA peace talks. United States says that a final accord is near. Turabi stays critical of accords.
16 October 2003	DUP is invited as observer of talks. Observers say that 80 to 90 percent is agreed in twenty days of mutual meetings. Six-year period will start on day of final signing.
17–18 October 2003	SLM claims GoS attacks on civilians in Darfur.
19 October 2003	Turabi calls for elections.
20 October 2003	Government attacks in northern Darfur. GoS claims "tribal attacks" in Western Darfur. Fifteen villages destroyed and 15,000 more displaced persons. Despite this problem, al-Beshir says he is serious about peace with the SPLA.
21 October 2003	SLM Darfur cites forty-seven cease-fire violations of the GoS. Colin Powell pushes for Sudan peace and will review sanctions when accord is signed. GoS promises more political freedoms after signed accords. Press stops referring to the war as a *jihad*. More travel freedom, less press censorship.
22 October 2003	Powell pushes for peace.
23 October 2003	The United Nations estimate that more than 500,000 refugees have fled fighting in Darfur to Chad. That is, 300,000 from northern Darfur and 200,000 from southern Darfur, but another 76,000 in the fall of 2003. The earlier cease-fire has totally collapsed. Rumors are that final accords will be reached by December 2003. PNC says longer. Final dates not clear. GoS says December possible.
24 October 2003	The SLA fears major offensive by Sudan government, especially if the peace accord goes forward with the SPLA. The SLA is looking for a comprehensive and democratic settlement. United Nations estimates that there are 3,000 dead in Darfur this year alone.
25 October 2003	Lam Akol forces quit the GoS and rejoin the SPLA. Garang reaction unknown.
29 October 2003	Sudan military helicopter crashes in neighboring Kordofan province. Twenty are reported killed. United States extends 1997 sanctions against Sudan that could have ended on 3 November. Thus, Sudan's reputation in Washington still not acceptable and the United States' Sudan Peace Act provisions are renewed because of lack of progress on human rights and peace negotiations.
30 October 2003	Stalled talks in Chad between GoS and the SLM of Darfur. Both are still positioning their demands.
1 November 2003	SLA charges GoS hitting Darfur targets with Antonov bombing raids in Northern Darfur. Talks are suspended.

8 November 2003	pro-GoS militias kill 421 and displace 60,000, says Reuters report. SLA rebels claim cease-fire violations, but call for international monitors of situation. GoS officials say they are "bandit" attacks for livestock water rights.
23 January 2004	Flogging of girl is suspended. GoS military continues counterattacks against Darfur rebels.
March 2004	*Janjaweed* militias mobilized against rural civilian populations in Darfur. Hassan al-Turabi detained by GoS.
May 2004	Principles of power-sharing are agreed on by SPLA and GoS.
September 2004	Colin Powell calls the situation in Darfur "genocide" following American domestic pressures; most African and Arab nations do not use this term.
9 January 2005	Comprehensive Peace Agreement signed between GoS and the SPLA. United Nations does not call the violent Darfur situation "genocide," nor does Amnesty International.
March 2005	UN sanctions are authorized for Darfur and accusations about war crimes are sent to the ICC.
June 2005	The GoS and the NDA sign a document of reconciliation. Al-Turabi is freed.
9 July 2005	John Garang is sworn in as vice president of Sudan following the CPA protocol.
1 August 2005	John Garang is killed in helicopter crash in the south.
October 2005	The Government of South Sudan is established.
May 2006	The Darfur Peace Agreement is signed in Abuja, but only one faction of the Darfur rebels signs.
August 2006	The GoS rejects the presence of UN peacekeeping forces in Darfur.
October 2006	Jan Pronk is expelled from Sudan.
November 2006	The AU mandate over Darfur is extended. Hundreds killed in southern clashes at Malakal.
2007	Sudan economy is growing at 10 percent per year because of oil revenues.
April 2007	GoS accepts the present of UN peacekeeping forces in Darfur.
May 2007	*Janjaweed* leaders are charged by the ICC with war crimes. United States applies sanctions against Sudan for Darfur war.
July 2007	United Nations and GoS accept total peacekeeping force strength at 26,000 for Darfur. This force is slowly mobilized and underequipped.
October 2007	The SPLM withdraws from the GNU relationship.
December 2007	The SPLM rejoins the GNU.
2008	AU/UN (UNAMID) forces in Darfur reach about 10,000 peacekeepers as United Nations takes over full authority. GoS military attacks UNAMID forces, but apologizes for the "error."

February 2008	United Nations asks for increase forces and logistical support for UNAMID.
March 2008	More helicopters are provided to UNAMID by Russia; tensions are rising in Abyei.
April 2008	Census for 2010 elections is initiated.
May 2008	JEM units cross western Sudan to stage major attack on Omdurman; scores are killed, wounded, and captured. SPLA Defense Minister is killed in plane crash. Major armed clashes unfold at Abyei.
June 2008	Salva Kiir and al-Beshir accept Hague arbitration over Abyei boundaries.
July 2008	Al-Beshir is charged by the ICC for war crimes, but not for genocide.
September 2008	Small-scale attacks continue in Darfur.
October 2008	Ukrainian freighter hijacked by Somali pirates with a load of tanks presumed to be heading to the GoS.
December 2008	GoS troops sent to southern Kordofan to protect oil workers under attack by JEM forces.
January 2009	Hassan al-Turabi rearrested by al-Beshir.
May 2009	Hundreds killed in southern Kordofan clashes over cattle trespasses.
June 2009	GoS accused of supplying arms to fuel Southern conflicts; this is denied.
July 2009	Hague arbitration grants Hegleig oil fields to the north.
August 2009	United Nations declares that the main fighting in Darfur is over.
October 2009	SPLM protests the allocation of intelligence and security powers in the Sudan Parliament.
December 2009	The North and South agree on the terms of the 2011 referendum.
January 2010	Al-Beshir states that he will accept the results of the 2011 Referendum, including the possibility of separation.
February 2010	The ICC charges against al-Beshir to be reviewed by the ICC.
23 February 2010	Peace agreement with more Darfur factions and the GoS. JEM prisoners held by the GoS are released, and GoS soldier prisoners held by JEM to be released.
11 April 2010	Elections unfold with Al-Beshir winning, major parties withdrawing and with irregularities reported.
January 2011	Referendum slated for North-South unity or separation.

Summary of Key Documents

Addis Ababa Accords (1972)
This agreement ended the first North-South civil war, with a unified Sudan having regional autonomy for the South. It integrated the military forces of the Anya-Nya and the government of Sudan.

Koka Dam Declaration (24 March 1986)
The SPLA and the northern parties, except NIF and DUP, agree to make a "new Sudan" without the September (Islamic) Laws. DUP joined in November 1988; NIF never joined,

Abuja I (26 May 1992)
The SPLA, SPLA-Nasir faction, and Government of Sudan meet in Nigeria to discuss the basic issues of national identity and the relationship of state to religion. This led to an impasse.

Abuja II (26 April–18 May 1993)
The SPLA and the Government of Sudan met again to try to address this central issue. They failed again, but the polarization made it clear what was at stake.

Machakos Protocol (20 July 2002)
This agreement, signed in Kenya, between the SPLA and the Government of Sudan, provided for common principles to solve the North-South conflict, especially with compromises about the relationship between state and religion that aborted the Abuja meetings. It also provided for the right of self-determination.

This protocol would become Chapter 1 of the 2005 Comprehensive Peace Agreement.

UN Resolutions (2003–2007)

1502, Humanitarian access need for Darfur	26 August 2003
1547, Report on conflict situation in Sudan	11 June 2004
1556, Disarm *janjaweed* in Darfur	30 July 2004
1564, Sanctions are threatened	18 September 2004
1574, North/South should refrain from violence	19 November 2004
1584, Extends UNAMIS mandate	10 March 2005
1588, Extends UNAMIS mandate	17 March 2005
1590, UNAMIS → UNMIS, force of 10,000	24 March 2005
1591, Sanctions against Government of Sudan	29 March 2005
1593, Refers certain combatants to the ICC	31 March 2005
1627, Welcome to the CPA	23 September 2005
1651, Extends panel of experts on UN 1591	21 December 2005
1665, Extends panel of experts on UN 1591	29 March 2006
1706, Expands Darfur UNMIS mandate	31 August 2006
1755, Extends UNMIS by six months	30 April 2007
1769, Hybrid forces expanded to 20,000	31 July 2007

Security Protocols (25 September 2003)
Wealth-Sharing Protocols (7 January 2004)
Protocols on Power-Sharing, Abyei, South Kordofan, and Blue Nile (26 May 2004)
The Naivasha Accords (31 December 2004)
Built upon the important Machakos Protocol, specific topic protocols, and general trust- and confidence-building, these would all be signed at Naivasha, Kenya as chapters in the Comprehensive Peace Agreement of 2005. These included additional protocols on Abyei, South Kordofan and Blue Nile, implementation modalities, and wealth-sharing.

The Comprehensive Peace Agreement (9 January 2005)
This agreement of 241 pages, 6 chapters, and annexes was signed by 'Ali Osman Muhammad Taha for the government of Sudan and by John Garang for the SPLA. Its first chapter was founded on the fundamental issues resolved with the Machakos Protocol of 2002 as well as the other Naivasha protocols of 2004. Not only would this be a route to peace, it would also prepare for national and democratic elections in 2009 (now 2010) and for a referendum on self-determination in 2011.

Darfur Peace Accord (5 May 2006)
This agreement of six chapters and an annex was roughly modeled after the 2005 CPA and had provisions for power- and wealth-sharing, consultation, ceasefire, and

implementation. The signature page provided for representatives of the two factions of the Sudan Liberation Army (Darfur) and the Justice and Equality Movement. The signatures of the Government of Sudan and the Minnawi faction of the SLA were there, but the 'Abd al-Wahed and JEM groups were missing. This failure meant that for four more years, the conflict continued until March 2010, assuming that the Qatari accords with Khalil Ibrahim hold and new fighting does not erupt.

Eastern Sudan Peace Accord (14 October 2006)

This agreement between the government of Sudan and the Eastern Front (Beja Congress and Free Lions) brought peace to this region in a document of 6 chapters and 35 articles that provided for disarmament, demobilization, power-sharing, normalization of relations, and other practical matters. It has held since being signed in Asmara, Eritrea.

Military and Demographic Data

ARMED FORCES OF SUDAN (ARMY, NAVY, AIR FORCE, POPULAR MILITIA)

Personnel	1988–89	1990	1995	2002	2004
Number in Military	57,700	72,800	112,500		104,000
Manpower Availability					
Males aged 15–49			6,806,588	8,739,982	9,032,830
Males fit for service			4,185,206	5,380,917	5,558,460
Males at military age			313,958	398,294	429,334

Budget (Defense & Security)	1983–4	1987–8	1985–6	1993–4	2001
	$260.6 m	$478.2 m	$473.1 m	$600 m USD	$3 b USD

(Sudan pounds unless otherwise noted.)
Sources: "Sudan—Statistical Survey," *The Middle East and North Africa, 1991,* London, 1990, p. 799; *Africa Contemporary Record,* 1989–90, Vol. 22, p. B459–460; Wikipedia, 2002 data; *Global Studies,* 6th ed., 1995; *CIA World Factbook,* 2007.

Army Equipment	1988	1991	2008
Main Battle Tanks			
(T-54/55), Digna, USSR	155	200	250

(*continued*)

(Type 59D), *al-Zubeir*, China	10	10	
(M-60A3), USA	20	20	unknown
Type 62			unknown
Type 63			unknown
Type 72, *al- Zubeir*, Iran, China			unknown
Type 85 M-11, *al-Bashir*, Russia			unknown
Type 88			unknown
Light Tanks (Type 62), China	60	70	unknown
Armored Reconnaissance Vehicles (ARVs)			
(AML-90), France	6	6	
Saladin, Britain	15	15	
Ferret, Britain	50	50	
BRDM-1/-2, USSR		30	
Armored Personnel Carriers (APCs)			
BTR-50/-152, USSR	40	40	
BTR-80A, Russia, *Shareef I IFV*			unknown
WZ551, China, *Shareef 2 IFV*			unknown
OT-62/64, Czechoslovakia	30	30	
M-113, USA	36	36	36
2Si, *SPG, Abu Fatma*, Russia			unknown
V-100/150 Commando, USA	80	80	100
Walid, Egypt	100	100	120
Artillery			
M-101, 105mm, USA		18	18
Model 56, 105mm, USA		6	
D-74, 122mm, USA		4	
M-1938, 122mm, USA	24	24	
Type 54/D-30,122mm, USSR/PRC	12	42	
M-46/Type 59-1,130mm, as above	36	27	
D-20, 152mm, Russia			4
M-114A1, 155mm, USA	12	12	
AMX Mk F-3, 155mm, France	11	6	
Multiple Rocket Launchers			
Al-Saqr-30	6		
BM-21, 122mm, Russia	4	4	
Anti-Tank Weapons			
Swingfire wire-guided, Egypt	18	4	
M-1942, 76mm guns, Russia	18	18	
M-1944, 100mm guns, Russia	20	20	
B-10 82mm recoilless rifles, Russia		30	
M-40A1, 106mm, recoilless, USA		100	

Mortars		
81mm		
82mm		
RT-61, 120mm	50	
M-38/43, 120mm	50	
M-43, 120mm, Russia		12
AM-49, 120mm, Russia	24	

Sources: The Military Balance, 1991–1992, London, 1991, p. 119; Photius Coutsoukis, 2004; Wikipedia, *Military of Sudan,* 2008; *Sudan Military,* Nation Master, 2004. Note: The Military Industry Corporation in Sudan is now self-sufficient in conventional arms: ammunition, machine guns, mortars, artillery, rocket and armored vehicles, UAVs, and tanks. It is likely the former obsolete and unserviceable equipment is most likely solved. Other military suppliers are China, Iran, Libya, and Russia.

Air Force Equipment	1991	2008
Fighter Ground Attack Aircraft		
F-5E/F, USA	9	
J-5, China	10	
J-6, China	9	
Fighter Aircraft		
MiG-21, USSR*	8	
MiG-23, USSR*	3	
J-6, China	6	
MiG-29, Russia		12
Counterinsurgency Aircraft		
BAC-167 Mk Strikemaster, Britain	3	
BAC Jet Provost Mk55, Britain	3	
Transport Aircraft		
C-130H Hercules, USA	5	
An-24, USSR	5	unknown
DHC-5D Buffalo, Canada	2	
C-212 Aviocar, Brazil	4	
EMB-110P, Brazil	6	
F-27 Friendship, Holland	1	
Falcon 20/50 Executive jet, France	2	
Maritime Reconnaissance Aircraft		
Casa C-212 Aviocar, Brazil	2	
Helicopters		
AB-212, Italy	11	

(continued)

IAR/SA-330, Puma, France/Romania	15	
Mi-4, USSR	4	
Mi-8, USSR	14	
Mi-24, USSR, armed	2	
Hind, USSR, armed		unknown
Training aircraft		
MiG-15U, USSR	4	
MiG-21U, USSR	4	
JJ-5, China	2	
JJ-6, China	2	

Source: *The Military Balance, 1991–1992*, London, 1991, p. 119; DMSD Market Intelligence, *Middle East and Africa*, 1990.
*Operational?; http://www.newsfromafrica.org, 2008.

Navy Equipment*	1988	1991
Patrol Craft		
Coastal, 70 tons, via Iran, Germany		2
Sewart, 10 tons, via Iran, USA		4
River, *Gihad* 19.5 tons, Yugoslavia	3	4
Amphibious Craft		
Sobat (DTM-221) LCU, 410 tons	2	2

Sources: *Jane's Fighting Ships*, 1991–1992, Coulsdon, UK, 1991, pp. 512–513.
*Of questionable serviceability

Navy Personnel	1980s	1990s
	700	1,800

Air Defense Equipment	1988	1991
Anti-Aircraft Guns		
M-167, Vulcan, 20mm, USA	present	unknown
M-163- Vulcan, 20mm, USA	present	unknown
ZU-23-2, 37mm, Egypt	present	unknown
M-1939, Type 63, 37mm, China	120	120
L-60, Bofors, 40mm, Sweden	60	60
KS-12, 85mm, Russia	present	unknown
KS-19, 100mm, Russia	present	unknown

Surface-to-Air Missiles
    SA-2, radar-guided, Russia   18
    SA-7 Manpad, short range Russia   unknown
    Redeye, USA   unknown

Sources: *The Military Balance, 1991–1992*, London, 1991, p. 119; *African Contemporary Record*, Vol. 22, 1989–90, p. 460.

Sudan Peoples' Liberation Army (SPLA) of "New Sudan"

SPLA Forces	1986*	1989	1991	2008
	12,500	20,000–30,000	50,000–60,000	unknown

*The SPLA was formed from the mutiny of Battalion 105 and 106 of the Sudan Army. This breakaway was led by John Garang, who became the founder of the SPLA. SPLA weapons include: Kalashnikovs (AK-47), 60 mm mortars, 14.5 mm anti-aircraft, grenades, pistols, antitank land mines, and SAM-7 (manpads). In 2007 to 2008, the SPLA has been modernizing the airport in Juba and has been acquiring as many as one hundred Russian tanks.
Source: *Africa Contemporary Record*, Vol. 22, 1989–90, p. 460; press agencies in 2008.

DEMOGRAPHIC DATA

Descriptive matter

Population
Area:	$32,505,810 \text{ km}^2$ ($967,500 \text{ mi}^2$)
Population	
1990	24,971,806
1995	30,120,420
2007	39,379,358 (estimate)
2010	43,045,000 (projected)
2025	60,602,000 (projected)
Crude Birth Rate:	35.3/1,000
Crude Death Rate:	15.2/1,000
Infant Mortality Rate:	91.7/1,000
Life Expectancy:	
Males	47.1 years
Females	48.8 years
Literacy:	60.9%

Sources: Population Reference Bureau; World Wide Web; *Time Almanac 2009*; CIA World Factbook 2008.

Economy
   GDP (2006): $97.47 b USD
   PCI $900 USD
   Sectoral Composition (2006)
      Agriculture, Fishing, Forestry, Mining   35.5%
      Manufacturing, Industry   24.8%
      Services   39.7%
   Labor Force Distribution
      Agriculture, Fishing, Forestry, Mining   80.0%
      Manufacturing, Industry   7.0%
      Services   13.0%
      Arable land   6.78% of total
   Budget (2006)
      Revenues $7.943 b USD
      Expenditures $10.1 b USD
   Trade:
      Imports (2006) $8,074,000,000 USD
                                      (China, EU, Saudi Arabia,
                                      Japan, India)
     [foods, manufactured items, refinery and transport equipment, medicines, chemical, textiles, wheat]
      Exports (2006) $5,657,000,000 USD
                                        (China, Japan, UAE, Saudi
                                      Arabia, Egypt)
     [oil and petroleum products, cotton, sesame, livestock, peanuts, gum arabic, and sugar]

Sources: Time Almanac 2009; CIA Factbook 2008.

Glossary

(Ar: Arabic; Dn: Dinka; Gr: Greek; Nb: Nubian; Sh: Shilluk)

'Abeed (Ar) — "slaves"; a pejorative "fighting" word or insult.

Aethiopia (Gr) — land of the "burnt faces," translated to Arabic as *Bilad as-Sudan.*

Akhwan, Akhwat (Ar) — "brothers," "sisters"; can have political application.

Ansar (Ar) — "faithful followers," especially in devoted religious sense, *Ansar al-Mahdi.*

'Arab (Ar) — literally "nomad"; or Arabic culture, food, dress, values, and language.

'Ayb (Ar) — "shame"; any shameful behavior; reproach.

Baladi (Ar) — "country" but can mean provincial, authentic, or traditional in a folk way.

Baqt (Ar) — corruption from Latin "pact"; an economic and/or treaty or truce agreement.

Baraka (Ar) — "blessing" or spiritual powers, endowed in people and places.

Bilad as-Sudan (Ar) — "the Land of the Blacks"; "Negro-land"; "Ethiopia"; West African *Sahel.*

Cieng (Dn) — conforming to ideal, orderly, or proper behavior and social relations.

Danaqla (Nb) — Nubian people from the city or kingdom of Dongola; non-Arab northerners.

Dar (Ar) — "house" or "abode," as in *Dar-Fur* ("the place of the Fur people").

Dar al-Kufur (Ar) — "land of the non-Muslims or nonbelievers."

Darb al-Arbaien (Ar) — "forty-day road"; trade route from savanna Sudan to the Egyptian oases.

Dheeng (Dn) — gentleman, handsome, prideful, kind, and aesthetically correct.

Durra (Ar) — "millet" or sorghum, staple grain of the savanna for bread and beer.

Faqi Feki (Fuqaha, Pl) (Ar) — an Islamic sage or holy man, possibly of a Sufi order.

Feddan (Ar) — unit of land measurement equal to 1.038 acres.

Fellata (variously *Fula, Peul, Fulani*, etc.) — a person of West African origins.

Fertit — region in southern Darfur region, noted for slave raiding.

Ghazwa (Ar) — "slave raid."

Hadd, Hudud (Ar) — "borders" or "edges"; physical punishments allowed by Islamic law.

Hafir, Hufara (Ar) — "excavations" or earth basins for water conservation.

Halal (Ar) — acceptable behavior, food, or clothing allowed by Islam.

Haram (Ar) — unacceptable behavior, food, or clothing; not allowed by Islam.

Hezib (Ar) — (political) "party."

Inqaz (Ar) — salvation, as in a political movement so titled.

Intifada (Ar) — "uprising" as in political or military resistance to injustice.

Irhabeen (Ar) — "terrorists."

Islam (Ar) — "peace" or "surrender" to the Greatness of God; the name of the religious faith.

Jama'a al-Islamiya (Ar) — "Islamic group," as in the Egyptian fundamentalist political group.

Jamhouriyeen (Ar) — "Republicans," i.e., Republican brothers, a reformist Islamic group.

Janjaweed (Ar) — "devilish horsemen"; progovernment militia active in Darfur and Kordofan.

Jebha (Ar) — "front," as in a unified political group.

Jellaba (Ar) — northern Sudanese ("wearers of *jellabiyas*"; can be disparaging).

Jihad (Ar) — "struggle" to improve self and community; can be personal, political, or military.

Jinn (Ar) — "spirits" responsible for mischievous acts in folk Islam.

Juur (Dn) — "foreigners," as in non-Dinka or Arabs.

Khalifa, Khulafa (Ar) — (legitimate) "successor" to maintain the political order.

Khalwa (Ar) — (Quranic) elementary "school" for teaching the basics of literacy and religious thought.

Khawaja (Ar) — "foreigners," especially Europeans.

Kush (Nb) — name for ancient Nubia; also *Ta-Seti*, "the land of the bow people."

Kutab (Ar) — (Quranic) school for the basics of religious literacy.

Mahdi (Ar) — (expected) "prophet," "divinely guided one," especially from Shi'a traditions.

Majlis (Ar) — "council," a consultative body to determine policy," as in *majlis ash-shayukh*.

Medan (Ar) — an urban "square" or metaphorical "meeting place" for idea and commerce.

Merissa (Nb, Ar) — fermented *durra* (sorghum) to make a folk beer.

Meroe (Nb, Gr) — ancient Nubian empire in north Sudan three centuries before and after Christ.

Muaskarat (Ar) — refugee camps.

Mundukuru (Dn) — disparaging term for (European) "foreigners."

Murahileen (Ar) — progovernment "militia" forces used in war against the South.

Naqba (Ar) — "catastrophe," as in major political setback; i.e., colonialism or occupation.

Nubia (Nb) — "gold"; i.e., "land of gold"; ancient region of northern and central Sudan.

Qadi (Ar) — "court judge" versed in Islamic law (*Shari'a*).

Qubba (Ar) — (domed) "tomb," especially of a holy man; a blessed place.

Razzia (Ar) — "slave raid," especially during the Turkish occupation of Sudan.

Reth (Sh) — king of the Shilluk.

Rif (Ar) — "countryside," "rural," "folk" tradition.

Sahel (Ar) — "border" or "edge," as in the border of the desert and grassland, or coast, *Sawaheel*.

Salafi (Ar) — radical reform movement advocating for the "pious fathers"; *Jihad* group in Egypt.

Sayed (Ar) — "mister" or "sir"; term of respect; generally, the traditional elites of northern Sudan.

Sharif (Ar) — "honorable"; by extension, those who claim descent from the Prophet Muhammad.

Sheikh (Ar) — "patrilineal leader"; someone honored by religion, age, and community respect.

Shi'a (Ar) — minority faith in Islam, followers of Imam 'Ali.

Shura (Ar) — (consultative) "council" or advisory group.

Sudd (Ar) — "barrier"; in southern Sudan, the vast swamp that blocked Arabs and Islam.

Sufi (Ar) — Islamic mystics who wore "wool" (suf, in Arabic) hats; refers also to popular of folk Islam.

Sultan (Ar) — literally "the power"; title for the regnant king or ruler of a Muslim territory.

Sunna (Ar) — the codified and accepted practices and behaviors for proper (majority) Muslims.

Sunni (Ar) — majority faith in Islam; followers of the descendants of the Prophet Muhammad.

Suq, Aswaq (Ar) — "marketplace" for social and economic encounters.

Takfir wa al-Hegira (Ar) — "repentance" and migration; name of fundamentalist Muslim group.

Tariqa, Turuq (Ar) — "religious brotherhood"; also "the way," especially for Sufi followers.

Toich (Dn) — flat, clay plains for cattle grazing.

Tuhur (Ar) — "cleansing," as in the practice of female circumcision; ethnic removal.

Umma (Ar) — "nation" or universal community of fellow Muslims.

Walid, Awlad (Ar) — "born"; "son"; "native," as in *awlad al-balad* ("born of the land").

Watan (Ar) — "nation," as in the modern political sense of nationalism.

Zariba (Ar) — "acacia thorn fence" or enclosure for livestock or irregular military defense.

Zinj, Zanuj (Ar) — East African of peoples of mixed African origins, e.g., African Americans.

Zurqa (Ar) — "blue" as in "blue-black"; disparaging racial term of contempt.

Bibliography

Abbadi, Saad. *The National Register of Current Research: 1982–1983*. National Documentation Centre.

Abdalla, Ismail. *Perspectives and Challenges in the Development of Sudanese Studies*. Edwin Mellen Press (1993), hardcover, 313 pages.

Abdin, Hasan. *Early Sudanese Nationalism, 1919–1925* (Sudan Library Series). Institute of African & Asian Studies, University of Khartoum (1985), unknown binding, 167 pages.

Ahmed, Abdel Ghaffar M. *Understanding the Crisis in Darfur: Listening to Sudanese Voices*. Bergen, Norway: University of Bergen.

Ahmad, Abdel Ghaffar Muhammad. *Shaykhs and Followers: Political Struggle in the Rufaa al-Hoi Nazirate in the Sudan*. Khartoum University Press (1974), unknown binding, 170 pages.

Ahmed, Osman Hassan. *Sixteen Sudanese Short Stories*. Washington, D.C.: Office of the Cultural Counselor, Embassy of the Democratic Republic of the Sudan (1981).

———. *Sudan & Sudanese: A Bibliography of American and Canadian Dissertations & Theses on the Sudan* (Sudanese Publications Series). Embassy of the Democratic Republic of the Sudan (1982), unknown binding, 153 pages.

al-Hayy, Muhammad Abd. *Cultural Policy in the Sudan* (Studies & Documents on Cultural Policies). United Nations Educational (1982), paperback, 52 pages.

Al Hussein, Asma Obeid Allah. *Guide to Understanding of Darfur Peace Agreement*. Abuja: Department of Publishing & Media Production.

Ali, Abbas Ibrahim Muhammad. *The British, the Slave Trade, and Slavery in the Sudan, 1820–1881*. Khartoum University Press (1972), unknown binding, 137 pages.

Ali, Hayder Ibrahim. *Darfur Report 2006*. Cairo: Sudanese Studies Center.

Alier, Abel. *Southern Sudan: Too Many Agreements Dishonoured* (Sudan Studies Series). Paul & Co Pub Consortium (1992), hardcover, 292 pages.

Al-Mak, Ali. *A City of Dust* (Sudanese Publications Series). Office of the Cultural Counsellor, Embassy of the Democratic Republic of the Sudan (1982), unknown binding, 40 pages.

Al Sadig, Salah Omer. *Sudanese Cultures through the Ages*. Khartoum: AZZA P.H.

Arifi, Salih Abdalla. *Local Government and Local Participation in Rural Development in the Sudan* (Monograph Series/Development Studies and Research Centre, Faculty of

Economic & Social Studies, University of Khartoum). Development Studies and Research Centre, Faculty of Economic and Social Studies, University of Khartoum (1978), unknown binding, 34 pages.

Arkell, A. J. *A History of the Sudan to A.D. 1821*. The Athlone Press (1955), 1st ed., hardcover.

Asad, Talal. *Anthropology and the Colonial Encounter*. Ithaca Press (1973), paperback, 288 pages.

Asher, Michael. *A Desert Dies*. St. Martin's Press (1986), hardcover.

Babikir, Mustapha. *Transformations Socio-economiques dans la Region de Kassala-Gedaref*. Cairo: Kassala-Gedaref Research Programme.

Badri, Haga Kashif. *Women's Movement in the Sudan*. New Delhi: Asia News Agency (1986).

Baker, Charles F. and Rosaile F. Baker. *Ancient Nubia* (Calliope World History for Young People). Cobblestone Publishing (1996), paperback, 49 pages.

Balamoan, G. Ayoub. *Migration Policies in the Anglo-Egyptian Sudan, 1884 to 1956* (*History of Human Tragedies on the Nile: 1884 to 1975*, Vol. 1). Harvard University Center for Population Studies (1976), unknown binding, 470 pages.

Ballard, Colin R. *Kitchener*. Dodd, Mead & Co (1930), unknown binding, 341 pages.

Bechtold, Peter K. *Politics in the Sudan: Parliamentary and Military Rule in an Emerging African Nation* (Praeger Special Studies in International Politics and Government). Praeger Publishers Inc. (1976), hardcover, 382 pages.

Bedri, Babikr. *The Memoirs of Babikr Bedri*. Oxford University Press (1969), hardcover, 272 pages.

Bennett, Ernest N. *Downfall of the Dervishes*. Greenwood Pub Group (1969), hardcover, 267 pages.

Bernal, Victoria. *Cultivating Workers*. Columbia University Press (1991), hardcover, 224 pages.

Beshir, Mohamed Omer. *Education in Africa: Two Essays*. Khartoum University Press (1974), unknown binding, 59 pages.

———. *Educational Policy and the Employment Problem in the Sudan* (Monograph Series). Development Studies and Research Centre, Faculty of Economic & Social Studies, University of Khartoum (1977), unknown binding, 68 pages.

———. *The Southern Sudan: From Conflict to Peace*. Barnes & Noble Books (1975), unknown binding, 188 pages.

Bleuchot, Herve. *Les Cultures Contre l'Homme?: Essai d'Anthropologie Historique du Droit Penal Soudanais* (French edition). Presses Universitaires d'Aix-Marseille, Faculte de Droit et de Science Politique (1994), unknown binding, 480 pages.

Bryan, M. A. *Distribution of the Nilotic and Nilo-Hamitic Languages of Africa*. London: Oxford University Press.

Bryan, Margaret Arminel. *Distribution of the Nilotic and Nilo-Hamitic Languages of Africa* (African languages). For the International African Institute by the Oxford University Press (1948), unknown binding, 60 pages.

Burr, J. Millard. *Darfur: The Long Road to Disaster*. Markus Wiener Publishers (2006), paperback, 340 pages.

Burr, Millard. *Revolutionary Sudan: Hasan Al-Turabi and the Islamist State, 1989–2000* (Social, Economic, and Political Studies of the Middle East and Asia). Brill Academic Publishers (2003), hardcover, 300 pages.

Bushra, el-Sayed. *An Atlas of Khartoum Conurbation*. Khartoum University Press (1976), hardcover, 95 pages.

Buurri al Lamaab. *A Suburban Village in the Sudan* (Cornell Studies in Anthropology). Cornell University Press (1964), 1st ed., hardcover, 296 pages.

Caillou, Alan. *Khartoum.* Signet Books (1966), mass market paperback.

———. *South from Khartoum: The Story of Emin Pasha.* New York: Hawthorn Books (1974).

Cass, Frank. *Civil Wars*, Vol. 5, No. 3. London: Frank Cass.

Church Orr International Ltd. *1969–79: A Decade of Progress.* Nairobi: 10th Anniversary of the May Revolution, Printing and Packaging Corporation Ltd.

Classified List of Publications: 1985. Khartoum: Khartoum University Press.

Collectif, Politique Africaine. N-066-le Soudan. Karthala (1997), reliure inconnue.

Collins, Robert O. *A History of Modern Sudan.* Cambridge University Press (2008), 1st ed., paperback, 360 pages.

———. *African History in Documents: Eastern African History* (African History Text and Readings, Vol. 2). M. Wiener Pub. (1990), paperback, 244 pages.

———. *Egypt & the Sudan.* Englewood Cliffs, NJ: Prentice-Hall (1967).

———. *The Nile.* Yale University Press (2002), 1st ed., hardcover, 260 pages.

Cookson, John A. U.S. *Army Area Handbook for the Republic of the Sudan Department of the Army Pamphlet No. 550-27.* Department of the Army, Foreign Areas Studies Division.

Cordell, Dennis D. *Dar Al-Kuti and the Last Years of the Trans-Sahara Slave Trade.* University of Wisconsin Press (1985), 1st ed., hardcover, 283 pages.

Crabit, Pierre. *Gordon: The Sudan and Slavery.* (1969), hardcover.

Cunnison, Ian. *Baggara Arabs: Power and the Lineage in a Sudanese Nomad Tribe.* Clarendon Press/Oxford University Press (1966), hardcover, 233 pages.

Daly, M. W. *Imperial Sudan: The Anglo-Egyptian Condominium 1934–1956.* Cambridge University Press (2003), paperback, 488 pages.

Daly, Martin. *Civil War in the Sudan.* I. B. Tauris (1993), hardcover, 224 pages.

Deng, Francis Mading. *Cry of the Owl.* Lilian Barber Pr (1989), 1st ed., paperback.

———. *Dinka Folktales: African Stories from the Sudan.* Holmes & Meier Publishers (1984), hardcover, 204 pages.

———. *Dinka of the Sudan* (Case Studies in Cultural Anthropology). Holt McDougal (1972), paperback, 270 pages.

———. *Dinka of the Sudan.* Waveland Press (1984), paperback, 174 pages.

———. *Seed of Redemption: A Political Novel.* Lilian Barber Pr (1986), hardcover, 304 pages.

———. *Tradition and Modernization: A Challenge for Law Among the Dinka of the Sudan.* Yale Univ Pr (1987), 2nd ed., paperback, 480 pages.

———. *War of Visions: Conflicts of Identities in the Sudan.* Brookings Institution Press (1995), paperback, 592 pages.

Department of Statistics. *First Population Census of Sudan: Town Planners' Supplement* (Vol. 1). Khartoum: The Republic of Sudan.

Department of Statistics, National Planning Division. *Foreign Trade Statistics: First Nine Months 1974.* Khartoum: Democratic Republic of Sudan.

———. *National Income Accounts and Supporting Tables (1971/72).* Khartoum: The Democratic Republic of the Sudan.

Die Sudanforschung in der Bundesrepublik Deutschland: Ergebnisse der Bremer Tagung 1993 (Institut fur Weltwirtschaft und internationales Management). Lit (1995), paperback, 405 pages.

Directory of the Republic of the Sudan 1957–58, Including Trade Index and Biographical Section. London: The Diplomatic Press and Publishing Co.

Doolittle, Duncan H. *A Soldier's Hero: General Sir Archibald Hunter.* Anawan Pub. Co (1991), unknown binding, 358 pages.

Draft of the National Charter, The Democratic Republic of Sudan.

Durham University Library. *A Summary Guide to the Sudan Archive.* Durham: Durham University.

El-Amin, Mohammed Nuri. The Emergence and Development of the Leftist Movement in the Sudan During the 1930s and 1940s (Occasional paper, University of Khartoum, Institute of African and Asian Studies). Institute of African and Asian Studies, University of Khartoum (1984), unknown binding, 159 pages.

Elbashir, Ahmed E. *The Democratic Republic of the Sudan in American Sources* (Sudanese Publication Series No. 12). Washington, D.C.: The Cultural Office, Embassy of the Democratic Republic of Sudan.

El-Bedawi, Mahjoub. *Selected Conference Papers, Sudan Studies Association: 1982–1984. Volume One: Social Sciences and Liberal Arts.* Washington, D.C.: Sudan Studies Association.

El-Bushra, El-Sayed. *Philosophical Society of the Sudan: Urbanization in the Sudan.* Proceedings of the Seventeenth Annual Conference, Khartoum.

El Gizouli, El Subki M. *The National Council for Research* (Sudan Public Relations Office, Periodical Bulletin: Issue 1). Khartoum: National Council for Research.

El Hassan, Ali Mohammed. *Essays on the Economy and Society of the Sudan* (Vol. 1). Khartoum: Economic and Social Research Council, NCR.

El-Singaby, Talaat. *La Republique Democratique du Soudan: Bilan des Recherches en France et en R.F.A.: Bibliographie Selective, 1900–1986* (Travaux et Documents de l'I.R.E.R.A.M) (French ed.). Centre d'Etudes et de Recherches sur l'Orient Arabe Contemporain (1987), paperback, 139 pages.

El-Tayeb, Salah El Din El Zein. *The Students' Movement in the Sudan: 1940–1970.* Khartoum University Press (1971), unknown binding, 76 pages.

Eltigani, Eltigani El Tahir. *War and Drought in Sudan: Essays on Population Displacement.* University Press of Florida (1995), hardcover, 114 pages.

El-Tigani, Mahgoub. *The Sudanese Human Rights Quarterly* (Issue No. 2). Cairo: Sudan Human Rights Organization.

Essays in Sudan Ethnography, Presented to Sir Edward Evans-Pritchard. Humanities Press (1972), unknown binding, 256 pages.

Evans-Pritchard, E. E. *The Nuer: A Description of the Modes of Livelihood and Political Institutions of a Nilotic People.* Oxford University Press (1969), 1st ed. American, paperback, 271 pages.

Ewald, Janet J. *Soldiers, Traders & Slaves.* University of Wisconsin Press (1990), hardcover, 288 pages.

Faculty of Economic & Social Studies, University of Khartoum. *Urbanisation and Exploitation: The Role of Small Centres.* Development Studies and Research Centre, Monograph Series No. 11. Khartoum: Khartoum University Press.

Faculty of Economic and Social Studies, University of Khartoum. *Sudan Society: Journal of Social Studies Society,* No. 3. Khartoum: Khartoum University Press.

———. *Sudan Journal of Economic and Social Studies,* Vol. 2, No. 1. Khartoum: Khartoum University Press.

Farwell, Byron. *Prisoners of the Mahdi.* W. W. Norton & Company (1989), paperback, 400 pages.

First, Ruth. *The Barrel of a Gun.* Penguin Books Ltd (1972), paperback, 528 pages.

Fluehr-Lobban, Carolyn, Richard A. Lobban, Jr., and Rober Kramer. *Historical Dictionary of the Sudan* (African Historical Dictionaries). The Scarecrow Press, Inc. (2002), 3rd ed., hardcover, 440 pages.

Forsbert, Malcolm. *Land Beyond the Nile*. Harper (1958), hardcover.

———. *Last Days on the Nile*. Lippincott (1966), paperback.

Fruzetti, Lina. *Culture and Change Along the Blue Nile: Courts, Markets, and Strategies for Development* (Westview Special Studies in Applied Anthropology). Westview Pr (Short Disc) (1990), ill. ed., paperback, 256 pages.

Funk, Kevin. *The Scramble for Africa: Darfur-Intervention and the USA*. Black Rose Books (2008), ill. ed., paperback, 290 pages.

GEO: A New View of Our World, Vol. 1 (February 1980). New York: Gruner Jahr (1979), unknown binding.

Ghazvinian, John. *Untapped: The Scramble for Africa's Oil*. Harcourt (2007), 1st ed., hardcover, 336 pages.

Goddard, John. *Kayaks Down the Nile*. *Brigham Young University Press* (1979), paperback, 318 pages.

Hall, Richard Seymour. *Lovers on the Nile: The Incredible African Journeys of Sam and Florence Baker*. Random House (1980), 1st ed., hardcover, 254 pages.

Hamilton, Ruth Simms. *African Urban Notes*, Vol. VI. East Lansing: Michigan State University.

Hassan, Yusuf Fadl. The Arabs and the Sudan: From the Seventh to the Early Sixteenth Century. Edinburgh: Edinburgh University Press (1967).

———. The Arabs and the Sudan: From the Seventh to the Early Sixteenth Century. Khartoum University Press (1973), unknown binding, 298 pages.

Hatch, John. *History of Britain in Africa from the Fifteenth Century to the Present*. Brookings (1969), hardcover.

Henderson, Larry Wills. *Egypt and the Sudan: Countries of the Nile*. T. Nelson (1971), 1st ed., hardcover, 221 pages.

Hill, Richard Leslie. *A Black Corps D'Elite: An Egyptian Sudanese Conscript Battalion with the French Army in Mexico, 1863–1867, and Its Survivors in Subsequent African H*. Michigan State University Press (1995), hardcover, 235 pages.

———. *Egypt in the Sudan, 1820–1881* (Middle Eastern Monographs, 2). Greenwood Press Reprint (1986), hardcover, 189 pages.

———. *Gordon: Yet Another Assessment* (SSSUK Occasional Publications Series). Sudan Studies Society of the United Kingdom (1987), paperback, 40 pages.

Hoagland, Edward. *African Calliope, a Journey to the Sudan*. Random House (1979), hardcover

Hodgkin, R. *Sudan Geography*. Longmans, Green (1951), hardcover.

Holt, P. M. *A History of the Sudan: From the Coming of Islam to the Present Day*. Longman (2000), 5th ed., paperback, 240 pages.

Holy, Ladislav. *Neighbours and Kinsmen*. C Hurst & Co Publishers Ltd (1974), hardcover, 198 pages.

Hopkins, Peter. *Kenana Handbook of Sudan*. Taylor and Francis (2007), 1st ed., hardcover, 256 pages.

Howell, John. *Local Government Politics in the Sudan*. Khartoum University Press (1978), paperback, 125 pages.

Hunwick, J. O. *Fontes Historiae Africanae, Commussion XXII*, No. 9/10 (Bulletin of Information, International Academic Union). Evanston: The Program of African Studies, Northwestern University.

Hyam, Ronald. *Reappraisals in British Imperial History* (Cambridge Commonwealth Series). Macmillan (1975), hardcover, 244 pages.

Idris, Helene Fatima. *Modern Developments in the Dinka Language*. Goteborg, Sweden: Goteborg University.

Ismail, Ellen T. Bukra. *Insha' Allah: A Look into Sudanese Culture*. E. Ismail-Schmidt (1988), 3rd ed., paperback, 88 pages.

Jacquard, Roland. *In the Name of Osama Bin Laden: Global Terrorism and the Bin Laden Brotherhood*. Duke University Press (2002), paperback, 320 pages.

Jok, Jok Madut. *Sudan: Race, Religion and Violence*. Oneworld Publications (2007), paperback, 352 pages.

————. *War and Slavery in Sudan (The Ethnography of Political Violence)*. University of Pennsylvania Press (2001), paperback, 224 pages.

Katsiaficas, George. *New Political Science, A Journal of Politics & Culture*, Vol. 23, No. 1. Glasgow: Bell & Bain Ltd.

Keen, David. *The Benefits of Famine: A Political Economy of Famine and Relief in Southwestern Sudan, 1983–1989*. Princeton University Press (1994), hardcover, 312 pages.

Khalid, Mansour. Speech delivered by Mansour Khalid, Minister of Foreign Affairs, at the Second Ambassadors Global Conference. 7 January 1974. The Democratic Republic of the Sudan, Ministry of Foreign Affairs.

Khalifa, Ahmad M. *The National Review of Social Sciences*, Vol. 4, No. 4. Cairo: The National Center for Social and Criminological Research.

————. *The National Review of Social Sciences*, Vol. 12, No. 2&3. Special Issue on Women. Cairo: The National Center of Social and Criminological Research.

Kok, Peter N. *Governance and Conflict in the Sudan, 1985–1995: Analysis, Evaluation and Documentation* (Mitteilungen). Deutsches Orient-Institut (1996), paperback, 382 pages.

Korn, David A. *Assassination in Khartoum: An Institute for the Study of Diplomacy Book*. Indiana University Press (1993), hardcover, 284 pages.

Krabacher, Thomas. *Global Studies: Africa*. McGraw-Hill/Dushkin (2008), 12th ed., paperback, 320 pages.

Langley, Andrew. *Explorers on the Nile (In Profile)*. Silver Burdett (1982), unknown binding, 64 pages.

Lewis, David L. *The Race to Fashoda: Colonialism and African Resistance*. Henry Holt & Co (P) (1995), paperback, 304 pages.

Lobban, Richard A. *Historical Dictionary of Ancient and Medieval Nubia* (Historical Dictionaries of Ancient Civilizations and Historical Eras). The Scarecrow Press, Inc. (2004), hardcover, 560 pages.

Lobban, Richard and Carolyn Fluehr-Lobban. *Sudan Studies Association Bulletin*, Vol. 9, No. 2–4, 1989. Baltimore: Morgan State University.

Mack, John. *Culture History in the Southern Sudan: Archaeology, Linguistics and Ethnohistory* (British Institute in Eastern Africa). British Institute in Eastern Af (1982), paperback, 178 pages.

MacLaren, Roy. *Canadians on the Nile 1882–1898*. Vancouver: Canada U. of British Columbia P (1978), hardcover.

Magnus, Philip. *Kitchener: Portrait of an Imperialist*. Penguin Books (1958), paperback.

Mahdi, Said Muhammad Ahmad. *A Guide to Land Settlement and Registration*. Khartoum University Press (1971), unknown binding, 92 pages.

Mahjoub, Jamal. *Navigation of a Rainmaker* (African Writers Series). Heinemann (1989), paperback, 192 pages.

Mahmoud, Mahgoub El-Tigani. *State Bureaucracy and Social Change: A Sociological Analysis of Politico-administrative Conflict in the Sudan* (n.d.).

———. *The Impact of Partial Modernization on the Emigration of Sudanese Professionals and Skilled Workers*. Providence: Brown University Press.

Mahmoud, Fatima Babiker. *The Sudanese Bourgeoisie: Vanguard of Development?* Zed Books (1984), hardcover, 170 pages.

Mamdani, Mahmood. *Saviors and Survivors: Darfur, Politics, and the War on Terror*. Pantheon (2009), hardcover, 416 pages.

Management of the Crisis in the Sudan. Centre for Development Studies, University of Bergen (1989), unknown binding, 178 pages.

Marcus, Harold G. (editor). *The Heroic Age in Sinnar* (Ethiopian Series Monograph No. 15, Committee on Northeast African Studies). Michigan State Univ African Studies (1985), paperback.

Martin, Percy F. *The Sudan in Evolution: A Study of the Economic, Financial, and Administrative Conditions of the Anglo-Egyptian Sudan*. Constable and Co (1921), unknown binding, 559 pages.

McGregor-Hastie, Roy. *Never to be Taken Alive*. Sidgwick and Jackson (1985), hardcover.

McHugh, Neil. *Holymen of the Blue Nile: The Making of an Arab-Islamic Community in the Nilotic Sudan, 1500–1850* (Islam and Society in Africa). Northwestern University Press (1994), 1st ed., hardcover, 280 pages.

Metz, Helen Chapin. *Sudan: A Country Study* (Area Handbook Series). Dept. of the Army (1992), 4th ed., hardcover, 370 pages.

Ministry of Culture and Information. *Jonglei Project (Phase 1)*. Khartoum: The Democratic Republic of the Sudan.

Ministry of Culture and Information, Sudan. *The Democratic Republic of the Sudan*. London: London Lithographic Limited.

Ministry of Finance, Planning and National Economy. *Foreign Trade Statistics: Democratic Republic of Sudan* (1976). Khartoum: Department of Statistics.

Ministry of Foreign Affairs. *Welcome to Sudan*. Tamaddon Printing Press: Khartoum

Ministry of Health Sudan. *Blue Nile Health Project: Annual Report, 1984*. Wad Medani, Sudan.

———. *Blue Nile Health Project: Annual Report, 1985*. Wad Medani, Sudan.

Ministry of Mineral Resources. *Annual Report: July 1961–June 1962*. Sudan Survey Department.

Mohamed, Abbas Ahmed. *White Nile Arabs: Political Leadership and Economic Change* (London School of Economics Monographs on Social Anthropology). Berg Publishers (1990), hardcover, 232 pages.

Moorehead, Alan. *The Blue Nile*. Harper Perennial (2000), paperback, 368 pages.

———. *The White Nile*. Harper Perennial (2000), paperback, 448 pages.

Nachtigal, Gustav. *Sahara and Sudan*. Barnes & Noble (1971), unknown binding.

Nalder, L. F. *A Tribal Survey of Mongalla Province*. Negro Universities (1970), hardcover.

Nasr, Ahmad A. *African Studies in Africa* (Sudan Library Series, 10). Khartoum: Institute of African & Asian Studies, University of Khartoum.

National Council for Research, Democratic Republic of Sudan. The National Register of Current Research (Supplement 1983–1985). Khartoum: National Documentation Centre.

Nimiery, Jaafar Mohamed H. E . Sudanese Socialist Union, First National Congress 25 January 1974, Opening Address of H. E President Jaafar Mohamed Nimery, President. Doc. No. C/I/1. Culture Printing Press.

Nobel, Peter. Refugee Law in the Sudan. With The Refugee Conventions and The Regulation of Asylum Act of 1974. Research Report No. 64. The Scandinavian Institute of African Studies: Uppsala Region, Sudan Southern Region. The Six-Year Plan of Economic and Social Development, 1977/78–1982/83. The Ministry (1977), unknown binding, 413 pages.

Nordenstam, Tore. *Sudanese Ethics*. Uppsala: Scandinavian Institute of African Studies (1968).

Novelli, Bruno. *A Grammar of the Karimojong Language* (Geographia Religionum) (German ed.). Dietrich Reimer (1985), paperback, 286 pages.

Numayri, Jafar Muhammad. Sudanese Socialist Union, Second National Congress, H. E. President Jaafar Mohamed Numieri's address on the plan for economic & social development, 1977/78–1982/83, Friday, 28 January 1977, Khartoum. Ministry of Culture and Information (1977), unknown binding, 34 pages.

Nyibil, Thaan. *Experiences in the Resistance Movement Against Arab Colonial Rule in Sudan*. Vantage Pr (1990), 1st ed., hardcover, 92 pages.

O'Brien, Jay. *The Political Economy of Development and Under Development: An Introduction*. Development Studies Book Series No. 2. Khartoum: Khartoum University Press.

Office of the Cultural Counsellor, Embassy of the Democratic Peoples' Republic of the Sudan. A Short Anthology of Sudanese Literature: Selections from Sudanese Literature (5). Brentwood: International Graphics Printing Service.

Palmisano, Antonio L. *Mito e Societa: Analisi della Mitologia dei Lotuho del Sudan* (Collana di Antropologia Culturale e Sociale) (Italian ed.). FrancoAngeli (1989), unknown binding, 286 pages.

Peace and Unity in the Sudan. Khartoum University Press (1978), paperback, 192 pages.

Petterson, Donald. *Inside Sudan: Political Islam, Conflict, and Catastrophe*. Basic Books (2003), rev. ed., paperback, 288 pages.

Pitamber, Sunita. *Sudan Economy Research* (Group Discussion Papers). Bremen: Institute for World Economics and International Management.

Public Relations Office, Sudan Government. *Sudan Almanac 1949*. Khartoum: McCorquodale & Co.

Rahim, Muddathir Abdel. *Imperialism & Nationalism in the Sudan: A Study in Constitutional & Political Development, 1899–1956* (Sudan Studies Series, No. 11). Khartoum University Press (1987), paperback, 275 pages.

Refugee Studies Centre. *Forced Migration Review*, Issue 31. Oxford: University of Oxford.

Rey, Charles Fernand. *In the Country of the Blue Nile*. Duckworth (1927), hardcover, 296 pages.

Roden, David. *The Twentieth Century Decline of Suakin* (Suakin Project Series). Sudan Research Unit, University of Khartoum (1970), unknown binding, 22 pages.

Rolandsen, Øystein. *Guerrilla Government: Political Changes in the Southern Sudan during the 1990s*. Nordic Africa Institute (2005), paperback, 170 pages.

Rone, Jemera. *Behind the Red Line: Political Repression in Sudan*. Human Rights Watch (1996), paperback, 343 pages.

———. *Civilian Devastation: Abuses by All Parties in the War in Southern Sudan*. Human Rights Watch (1991), paperback, 294 pages.

————. *Sudan, Oil, and Human Rights*. Human Rights Watch (2003), 1st ed., hardcover, 754 pages.

Ryle, J. *Warriors of the White Nile (Peoples of the Wild)*. Silver Burdett Press (1982), hardcover, 176 pages.

Saalakhan, El-Hajj Mauri'. *Target Sudan (What's Really Behind the Crisis in Darfur?)*. The Peace and Justice Foundation (2004), paperback, 143 pages.

Salih, Abdelrahim Mohammed. *The Manasir of Northern Sudan: Land and People: A Riverain Society and Resource Scarcity*. R. Koppe (1999), paperback, 282 pages.

Salih, al-Tayyib. *Tayeb Salih Speaks: Four Interviews with the Sudanese Novelist* (Sudanese Publication Series). Office of the Cultural Counsellor, Embassy of the Democratic Republic of the Sudan (1982), unknown binding, 56 pages.

Salih, Tayeb. *Season of Migration to the North* (New York Review Books Classics). NYRB Classics (2009), paperback, 184 pages.

————. *Tayeb Salih's Season of Migration to the North: A Casebook*. Syracuse Univ Pr (Sd) (1986), paperback.

Salvadorini, Bernardi and Bono Novati. Africa Rivista Trimestrale di Studi e Documentazione dell'Istituto Italiano per l'Africa e l'Oriente. USPI (1959), paperback.

Santandrea, Stefano. *A Popular History of Wau from Its Foundation to about 1940*. Rome.

Seeley, J. A. *Famine in Africa: A Guide to Bibliographies and Resource Centres* (Cambridge African Occasional Papers). African Studies Centre, University of Cambridge (1986), hardcover, 86 pages.

————. *Famine in Sub-Saharan Africa: A Select Bibliography (Excluding the Sahel) from 1978* (Cambridge African Occasional Papers). African Studies Centre, University of Cambridge (1986), unknown binding, 176 pages.

Sharf, Frederic. *Omdurman 1898*. Greenhill Books (2006), 1st ed., hardcover, 240 pages.

Shepherd, George W. "Shari'a Law and Strife in the Sudan: Is Peace Possible?" (*Africa Today*, Vol. 36, No. 3&4). Denver: University of Denver.

Sherif, Negm el Din Mohamed. *A Short Guide to the Antiquities Garden, Sudan National Museum by Negm el Din Mohamed Sherif*. Antiquities Service, Ministry of Sudan (1977), paperback.

Shibeika, Mekki. *The Independent Sudan*. New York: R. Speller (1959).

Sidahmed, Salam. *Sudan (Contemporary Middle East)*. RoutledgeCurzon (2005), 1st ed., hardcover, 208 pages.

Sikainga, Ahmad Alawad. *Slaves into Workers: Emancipation and Labor in Colonial Sudan* (CMES Modern Middle East Series). University of Texas Press (1996), 1st ed., hardcover, 304 pages.

Sin, Abu M. E. *The Future of Sudan's Capital Region: A Study in Development and Change*. Khartoum: Khartoum University Press.

Smith, Wilbur. *The Triumph of the Sun*. Thomas Dunne Books (2005), hardcover, 512 pages.

Social Studies Society. *Sudan Society 1969*. Khartoum: Khartoum University Press.

Soslah, Gunnar M. *How to Survive Development: The Story of New Halfa* (Monograph Series—Development Studies and Research Centre, University of Khartoum). Development Studies and Research Centre, Faculty of Economic & Social Studies, University of Khartoum (1977), unknown binding.

Spaulding, Jay. *After the Millennium: Diplomatic Correspondence from Wadai and Dar Fur on the Eve of Colonial Conquest. 1885–1916*. Northeast African Studies Series, Monograph No. 18. East Lansing: Michigan State University Press.

————. *Public Documents from Sinnar* (African Historical Sources). Michigan State Univ Pr (1989), hardcover, 426 pages.

Steevens, George Warrington. *With Kitchener to Khartoum*. Edinburgh and London: William Blackwood and Sons (1898), 11th ed., hardcover.

Stiansen, Endre. *Kordofan Invaded: Peripheral Incorporation and Social Transformation in Islamic Africa*. Leiden, Netherlands: Koninklijke Brill.

Sudan Almanac 1952. Khartoum: Public Relations Branch Sudan Government (1952), unknown binding.

Sudan Field Office, Save the Children Federation. *U.S. Baseline Report: Um Ruwaba District, North Kordofan Province, Sudan*. El Tamaddon Printing Press, Ltd.

Sudan Notes and Records. [S.l., s.n.], 1998.

Sudan Society: Journal of the Social Studies Society. (1972), hardcover.

Suliman, Ali Ahmed. *Issues in the Economic Development of the Sudan*. Khartoum University Press (1975), unknown binding, 154 pages.

Svoboda, Terese. "Cleaned the Crocodile's Teeth." Nuer Song. Greenfield Review Press (1985), 1st ed., paperback, 104 pages.

Sylvester, Anthony. *Sudan Under Numeiri*. The Bodley Head Ltd (1977), hardcover, 240 pages.

Taddia, Irma. *Fonti Comboniane per la Storia dell'Africa Nord-Orientale*. Bologna: Universita degli Studi di Bologna, Dip Artimento di Politica Istituzioni Storia (1986).

Tayib, Abdulla El. *Heroes of Arabia*. Khartoum University Press (1976), unknown binding, 60 pages.

Taylor, John. *Egypt and Nubia* (British Museum Paperbacks). Harvard University Press (1991), paperback, 72 pages.

The Central Office of Information, The Republic of the Sudan. *Sudan Almanac, 1968: An Official Hand-Book*. Khartoum: Government Printing Press.

The Judiciary, Khartoum. *Sudan Law Journal and Reports (1972)*. Khartoum: Offset Printing Press.

The Opening of the Nile Basin: Writings by Members of the Catholic Mission to Central Africa on the Geography and Ethnography of the Sudan, 1842–1881. Barnes & Noble Books (1975), unknown binding, 330 pages.

The Republic of the Sudan. *Population and Housing Survey, 1964/66*. Khartoum: Department of Statistics.

The Shrinking Deadlock?: Developments in East/West Relations and Africa: Papers from the International Conference on East/West Relations and Africa. Beitrage zur doppelten Entkolonialisierung. Verlag fur Interkulturelle Kommunikation (1992), unknown binding, 101 pages.

The Sudan: A Record of Progress (1898–1947). The Sudan Government.

The Sudanese Socialist Union. *National Unity and the Emergence of a Just Society in the Sudan*. Nairobi: Printing and Packaging Corporation Ltd.

Theobald, Alan Buchan. *'Ali Dinar, Last Sultan of Darfur, 1898–1916*. Longmans (1965), unknown binding, 243 pages.

Thomas, Frederic C. *Slavery and Jihad in the Sudan: A Narrative of the Slave Trade, Gordon and Mahdism, and Its Legacy Today*. IUniverse (2009), paperback, 256 pages.

Trench, Charles Chenevix. *The Road to Khartoum: A Life of General Charles Gordon*. Carroll & Graf Publishers (1989), paperback, 320 pages.

Udal, John O. *The Nile in Darkness*. M. Russell (1998), ill. ed., hardcover, 681 pages.

Universita degli Studi: Istituto di Studi Africani e Orientali. *Orientalia Karalitana: Quaderni dell'Istituto di Studi Africani e Orientali*. Cagliari, Universita degli Studi, Stampa (1987).

University of Africa. *Sudan Today.* University Press of Africa (1971), hardcover.

University of Edinburgh: Centre of African Studies. *Post Independence Sudan: Proceedings of a Seminar Held in the Centre of African Studies, University of Edinburgh, 21 and 22 November 1980.* Edinburgh, Centre of African Studies, University of Edinburgh, W0 1-1981.

University of Khartoum. *Institute of African and Asian Studies 1984–86.* Khartoum: Khartoum University Press.

————. *Institute of African and Asian Studies: Prospectus (1981–82).* Khartoum: Khartoum University Press.

Uzoigwe, G. N. *Britain and the Conquest of Africa: The Age of Salisbury.* University of Michigan Press (1974), hardcover, 416 pages.

Vivekananda, Franklin. *Scandinavian Journal of Development Alternatives and Area Studies,* Vol. 19, No. 2&3 (June and September 2000). Stockhom: Scandinavian Journal of Development Alternatives and Area Studies.

Voll, John Obert. *Historical Dictionary of Sudan* (African Historical Dictionaries Series, No. 17). Scarecrow Pr (1978), hardcover, 193 pages.

————. *Sudan: State and Society in Crisis.* Indiana University Press (1991), paperback, 188 pages.

Waal, Alex de. *War in Darfur and the Search for Peace* (Studies in Global Equity, Darfur). Global Equity Initiative, Harvard University (2007), paperback, 431 pages.

Warburg, Gabriel R. *Historical Discord in the Nile Valley* (Series in Islam and Society in Africa). Northwestern University Press (1992), 1st ed. ed, hardcover, 210 pages.

Warburg, Gabriel. *Islam, Nationalism and Communism in a Traditional Society: The Case of Sudan.* Routledge (1978), ann. ed., hardcover, 253 pages.

————. *Islam, Sectarianism, and Politics in Sudan since the Mahdiyya.* Hurst & Co. (2003), hardcover, 252 pages.

Warner, Philip. *Dervish: The Rise and Fall of an African Empire* (Wordsworth Military Library). Wordsworth Military Library (2000), paperback, 235 pages.

Wayne, Scott. *Egypt and the Sudan* (Lonely Planet Travel Survival Kit). Lonely Planet Publications (1990), 2nd ed., paperback, 440 pages.

————. *Lonely Planet Egypt and the Sudan: A Travel Survival Kit.* Lonely Planet Publications (1987), paperback, 392 pages.

Whitman, Anthony Lake and Christine Todd. *More than Humanitarianism: A Strategic U.S. Approach toward Africa* (Independent Task Force Report). Council on Foreign Relations Press (2006), paperback, 148 pages.

Wilding, Dietrich. *Sudan: Ancient Kingdom of the Nile.* Flammarion (1997), hardcover, 400 pages.

Willis, Justin. *Sudan Studies: Official Newsletter of the Sudan Studies Society of the United Kingdom.* Issues 1–4 (2/1987–4/1988), 6–7 (6/1989–1/1980), 9–10 (12/1990–5/1991), 16–23 (12/1994–3/1999), 26–27 (2001), 39 (1/2009). Durham: SSSUK.

Winks, Robin W., ed. *British Imperialism: Gold, God, Glory.* Holt, Rinehart and Winston (1964), paperback.

Wohlmuth, Karl. *African Development Perspectives Yearbook* (Abstracts, Vol. 1–7). Bremen: University of Bremen.

————. *Alternative Economic Strategies for the Sudan* (Discussion Papers/Sudan Economy Research Group). University of Bremen, Sudan Economy Research Group (1992), unknown binding, 67 pages.

Woodward, Peter. *Sudan after Nimeiri* (Routledge/Soas Series on Contemporary Politics and Culture in the Middle East). Routledge (1991), 1st ed., hardcover, 240 pages.

Yacoub, el Sammani A. *Scientific and Technical Potential "STP" in the Sudan: A Summary of Results*. National Council for Research Khartoum (1974), unknown binding, 64 pages.

Young, Helen. *Darfur: Livelihoods Under Siege*. Medford: Feinstein International Famine Center.

———. *Livelihoods, Power and Choice: The Vulnerability of the Northern Rizaygat, Darfur, Sudan*. Medford: Feinstein International Center.

Young, William Charles. *The Rashaayda Bedouin: Arab Pastoralists of Eastern Sudan* (Case Studies in Cultural Anthropology). Houghton Mifflin Harcourt P (1995), paperback, 157 pages.

Yousif, Yousif Babiker. *Food and Nutrition in the Sudan*. National Council for Research, Tamaddon Press.

Ziegler, Peter. *Omdurman* (Pen & Sword Military Classics). Pen and Sword (2003), paperback, 240 pages.

Index

About the Author

DR. RICHARD A. LOBBAN, JR. is the former Chair of Anthropology at Rhode Island College, where he taught for thirty-six years and was also the Director the Program of African and Afro-American Studies. He is now Professor Emeritus. He is the Executive Director of the Sudan Studies Association and has published scores of articles, reviews, chapters, edited works, and books on Sudan, including his two-volume Sudan references—*Historical Dictionary of Sudan* and *Historical Dictionary of Ancient and Medieval Nubia*—and he translated the works on Sudan by the French traveler Pierre Tremaux. He has also researched in Tunisia, Egypt, Cape Verde, and Guinea-Bissau. He was President of the Narragansett Society of the Archaeological Institute of America. He has a continuing excavation in Sudan and leads archaeological tours to Egypt and Sudan. Since retiring, he is Adjunct Professor of African Studies at the Naval War College and Adjunct Professor at Carnegie Mellon University.